ACCA

PAPER P1

PROFESSIONAL ACCOUNTANT

In this June 2007 new edition

- We discuss the **best strategies** for revising and taking your ACCA exams

- We show you how to be well prepared for the **December 2007 exam**

- We give you **lots of great guidance** on tackling questions

- We show you how you can **build your own exams**

- We provide you with **three** mock exams including the **Pilot paper**

- We provide the **ACCA examiner's answers** as well as our own to key exam questions and the Pilot Paper as an additional revision aid

Our **i-Pass** product also supports this paper.

FOR EXAMS IN DECEMB

D1340785

BPP
LEARNING MEDIA

First edition June 2007

ISBN 9780 7517 3366 2

British Library Cataloguing-in-Publication Data
A catalogue record for this book
is available from the British Library

Published by

BPP Learning Media Ltd
BPP House, Aldine Place
London W12 8AA

www.bpp.com/learningmedia

Printed in Great Britain by
Hobbs The Printers
Brunel Road
Totton
Hampshire SO40 3WX

Your learning materials, published by BPP Learning Media Ltd, are printed on paper sourced from sustainable, managed forests.

We are grateful to the Association of Chartered Certified Accountants for permission to reproduce past examination questions. The suggested solutions in the exam answer bank have been prepared by BPP Learning Media Ltd, unless where otherwise stated.

Contents

Question index

The headings in this checklist/index indicate the main topics of questions, but questions often cover several different topics.

	Marks	Time allocation Mins	Page number Question	Page number Answer

Mock exam 1

Questions 30 to 33

Mock exam 2

Questions 34 to 37

Mock exam 3 (Pilot paper)

Questions 38 to 41

Planning your question practice

Our guidance from page 41 shows you how to organise your question practice, either by attempting questions from each syllabus area or **by building your own exams** – tackling questions as a series of practice exams.

Topic index

Listed below are the key Paper P1 syllabus topics and the numbers of the questions in this Kit covering those topics.

If you need to concentrate your practice and revision on certain topics or if you want to attempt all available questions that refer to a particular subject, you will find this index useful.

Syllabus topic	Question numbers
Risk culture	18
Risk management	7, 12, 14-18, 28, Mock 1 Q3, Mock 1 Q4, Mock 2 Q4
Risk monitoring	17, Mock 1 Q4
Sarbanes-Oxley	29
Shareholders	28, Mock 1 Q2
Social issues	21
Social responsibility	7, 21, Mock 1 Q1
Stakeholders	4, 26, Mock 1 Q1, Mock 3 Q4
Strategic risks	Mock 2 Q1
Sustainability	Mock 1 Q1

Using your BPP Practice and Revision Kit

Tackling revision and the exam

You can significantly improve your chances of passing by tackling revision and the exam in the right ways. Our advice is based on feedback from ACCA examiners.

- We look at the dos and don'ts of revising for, and taking, ACCA exams
- We focus on Paper P1; we discuss revising the syllabus, what to do (and what not to do) in the exam, how to approach questions and ways of obtaining easy marks

Selecting questions

We provide signposts to help you plan your revision.

- A full **question index**
- A **topic index** listing all the questions that cover key topics, so that you can locate the questions that provide practice on these topics, and see the different ways in which they might be examined
- **BPP's question plan** highlighting the most important questions and explaining why you should attempt them
- **Build your own exams**, showing how you can practise questions in a series of exams

Making the most of question practice

At BPP we realise that you need more than just questions and model answers to get the most from your question practice.

- Our **Top tips** provide essential advice on tackling questions, presenting answers and the key points that answers need to include
- We show you how you can pick up **Easy marks** on questions, as we know that picking up all readily available marks often can make the difference between passing and failing
- We include **marking guides** to show you what the examiner will reward
- We refer to the **2007 BPP Study Text** for detailed coverage of the topics covered in each question
- In a bank at the end of this Kit we include the **examiner's answers** to the Pilot paper and other questions. Used in conjunction with our answers they provide an indication of all possible points that could be made, issues that could be covered and approaches to adopt

Attempting mock exams

There are three mock exams that provide practice at coping with the pressures of the exam day. We strongly recommend that you attempt them under exam conditions. **Mock exams 1 and 2** reflect the question styles and syllabus coverage of the exam; **Mock exam 3** is the Pilot paper. To help you get the most out of doing these exams, we not only provide help with each answer, but also guidance on how you should have approached the whole exam.

Passing ACCA exams

Revising and taking ACCA exams

To maximise your chances of passing your ACCA exams, you must make best use of your time, both before the exam during your revision, and when you are actually doing the exam.

- Making the most of your revision time can make a big, big difference to how well-prepared you are for the exam

- Time management is a core skill in the exam hall; all the work you've done can be wasted if you don't make the most of the three hours you have to attempt the exam

In this section we simply show you what to do and what not to do during your revision, and how to increase and decrease your prospects of passing your exams when you take them. Our advice is grounded in feedback we've had from ACCA examiners. You may be surprised to know that much examiner advice is the same whatever the exam, and the reasons why many students fail don't vary much between subjects and exam levels. So if you follow the advice we give you over the next few pages, you will **significantly** enhance your chances of passing **all** your ACCA exams.

How to revise

☑ Plan your revision

At the start of your revision period, you should draw up a **timetable** to plan how long you will spend on each subject and how you will revise each area. You need to consider the total time you have available and also the time that will be required to revise for other exams you're taking.

☑ Practise Practise Practise

The **more exam-standard questions** you do, the **more likely you are to pass** the exam. Practising full questions will mean that you'll get used to the time pressure of the exam. When the time is up, you should note where you've got to and then try to complete the question, giving yourself practice at everything the question tests.

☑ Revise enough

Make sure that your revision covers the breadth of the syllabus, as all topics could be examined in a compulsory question. However it is true that some topics are **key** – they are likely to appear often or are a particular interest of the examiner – and you need to spend sufficient time revising these. Make sure you also know the **basics** – the fundamental calculations, proformas and report layouts.

☑ Deal with your difficulties

Difficult areas are topics you find dull and pointless, or subjects that you found problematic when you were studying them. You mustn't become negative about these topics; instead you should build up your knowledge by reading the **Passcards** and using the **Quick Quiz** questions in the Study Text to test yourself. When practising questions in the Kit, go back to the Text if you're struggling.

☑ Learn from your mistakes

Having completed a question you must try to look at your answer critically. Always read the **Top tips guidance** in the answers; it's there to help you. Look at **Easy marks** to see how you could have quickly gained credit on the questions that you've done. As you go through the Kit, it's worth noting any traps you've fallen into, and key points in the **Top tips** sections, and referring to these notes in the days before the exam. Aim to learn at least one new point from each question you attempt, a technical point perhaps or a point on style or approach.

☑ Read the examiners' guidance

ACCA's website contains articles by examiners which you **must** read, as they may form the basis of questions on any paper after they've been published.

Read through the examiner's answers included at the back of the Kit. In general these are far longer and more comprehensive than any answer you could hope to produce in the exam, but used in conjunction with our more realistic solutions, they provide a useful revision tool, covering all possible points and approaches.

☑ Complete all three mock exams

You should attempt the **Mock exams** at the end of the Kit under **strict exam conditions**, to gain experience of selecting questions, managing your time and producing answers.

How NOT to revise

☒ Revise selectively

Examiners are well aware that some students try to forecast the contents of exams, and only revise those areas that they think will be examined. Examiners try to prevent this by doing the unexpected, for example setting the same topic in successive sittings.

☒ Spend all the revision period reading

You cannot pass the exam just by learning the contents of Passcards, Course Notes or Study Texts. You have to develop your **application skills** by practising questions.

☒ Audit the answers

This means reading the answers and guidance without having attempted the questions. Auditing the answers gives you **false reassurance** that you would have tackled the questions in the best way and made the points that our answers do. The feedback we give in our answers will mean more to you if you've attempted the questions and thought through the issues.

☒ Practise some types of question, but not others

Although you may find the numerical parts of certain papers challenging, you shouldn't just practise calculations. These papers will also contain written elements, and you therefore need to spend time practising written question parts.

☒ Get bogged down

Don't spend a lot of time worrying about all the minute detail of certain topic areas, and leave yourself insufficient time to cover the rest of the syllabus. Remember that a key skill in the exam is the ability to **concentrate on what's important** and this applies to your revision as well.

☒ Overdo studying

Studying for too long without interruption will mean your studying becomes less effective. A five minute break each hour will help. You should also make sure that you are leading a **healthy lifestyle** (proper meals, good sleep and some times when you're not studying).

How to PASS your exams

☑ Prepare for the day

Make sure you set at least one alarm (or get an alarm call), and allow plenty of time to get to the exam hall. You should have your route planned in advance and should listen on the radio for potential travel problems. You should check the night before to see that you have pens, pencils, erasers, watch, calculator with spare batteries, also exam documentation and evidence of identity.

☑ Select the right questions

You should select the optional questions you feel you can answer **best**, basing your selection on the topics covered, the requirements of the question, how easy it will be to apply the requirements and the availability of easy marks.

☑ Plan your three hours

You need to make sure that you will be answering the correct number of questions, and that you spend the right length of time on each question – this will be determined by the number of marks available. Each mark carries with it a **time allocation** of **1.8 minutes**. A 25 mark question therefore should be selected, completed and checked in 45 minutes. With some papers, it's better to do certain types of question first or last.

☑ Read the questions carefully

To score well, you must follow the requirements of the question, understanding what aspects of the subject area are being covered, and the tasks you will have to carry out. The requirements will also determine what information and examples you should provide. Reading the question scenarios carefully will help you decide what **issues** to discuss, **techniques** to use, **information** and **examples** to include and how to **organise** your answer.

☑ Plan your answers

Five minutes of planning plus twenty-five minutes of writing is certain to earn you more marks than thirty minutes of writing. Consider when you're planning how your answer should be **structured,** what the **format** should be and **how long** each part should take.

Confirm before you start writing that your plan makes **sense,** covers **all relevant points** and does not include **irrelevant material.**

☑ Show evidence of judgement

Remember that examiners aren't just looking for a display of knowledge; they want to see how well you can **apply** the knowledge you have. Evidence of application and judgement will include writing answers that only contain **relevant** material, using the material in scenarios to **support** what you say, **criticising** the **limitations** and **assumptions** of the techniques you use and making **reasonable recommendations** that follow from your discussion.

☑ Stay until the end of the exam

Use any spare time to **check and recheck** your script. This includes checking you have filled out the candidate details correctly, you have labelled question parts and workings clearly, you have used headers and underlining effectively and spelling, grammar and arithmetic are correct.

How to FAIL your exams

☒ Don't do enough questions

If you don't attempt sufficient questions on the paper, you are making it harder for yourself to pass the questions that you do attempt. If for example you don't do a 20 mark question, then you will have to score 50 marks out of 80 marks on the rest of the paper, and therefore have to obtain 63% of the marks on the questions you do attempt. Failing to attempt all of the paper is symptomatic of poor time management or poor question selection.

☒ Include irrelevant material

Markers are given detailed mark guides and will not give credit for irrelevant content. Therefore you should **NOT** braindump all you know about a broad subject area; the markers will only give credit for what is **relevant**, and you will also be showing that you lack the ability to **judge what's important.** Similarly forcing irrelevant theory into every answer won't gain you marks, nor will providing uncalled for features such as situation analyses, executive summaries and background information.

☒ Fail to use the details in the scenario

General answers or reproductions of Kit answers that don't refer to what is in the scenario in **this** question won't score enough marks to pass.

☒ Copy out the scenario details

Examiners see **selective** use of the right information as a key skill. If you copy out chunks of the scenario which aren't relevant to the question, or don't use the information to support your own judgements, you won't achieve good marks.

☒ Don't do what the question asks

Failing to provide all the examiner asks for will limit the marks you score. You will also decrease your chances by not providing an answer with enough **depth** – producing a single line bullet point list when the examiner asks for a discussion.

☒ Present your work poorly

Markers will only be able to give you credit if they can read your writing. There are also plenty of other things that will make it more difficult for markers to reward you. Examples include:

- Not using black or blue ink
- Not showing clearly which question you're attempting
- Scattering question parts from the same question throughout your answer booklet
- Not showing clearly workings or the results of your calculations

Paragraphs that are too long or which lack headers also won't help markers and hence won't help you.

Using your BPP products

This Kit gives you the question practice and guidance you need in the exam. Our other products can also help you pass:

- **Learning to Learn Accountancy** gives further valuable advice on revision

- **Passcards** provide you with clear topic summaries and exam tips

- **Success CDs** help you revise on the move

- **i-Pass CDs** offer tests of knowledge against the clock

- **Learn Online** is an e-learning resource delivered via the Internet, offering comprehensive tutor support and featuring areas such as study, practice, email service, revision and useful resources

You can purchase these products by visiting www.bpp.com/mybpp.

Visit our website www.bpp.com/acca/learnonline to sample aspects of Learn Online free of charge. Learn Online is hosted by BPP Professional Education.

Passing P1

Revising P1

Topics to revise

Firstly we must emphasise that you will need a good knowledge of the **whole syllabus**. Any part of the syllabus could be tested within compulsory Question 1. Having to choose two out of three optional questions does not really represent much choice if there are areas of the syllabus you are keen to avoid. Although (like all syllabuses) this syllabus may have seemed a lot when you were studying, we actually believe that it is not as large as some of the syllabuses you have previously studied.

That said, there are certain topics that are stressed in the syllabus and by the examiner, and therefore are core:

- Concepts underpinning corporate governance
- Different categorisations of stakeholders
- The agency problem
- Features of, and arguments for and against, principles vs rules based approaches
- Sarbanes-Oxley
- Corporate governance best practice in relation to the board, board committees, remuneration and reporting
- Elements of control environment
- The main control procedures
- Risk analysis framework
- The main strategies for dealing with risks
- The key ethical positions
- Kohlberg's framework
- Gray, Owen, Adams seven positions on corporate social responsibility
- Meaning of sustainability

Your knowledge of other topic areas needs to demonstrate breadth. You need to have a good idea of:

- The range of stakeholders an organisation can have
- The different types of risks (not just financial) that it can face
- The elements of control and risk management systems
- The impact of culture
- The main elements of corporate and professional codes
- The main areas discussed in corporate social responsibility debates

It's also useful to keep reading the business pages during your revision period and not just narrowly focus on the syllabus. Remember that the examiner has stressed that this paper is about how organisations respond to real-world issues, so the more you read, the more practical examples you will have of how organisations have tackled real-life situations.

Question practice

You should use the Passcards and any brief notes you have to revise these topics, but you mustn't spend all your revision time passively reading. Question practice is vital; doing as many questions as you can in full will help develop your ability to analyse scenarios and produce relevant discussion and recommendations. The question plan on page 42 tells you what questions cover so that you can choose questions covering a variety of organisations and risk situations.

You should make sure you leave yourself enough time during your revision to practise 50 mark Section A questions as you cannot avoid them, and the scenarios and requirements of Section A questions are more complex. You should also leave yourself enough time to do the three mock exams.

Passing the P1 exam

Displaying the right qualities

The examiner will expect you to display the following qualities.

Qualities required	
Fulfilling the higher level question requirements	This means that when you are asked to show higher level skills such as **assessment or evaluation**, you will only score well if you demonstrate them. Merely describing something when you are asked to evaluate it will not earn you the marks you need.
Identifying the most important features of the organisation and its environment	You must use your **technical knowledge and business awareness** to identify the key features of the scenario.
Sorting the information in the scenario	You will get a lot of information, particularly in the Section A scenario, and will be expected to **evaluate how useful** it is and **use it** to support answers such as comparisons and discussions.
Selecting relevant real-life examples	You will gain credit for using **good examples.**
Using the governance and ethical frameworks	Remember that the examiner has emphasised the importance of accountants showing awareness of their responsibilities. You may be expected to **apply the frameworks** to determine what the problem is (for example which stakeholders should be considered) and to identify appropriate solutions.
Criticising the approaches you use	You may be expected not only to use guidance such as **corporate governance codes** or **principles-based ethical guidance**, but also criticise the approaches you use.
Arguing well	You may be expected to discuss both sides of a case, or present an argument in favour or against something. You will gain marks for the **quality** and **logical flow of your arguments**.
Making reasonable recommendations	The measures you recommend must be **appropriate** for the organisation; you may need to discuss their strengths and weaknesses, as there may be costs of adopting them. The recommendations should clearly state what has to be done.

Avoiding weaknesses

Our experience of, and examiner feedback from, other higher level exams enables us to predict a number of weaknesses that are likely to occur in many students' answers. You will enhance your chances significantly if you ensure you avoid these mistakes:

- **Failing to provide what the question verbs require** (discussion, evaluation, recommendation) or to write about the topics specified in the question requirements

- **Repeating the same material** in different parts of answers

- **Stating theories and concepts** rather than applying them

- **Quoting chunks of detail** from the question that don't add any value

- **Forcing irrelevancies into answers**, for example irrelevant definitions or theories, or examples that don't relate to the scenario

- **Giving long lists or writing down all that's known** about a broad subject area, and not caring whether it's relevant or not

- **Focusing too narrowly on one area** – for example only covering financial risks when other risks are also important

- **Letting your personal views prevent you from answering the question** – the question may require you to construct an argument with which you personally don't agree

- **Unrealistic or impractical recommendations**

- **Vague recommendations** - instead of just saying improve risk management procedures, you should discuss precisely **how** you would improve them

- **Failing to answer sufficient questions** because of poor time management

- **Not answering all parts of optional questions**

Using the reading time

We recommend that you spend the first part of the 15 minutes reading time choosing the Section B questions you will do, on the basis of your knowledge of the syllabus areas being tested and whether you can fulfil all the question requirements. Remember that Section B questions can cover different parts of the syllabus, and you should be happy with all the areas that the questions you choose cover. We suggest that you should note on the paper any ideas that come to you about these questions.

However don't spend all the reading time going through and analysing the Section B question requirements in detail; leave that until the three hours writing time. Instead you should be looking to spend as much of the reading time as possible looking at the Section A scenario, as this will be longer and more complex than the Section B scenarios and cover more of the syllabus. You should highlight and annotate the key points of the scenario on the question paper.

Choosing which questions to answer first

Spending most of your reading time on the Section A scenario will mean that you can get underway with planning and writing your answer to the Section A question as soon as the three hours start. It will give you more actual writing time during the one and a half hours you should allocate to it and it's writing time that you'll need. Comments from examiners of other syllabuses that have similar exam formats suggest that students appear less time-pressured if they do the big compulsory question first.

During the second half of the exam, you can put Section A aside and concentrate on the two Section B questions you've chosen.

However our recommendations are not inflexible. If you really think the Section A question looks a lot harder than the Section B questions you've chosen, then do those first, but **DON'T run over time on them.** You must leave yourself an hour and a half to tackle the Section A question. When you come back to it, having had initial thoughts during the reading time, you should be able to generate more ideas and find the question is not as bad as it looks.

Tackling questions

Scenario questions

You'll improve your chances by following a step-by-step approach to Section A scenarios along the following lines.

Step 1   Read the requirement

You need to identify the knowledge areas being tested and what information will therefore be significant.

Step 2   Identify the action verbs

These convey the level of skill you need to exhibit and also the structure your answer should have. A lower level verb such as define will require a more descriptive answer; a higher level verb such as evaluate will require a more applied, critical answer.

The examiner has stressed that **higher level requirements and verbs** will be most significant in this paper, for example critically evaluating a statement and arguing for or against a given idea or position.

Action verbs that are likely to be frequently used in this exam are listed below, together with their intellectual levels and guidance on their meaning.

Intellectual level		
1	**Define**	Give the meaning of
1	**Explain**	Make clear
1	**Identify**	Recognise or select
1	**Describe**	Give the key features
2	**Contrast**	Make a comparison between things on the basis of the differences between them
2	**Analyse**	Give reasons for the current situation or what has happened
3	**Assess**	Determine the strengths/weaknesses/importance/ significance/ability to contribute
3	**Discuss**	Examine in detail by using arguments for and against
3	**Construct the case**	Present the arguments in favour, supported by evidence
3	**Evaluate**	Determine the value of
3	**Recommend**	Advise the appropriate actions to pursue in terms the recipient will understand

Step 3   Identify what each part of the question requires

When planning, you will need to make sure that you aren't reproducing the same material in more than one part of the question.

Also you're likely to come across part questions with two requirements that may be at different levels; a part question may for example ask you to explain X and discuss Y. You must ensure that you **fulfill both requirements** and that your discussion of Y shows greater depth than your explanation of X (for example by identifying problems with Y or putting the case for and against Y).

Step 4   Check the mark allocation to each part

This shows you the depth anticipated and helps allocate time.

Step 5   Read the scenario through quickly, highlighting key data

In the front pages of the text we discussed what the key data would be for questions covering different areas of the syllabus:

Corporate governance	• Weaknesses in arrangements described
	• Relating arrangements described to governance best practice
Control systems	• Adequacy of control systems (what's missing)
	• Appropriateness of control systems (do they address key risks/problems)
	• Overall control environment/culture and influence on effectiveness of control processes
Risks	• Most significant risks (strategic/relate to key changes)
	• Most significant uncertainties
	• Consequences of risks materialising
	• Evidence of risk awareness in organisation
	• Factors determining risk response (risk appetite, size of organisation)
Ethics	• Ethical issues at stake
	• Ethical position of organisation
	• Ethical position of individuals
	• Factors that determine ethical positions

Step 6   Read the scenario carefully

Put points under headings related to requirements (eg by noting in the margin to what part of the question the scenario detail relates).

Step 7   Consider the consequences of the points you've identified

Remember that in the answer you will often have to provide recommendations based on the information you've been given. Consider also that you may have to criticise the code, framework or model that you've been told to use. You may have to bring in wider issues or viewpoints, for example the views of different stakeholders.

Step 8   Write a plan

You may be able to do this on the question paper as often there will be at least one blank page in the question booklet. However any plan you make should be reproduced in the answer booklet when writing time begins.

Consider carefully when planning your answer to Section A the sorts of issues that will earn you professional marks. How should you present your answer? Do the arguments you use have a logical flow and are they supported by material from the scenario?

Step 9   Write the answer

Make every effort to present your answer clearly. The pilot paper and other questions suggest that the examiner will be looking for you to make a number of clear points. The best way to demonstrate what you're doing is to put points into separate paragraphs with clear headers.

Discussion questions

Remember that **depth of discussion** will be important. Discussions will often consist of paragraphs containing 2-3 sentences. Each paragraph should:

- **Make a point**
- **Explain the point** (you must demonstrate **why** the point is important)
- **Illustrate the point** (with material or analysis from the scenario, perhaps an example from real-life)

Gaining the easy marks

Knowledge of the core topics that we list under topics to revise should present you with some easy marks. The pilot paper suggests that there will be some marks available on certain part questions for definitions, explanations or descriptions that don't have to be related to the scenario. However don't assume that you can ignore all the scenarios and still pass!

As P1 is a Professional level paper, 4 or 5 **professional level marks** will be awarded. Some of these should be easy to obtain. The examiner has stated that some marks may be available for presenting your answer in the form of a letter, presentation, memo, report or briefing notes. You may also be able to obtain marks for the style and layout of your answer.

Exam information

Format of the exam

		Number of marks
Section A:	1 compulsory case study	50
Section B:	Choice of 2 from 3 questions (25 marks each)	50
		100

Section A will be a compulsory case study question with typically four or five sub-requirements relating to the same scenario information. The question will usually assess and link a range of subject areas across the syllabus. It will require students to demonstrate high-level capabilities to understand the complexities of the case and evaluate, relate and apply the information in the case study to the requirements.

The case study will be between 400 and 700 words long. The examiner has stressed the importance of reading the case in detail, taking notes as appropriate and getting a feel for what the issues are. Scenarios may be drawn from any situation involving aspects of governance; this is likely to be, but need not be, in an organisational setting.

Professional marks will be available in Section A for presentation, logical flow of argument and quality of argument.

Section B questions are more likely to assess a range of discrete subject areas from the main syllabus section headings; they may require evaluation and synthesis of information contained within short scenarios and application of this information to the question requirements.

Although one subject area is likely to be emphasised in each Section B question, students should not assume that questions will be solely about content from that area. Each question will be based on a shorter case scenario to contextualise the question.

The paper will have a global focus; no numerical questions will be set.

Additional information

The Study Guide provides more detailed guidance on the syllabus.

Pilot paper

Section A

1   Corporate governance arrangements; acquisition risks; board structure; non-executive directors; environmental reporting

Section B

2   Directors' remuneration; remuneration committee; conflicts of interest

3   Professional ethics; integrity; deontological and consequentialist approaches

4   Internal control systems; reputation risks; ethical responsibilities

The Pilot paper is Mock exam 3 in this Kit.

Supplementary questions

Useful websites

The websites below provide additional sources of information of relevance to your studies for *Strategic Financial Management*.

- www.accaglobal.com

  ACCA's website. Includes student section.

- www.bpp.com

  Our website provides information about BPP products and services, with a link to the ACCA website.

- www.ft.com

  This website provides information about current international business. You can search for information and articles on specific industry groups as well as individual companies.

- www.economist.com

  Here you can search for business information on a week-by-week basis, search articles by business subject and use the resources of the Economist Intelligence Unit to research sectors, companies or countries.

- www.strategy-business.com

  This website includes articles from *Strategy & Business*.

- www.invweek.co.uk

  This site carries business news and articles on markets from Investment Week and International Investment.

- www.pwcglobal.com/uk

  The PricewaterhouseCoopers website includes UK Economic Outlook.

- www.bbc.co.uk

  The website of the BBC carries general business information as well as programme-related content.

Articles

EXAMINER'S APPROACH TO PAPER P1, PROFESSIONAL ACCOUNTANT

by **David Campbell**
22 Feb 2007

Paper P1, *Professional Accountant* is a new compulsory paper in the Essentials module at the Professional level of the ACCA Qualification. It is an exciting, challenging, and innovative paper that aims to enrich students' understanding of a number of important issues as they prepare to take their place as members of the professional accounting community.

Following in-depth consultation on the development of the new ACCA Qualification and guidance on ethics and governance teaching from IFAC and others, it was decided to create a new paper – Professional Accountant – to examine a number of areas relevant to the broad themes of professionalism, responsibility, accountability, and ethics. In terms of syllabus content, these themes are handled in the context of corporate governance, internal control, risk, and professional and business ethics. These areas form the basis of the new Paper P1 syllabus.

Content from a number of other parts of the new ACCA Qualification is relevant to the Paper P1 syllabus (refer to the 'linked papers' diagram in the *Syllabus*). Most obviously, it forms a prominent part of the qualification's emphasis on ethics. Professionalism and ethics are both at the heart of the new ACCA Qualification. They are covered in 11 of the 16 exam papers – including all papers at Professional level – and three of the Essentials performance objectives as part of the practical experience requirement. Underpinning the syllabus and the practical experience is the Professional Ethics module. The aim of the Professional Ethics module is to give students exposure to a range of ethical perspectives and can be completed once eligible to take Paper P1. Ideally, the Professional Ethics module should be taken at the same time as – or soon after – completing Paper P1. In addition, the Paper P1 syllabus builds on and develops content studied previously in Paper F1, *Accountant in Business* and Paper F8, *Audit and Assurance*.

It is important to study an ACCA-approved textbook for Paper P1. They are written especially for the syllabus, and are reviewed by the examiner, making them invaluable in terms of coverage and insight into what is examinable. The syllabus for Paper P1, possibly more than any of the other papers, is eclectic in nature and draws on material from a number of different disciplines. Students are strongly encouraged to read around the subject area, especially those students new to the content of the syllabus. A number of recommended books are listed at the end of the *Study Guide*.

Syllabus and relational diagram
Although the syllabus contains five areas (refer to the 'relational diagram' in the *Syllabus*), it is important to understand that all of these, taken together, comprise a logical 'whole'. All areas are interconnected and, in total, the syllabus represents a set of issues essential to the understanding of how accounting – especially in a business context – contributes to, and is underpinned by, governance and ethics. Although these have always been important to the accountancy profession, a number of well-publicised recent corporate failures and scandals have highlighted the need for sound governance and ethical behaviour. Society invests a great deal of trust in its professions and it is crucial that accounting professionals repay that trust and maintain the level of respect and regard in which they have been traditionally held. Accordingly, accountants need to be aware of their responsibilities to investors, to society, and to the highest standards of

professional probity and competence. The content of the Paper P1 syllabus will help students explore and develop these themes.

Part A of the syllabus focuses of corporate governance, responsibility, and accountability. This means exploring aspects of, for example, the agency relationship between directors and shareholders, the meaning of governance, the role and types of directors, issues of responsibility, and the meaning and limits of accountability. It aims to introduce these important themes while also encouraging students to think about the ethical assumptions made by accountants collectively as a profession.

The next three parts of the syllabus – B, C and D – focus specifically on issues that have, in recent corporate failures, been the most problematic. These include internal control, the identification and assessment of risk, and controlling and mitigating risk. The Paper P1 syllabus singles these out for separate consideration because, although they are integral to corporate governance as a whole, they play a crucial part in an accountant's responsibility to act in the public interest and in the interests of shareholders.

Sound systems of internal analysis, control, and audit underpin all effective corporate governance systems. Effective management at the strategic level rests on the assumption that internal activities can be controlled, verified, and reported on internally. If management loses control of internal systems and procedures, any claim of sound governance is lost – as was the case at Baring's Bank, when a single uncontrolled trader lost large amounts of money on derivatives markets. The same is true of risk. Being aware of all possible risks, understanding their potential impact, as well as the probability of occurrence, are important safeguards for investors and other stakeholders.

All of these preceding sections are underpinned by Paper P1's important consideration of both professional and business ethics – Part E of the syllabus. Ethical assumptions underpin and 'surround' any profession and system of governance. The accountancy profession, just as in medicine or law, is governed by certain ethical frameworks that inform practice and guide practitioners. This part of the Paper P1 syllabus explores some of these assumptions, while also looking at some of the ethical theories that help to explain them. This part of the syllabus will always be assessed to some degree in the compulsory section of the exam but not necessarily exclusively in that section.

Study Guide and intellectual levels

The *Study Guide*, which breaks the syllabus down into separate sections, is on the ACCA website. The superscript numbers at the end of each objective in the *Study Guide* indicate the level at which students should understand a particular subject or topic area. These levels of understanding, known as cognitive levels, are important as they indicate the depth to which each part of the syllabus may be examined.

Because Paper P1 is at the Professional level, the higher cognitive challenges – represented by the number 3 – are prominent. This means that this paper is more likely to use higher levels of questioning; whereas level 1 tasks might concern knowledge and comprehension (such as 'list', 'define', 'identify', 'calculate'), levels 2 and 3 are more challenging. Level 2 tasks concern application and analysis ('contrast', 'explain', 'discuss', and so on), and level 3 tasks concern synthesis and evaluation. Level 3 requirements might therefore include 'construct', 'evaluate', 'assess', 'formulate', or 'advise'.

It is likely that each Paper P1 exam will contain several questions at levels 2 and 3, and the *Study Guide* reflects this emphasis on higher cognitive levels. It is important to realise that if *Study Guide* sections require learning at levels 2 or 3, then it is possible that the exam will test that area at that cognitive level. The marking scheme will reflect this, and answers that do not attempt to answer at the higher cognitive level will be rewarded accordingly. If, therefore, a question asks a candidate to 'assess' or 'evaluate' an argument or a statement, answers that merely 'describe' will not be well rewarded.

Ethical and governance codes

Paper P1 covers two areas that, in some countries, are underpinned by 'codes' or 'guidelines' that attempt to regulate practice. In the light of recent corporate governance failures, governments and professional bodies have introduced these codes so as to reduce the 'freedom of movement' for managers, and to make their duties and responsibilities unambiguous in certain circumstances. The UK was among the first to introduce such initiatives, with the Cadbury Code back in 1992, but the intervening years have seen many other codes springing up in different parts of the world. Some apply to single jurisdictions, such as in Singapore, the UK, and the US, while other codes are intended to apply internationally. IFAC's and ACCA's Codes of Ethics are examples of ethical codes, while the Organisation for Economic Co-operation and Development (OECD) and International Corporate Governance Network (ICGN) both have international codes of corporate governance.

In the Paper P1 *Study Guide*, I have highlighted the fact that whereas a general knowledge of codes is important, line-by-line detail is not required. While the UK codes (such as the Combined Code, first published in 2003) provide a good summary of provisions in corporate governance, other countries and agencies have also produced equivalent guidelines. Students may be required to demonstrate familiarity with a code when answering a question, but it will be acceptable to refer to a local code if more appropriate, or to one of the international codes. ACCA's Code of Ethics applies broadly, and IFAC's Code of Ethics applies to all professional accountants whose professional bodies are members of IFAC (such as ACCA). If students live in a jurisdiction with its own code of ethics (such as the ICPAS code in Singapore), it will be acceptable to refer to that code where appropriate.

Explicit reference is made in the *Study Guide* to Sarbanes–Oxley, which is the legal underpinning of corporate governance in the US. Sarbanes–Oxley is the most influential corporate governance instrument of recent times and has changed practice globally, mainly because of the international dominance of US business.

Exam format

The exam will contain two sections. Section A will contain Question 1, which will be worth a total of 50 marks and which will be compulsory. It will be based on a case study scenario of several hundred words. The requirements will include several distinct tasks (listed as (a), (b), (c), etc) and will sample the syllabus quite broadly. Question 1 might contain elements of governance, risk, internal control, and will include some aspect of ethics.

One of the features of the Professional level exam papers is the awarding of 'professional marks'. These are marks allocated not for the content of an answer, but for the degree of professionalism with which certain parts of the answer are presented. They will usually be awarded in Section A (the compulsory part of the exam paper) and will total 4 to 6 marks.

It may be, for example, that one requirement asks you to present your answer in the form of, say, a letter, a presentation, a memo, a report, briefing notes, or similar. Some marks may be awarded for the form of the answer in addition to the content of the answer. This might be for the structure, content, style and layout, or the logical flow of arguments in your answer. You should assume that if the question asks for a specific format of answer that some marks may be awarded for an effective presentation of that format.

Section B will contain three questions (Questions 2, 3 and 4) and students will be invited to attempt two from the three questions set. Each question in Section B will, accordingly, be worth a total of 25 marks. In contrast to Question 1, it is likely that the questions in Section B will explore one part of the syllabus in a little more depth. Students should not assume, however, that each question in Section 2 will examine only one part of the syllabus. It is more likely that each will contain an emphasis on one part of the syllabus, while including content from other parts as well. All of the three questions in Section B will be based on a short scenario.

The *Pilot Paper*, which is on the ACCA website, is an illustration of the way the future papers will look and feel. In addition to the *Pilot Paper* – which students will want to study in some depth and eventually attempt – additional pilot questions will also be published.

David Campbell is examiner for Paper P1

new ACCA Qualification

intellectual levels

Gareth Owen explains how the design of the new ACCA Qualification can help students learn more effectively.

testing, testing, one, two, three

☑ **For the new ACCA Qualification, all** *Study Guides* **refer to three intellectual levels. These represent the three bands of intellectual or cognitive ability required to study a particular subject or topic area.**

It is recommended best practice in accounting education to give students as much guidance as possible on how much study is required in order to achieve syllabus aims and objectives. Students therefore need to be aware of the depth at which they will be assessed in any given area. This article explains how the system of intellectual levels should be used in relation to the ACCA syllabus, and looks in detail at the *Study Guides*.

WHAT ARE INTELLECTUAL LEVELS?
In the 1950s, educational psychologist Benjamin Bloom identified six main cognitive domains relating to study:
☐ knowledge
☐ comprehension
☐ application
☐ analysis
☐ synthesis
☐ evaluation.

According to Bloom, the level of cognitive difficulty increases from the recall of knowledge to the evaluation of complex ideas and situations resulting in appropriate decisions or recommendations.

Best practice suggests that professional accounting syllabuses should use three (rather than six) broad bands of cognitive difficulty to help students and their teachers gauge how much preparation is needed, and the level of difficulty they may encounter, in meeting various educational capabilities.

ACCA had adopted three ascending levels of cognitive difficulty, where 1 represents knowledge and comprehension, 2 is application and analysis, and 3 is synthesis and evaluation. These cognitive bands consolidate Bloom's six-level taxonomy.

WHAT KINDS OF CAPABILITIES ARE RELATED TO THESE LEVELS?
Level 1
Knowledge and comprehension require demonstration of the following capabilities:
☐ retention and recall of knowledge
☐ understanding of major accounting and business ideas, techniques, and theories
☐ use of knowledge and techniques in new but familiar situations
☐ recognition of fundamental cause and effect in accounting.

Level 2
Application and analysis require demonstration of the following capabilities:
☐ analysis of unfamiliar situations to prepare reports and solve problems using relevant concepts and theories

☐ recognition of subtle or hidden information patterns and trends within financial and other information, and the ability to interpret these
☐ the ability to infer from given information and draw conclusions.

Level 3
Synthesis and evaluation require demonstration of the following capabilities:
☐ creation of new ideas from, or new insights into, existing knowledge
☐ generalisation, comparison, and discrimination using complex and unstructured information
☐ assessment and evaluation of complex information
☐ use of reasoned argument to infer and make judgements
☐ presentation and justification of valid recommendations.

Do the modules of the syllabus correspond to the intellectual levels?
The new ACCA Qualification syllabus is divided into two main levels, each containing two modules: the Fundamentals level contains the Knowledge and Skills modules, and the Professional level contains the Essentials and Options modules. While both modules in the Professional level are broadly assessed at the same cognitive level, the Skills module papers are set at a higher

intellectual level than the Knowledge module papers. This is also reflected in the time allowed for the respective exams within these modules.

While there are three broad levels within the syllabus, these do not always match the cognitive levels described above. Therefore, it is not the case that every capability in the Knowledge module is assessed at Level 1, and that all Professional level capabilities are assessed at Level 3.

How does learning develop throughout the qualification?
As students progress through the qualification,

they both broaden and deepen their capabilities at all stages.

The Knowledge module is predominantly about the breadth and comprehension of knowledge, although there may also be some application or simple analysis. Students would therefore expect to see most capabilities set at Level 1, although in some subject areas there may be a few Level 2 requirements, particularly if the area is not developed further in subsequent papers.

In the Skills module, students should expect to see mostly Level 2 capabilities being assessed, but also to find a number of Level 1 capabilities which will be built on. In some

exceptional cases, some Level 3 capabilities will be identified, particularly in areas which are not being taken further at the Professional level.

This shows that even within the higher level modules there is still a need to acquire and comprehend new knowledge before more difficult capabilities relating to this new knowledge can be assessed.

At the Professional level, students should still expect to find a few Level 1 capabilities, as new knowledge is introduced, and before this knowledge can be applied, analysed, synthesised, and evaluated.

Figure 1 shows, in broad terms, the proportion of capabilities assessed at each

new ACCA Qualification module

intellectual level within each discrete module or modules.

FIGURE 1: APPROXIMATE DISTRIBUTION OF LEVEL 1, 2 AND 3 CAPABILITIES IN THE NEW ACCA QUALIFICATION SYLLABUS

Knowledge module	Skills module	Professional level

☒ Level 1
☒ Level 2
☐ Level 3

Which verbs are associated with which levels?

Bloom and other academics have suggested the types of verbs associated with each cognitive level, and these are listed in **Table 1** below. Some of the verbs Bloom lists are not relevant to a professional accountancy qualification, so only relevant verbs are included.

Please note that certain verbs (such as describe, explain, calculate) and other verbs found within the *Study Guides*, may be designated at different levels. This recognises that these verbs need to reflect the varying intellectual demands these requirements may make on students in different situations. For example, under one subject area, a sub-objective might be '*Explain* the structure of a T account[1]'. Another could be: '*Explain* how a warrant works as a derivative financial instrument[2]'. Not all the verbs listed in **Table 1** will necessarily be used by examiners in their question requirements, nor is this an exhaustive list. The verbs given are merely indicative of the capabilities examiners want students to acquire from the *Study Guide*, in order to meet a range of exam requirements.

The *Study Guide* will often contain more verbs than an examiner would ever use in an exam. This, however, does not mean that students shouldn't develop these capabilities. An example is given below.

In Paper F1, *Accountant in Business* learning outcome A1(b) asks students to describe various organisational structures as follows: 'Describe the different ways in which organisations may be structured: entrepreneurial, functional, matrix, divisional, departmental, by geographical area, and by product.'

However, an objective test question might be written as follows: 'Which of the following forms of organisational structure always requires staff to report to both functional and product managers?
a Divisional
b Departmental
c Matrix (correct answer)
d Entrepreneurial'

To answer the question correctly, the student must understand the nature, scope, and definition of each type of organisational structure. This would have been taught and learned through reading, and possibly writing, an explanation of each. Therefore, although this capability would not need explicit demonstration in the examination, the examiner will assume the successful student has this capability.

Should I refer to the *Study Guide* and to the intellectual levels when using examinable documents?

It is important that students should refer closely to both the *Study Guide* and the designated intellectual level of each capability when looking at examinable documents. This helps in two ways:
☐ If a document such as an accounting standard or a statute is listed, then students can refer to the area in the *Study Guide* relating to the content of that document, to identify the specific areas to be covered.
☐ By noting the intellectual levels and the verbs used, better guidance is given about the breadth and depth of knowledge required for each aspect.

Should I be worried about the inclusion of intellectual levels?

No one should worry about the inclusion of references to intellectual levels within the *Study Guides*. This new feature is intended to help students and tuition providers tailor their learning and determine the depth required to study various aspects of the syllabus.

The inclusion of intellectual levels is not intended to be prescriptive, and examiners have the freedom to assess the syllabus as they decide. However, they will need to refer to the *Study Guide* when setting their exams.

It is hoped that the inclusion of intellectual levels within the *Study Guides* will help examiners and students match each other's expectations more closely when setting and taking ACCA examinations. ▨

Gareth Owen is qualifications development manager at ACCA

TABLE 1: TYPICAL VERBS ASSOCIATED WITH INTELLECTUAL LEVELS

Level 1	List, define, describe, explain, select, calculate, identify, compare
Level 2	Apply, compare, analyse, compute, derive, reconcile, prepare, interpret, value, contrast, relate, classify, solve, implement
Level 3	Formulate, modify, rearrange, create, compose, design, develop, highlight, summarise, assess, evaluate, justify, decide, infer, advise, recommend, discuss, report

Planning your question practice

Planning your question practice

We have already stressed that question practice should be right at the centre of your revision. Whilst you will spend some time looking at your notes and Paper P1 Passcards, you should spend the majority of your revision time practising questions.

We recommend two ways in which you can practise questions.

- Use **BPP's question plan** to work systematically through the syllabus and attempt key and other questions on a section-by-section basis

- **Build your own exams** – attempt questions as a series of practice exams

These ways are suggestions and simply following them is no guarantee of success. You or your college may prefer an alternative but equally valid approach.

BPP's question plan

The BPP plan below requires you to devote a **minimum of 30 hours** to revision of Paper P1. Any time you can spend over and above this should only increase your chances of success.

Step 1   **Review your notes** and the chapter summaries in the Paper P1 **Passcards** for each section of the syllabus.

Step 2   **Answer the key questions** for that section. These questions have boxes round the question number in the table below and you should answer them in full. Even if you are short of time you must attempt these questions if you want to pass the exam. You should complete your answers without referring to our solutions.

Step 3   **Attempt the other questions** in that section. For some questions we have suggested that you prepare **answer plans** rather than full solutions. Planning an answer means that you should spend about 40% of the time allowance for the questions brainstorming the question and drawing up a list of points to be included in the answer.

Step 4   Attempt **Mock exams 1, 2 and 3** under strict exam conditions.

Syllabus section	2007 Passcards chapters	Questions in this Kit	Comments	Done ☑
Governance and responsibility	1 - 3	1	Prepare an answer plan for this question.	☐
		2	Answer in full. This question tests your knowledge of audit committees and your ability to make practical recommendations about remuneration arrangements.	☐
		3	Answer in full. This is a good example of a what's wrong with these corporate governance arrangements and how can they be improved question.	☐
		4	Answer in full. This question covers the issue of stakeholder involvement in organisations, stressed by the examiner as being very important.	☐
		5	Prepare an answer plan for this question.	☐
		6	Answer in full. This question was an extra example question published by the examiner, so should be a very good example of the style of question that he will ask.	☐
Internal control and review	4 - 5	7	Answer in full. This is a wide-ranging question, testing not only your knowledge of different areas of the syllabus, but your ability to make links between them.	☐
		8	Prepare a plan for this question.	☐
		9	Answer in full. This question focuses on important higher-level supervision and monitoring of internal control.	☐
		10	Answer in full. A good test of your knowledge of audit committees.	☐
		11	Answer in full. Most questions covering internal audit are likely to include independence issues; this question offers a good opportunity to discuss those issues.	☐
		12	Jot down the main issues you would discuss in this question.	☐
		13	Answer in full. Another example supplementary question that the examiner has issued.	☐

Syllabus section	2007 Passcards chapters	Questions in this Kit	Comments	Done ☑
Identifying, assessing and controlling risks	6 - 9	14	Answer in full. This question is a good test of your ability to recommend realistic risk management policies for an organisation.	☐
		15	Answer in full. A good question to practise, since it doesn't cover a conventional business. A reminder that not all exam questions will be about companies.	☐
		16	Answer in full. This question covers a wide range of the risks that businesses face.	☐
		17	Jot down some ideas for this question.	☐
		18	Answer in full. Another question involving an organisation that isn't a business and hence requiring more thought about the risks it faces.	☐
		19	Prepare a plan for this question.	☐
Professional values and ethics	10 - 12	20	Prepare an answer plan, seeing if you can generate enough discussion points (about 10-12).	☐
		21	Answer in full. This question covers the important issue of how an organisation determines what goes into a voluntary report.	☐
		22	Answer in full. This question covers a number of important ethical and social responsibility issues.	☐
		23	Answer in full. This is a good question demonstrating how codes of conduct work (or don't work) in practice.	☐
		24	Answer in full. This question covers several important issues and is a good example of how a shorter optional question might range across the syllabus.	☐
		25	Prepare a plan for this question.	☐
		26	Answer in full. A supplementary question issued by the examiner.	☐
		27-29	Answer in full. Answer these wide-ranging case study questions to give yourself practice in tackling lengthy questions.	☐

Build your own exams

Having revised your notes and the BPP Passcards, you can attempt the questions in the Kit as a series of practice exams.

	Practice exams		
	1	2	3
Section A			
1	27	28	29
Section B			
2	2	10	6
3	13	14	9
4	22	26	21

- Whichever practice exams you use, you must attempt **Mock exams 1, 2 and 3** at the end of your revision.

Questions

GOVERNANCE AND RESPONSIBILITY

Questions 1 to 6 cover governance and responsibility, the subject of Part A of the BPP Study Text for Paper P1.

1 Remuneration

45 mins

(a) As a consequence of the corporate governance codes, there is increasing disclosure in the accounts of listed companies of the procedures for determining the remuneration of directors, and the actual remuneration.

The following statements are quoted from recent accounts:

'The (two) non-executive directors constitute the remuneration committee.'

'No member of the committee has a personal financial interest, other than as a shareholder, in the matters to be decided. There are no conflicts of interest arising from cross directorships....'

'The Chairman has a service contract with a notice period of three years. This was originally drawn up in 20X2 and was considered at that time to afford protection for the Group against the loss of the services of a key executive. ....the Board does not intend to seek to vary the terms.'

Required

Analyse the significance for corporate governance of each of the above three statements. **(11 marks)**

(b) Under contractual remuneration arrangements, the Chief Executive of X Group received in 20X6, as disclosed in the annual report and accounts:

	£
Salary	516,000
Bonus	50,000
Employee profit-sharing scheme	8,000
Benefits	21,000

He has a three-year rolling contract. The Group contribution to his pension scheme was £85,000.

The bonus is determined by the remuneration committee, and is non-pensionable. It is based on the committee's assessment of the annual performance of the company and the individual's contribution thereto. The bonus may not exceed 25% of salary. Participation in the employee profit-sharing scheme is limited to £8,000. The benefits relate to the use of a company car and accommodation.

In addition to the above, the contract provides that the Chief Executive can receive, as part of his remuneration package, the following.

(i) A conditional allocation of ordinary shares, which may be approved annually by the Remuneration Committee, based on a percentage of salary not exceeding 50%.

Shares are held by trustees during the measurement period of three years.

Vesting (formal ownership and possession) of the shares is subject to a performance test at the end of the period. The test involves ranking the total shareholder return (TSR) against those of other top 100 companies (FT-SE 100).

(1) An upper quartile ranking will produce 100% vesting, a lower quartile zero.

(2) The calculation of intermediate points is linear.

The shares required are purchased in the market. Conditional allocations are expected to be at 50% of salary (the maximum).

(ii)   Share options may be granted, at the market price at the date of grant. The maximum share options granted in a three-year period cannot exceed four times annual salary.

These cannot be exercised for three years, and can be exercised only if the percentage growth of the TSR of the company equals or exceeds that of the average of the FT-SE 100 companies.

Required

Analyse and explain the motivational effect on the Chief Executive of each element of the remuneration package, and of the total package.   **(14 marks)**

(Total = 25 marks)

2 Nerium Engineering   45 mins

Nerium Engineering is a recently-listed company that has just appointed a new non-executive director to its main board of directors. At the first board meeting that the non-executive director attended, he was asked to become a member of the audit and remuneration committees, and is unsure whether to accept either or both appointments. He has therefore sought your advice.

The audit committee has only just been established and its terms of reference have yet to be finally agreed. The non-executive director is unsure what such a role might involve and, as a qualified engineer without a detailed understanding of finance, he is also unsure as to whether he is the right person for such a committee.

The remuneration committee has by contrast been established for just over two years. The director understands the main role of the remuneration committee but is worried about the responsibilities that he will be taking on. In particular he is concerned about widespread condemnation of 'fat cat' salaries and rewards, and criticisms of situations where senior executives have been forced to resign when their company has performed very badly but have taken a large pay-off when they leave. The non-executive director is worried that in some cases, non-executive directors on remuneration committees have been accused of failing to do their job properly by allowing excessive remuneration packages. He has been pondering the following quote from the UK Combined Code:

'Levels of remuneration should be sufficient to attract, retain and motivate directors of the quality required to run the company successfully, but a company should avoid paying more than is necessary for this purpose. A significant proportion of executive directors' remuneration should be structured so as to link rewards to corporate and individual performance.'

Required

Write a report to the non-executive director that:

(a)   Explains the possible role and responsibilities of the audit committee and the main qualities that a member of such a committee should possess   **(12 marks)**

(b)   Describes the basic principles that should be applied to test the acceptability of a performance measure
                                                                                                  (5 marks)

(c)   Discusses the bases that might be used for measuring the performance of senior executives, with a view to establishing a remuneration system that rewards individuals for achievement   **(8 marks)**

(Total = 25 marks)

3 MegaMart

45 mins

MegaMart plc is a medium sized retailer of fashion goods with some 200 outlets spread throughout the UK. A publicly quoted company on the London Stock Market, it has pursued a growth strategy based on the aggressive acquisition of a number of smaller retail groups. This growth has gone down well with shareholders, but a significant slowdown in retail sales has resulted in falling profits, dividends and, as a consequence, its share price. MegaMart had been the creation of one man, Rex Lord, a high profile entrepreneur, convinced that his unique experience of the retail business gained through a lifetime working in the sector was sufficient to guide the company through its current misfortunes. His dominance of the company was secured through his role as both Chairman and Chief Executive of the company. His control of his board of directors was almost total and his style of management such that his decisions were rarely challenged at board level. He felt no need for any non-executive directors drawn from outside the company to be on the board. Shareholders were already asking questions on his exuberant lifestyle and lavish entertainment, at company expense, which regularly made the headlines in the popular press. Rex's high profile personal life also was regularly exposed to public scrutiny and media attention.

As a result of the downturn in the company's fortunes some of his acquisitions have been looked at more closely and there are, as yet, unsubstantiated claims that MegaMart's share price had been maintained through premature disclosure of proposed acquisitions and evidence of insider trading. Rex had amassed a personal fortune through the acquisitions, share options and above average performance related bonuses, which had on occasion been questioned at the Shareholders' Annual General Meeting. His idiosyncratic and arrogant style of management had been associated with a reluctance to accept criticism from any quarter and to pay little attention to communicating with shareholders.

Recently, there has been concern expressed in the financial press that the auditors appointed by MegaMart, some twenty years ago, were also providing consultancy services on his acquisition strategy and on methods used to finance the deals.

Required

(a)   Analyse the corporate governance issues raised by the management style of Rex Lord.   **(15 marks)**

(b)   Rex Lord has consistently resisted the appointment of independent, non-executive directors to the board of MegaMart plc. Assess the advantages that the company might gain through the appointment of such directors.   **(10 marks)**

(Total = 25 marks)

4 Stakeholders

45 mins

Your 18 year old niece is about to begin a business studies course at university. To help her, you have managed to secure her a guest ticket at a conference that you have helped to organise. In a keynote speech at the conference, a junior government minister referred to the impact stakeholder theory has had and the importance of businesses showing responsibility towards all their stakeholders.

Your niece is confused as she thought that businesses were basically responsible to their owners/shareholders and therefore would seek to maximise profits. She wonders how, if there are interested parties other than shareholders whom the business must respect, what the consequences will be and how a business decides whose interests are most important.

Required

(a)   Explain how methods of classifying stakeholders can illustrate:

   (i)   Their level of involvement with the business

   (ii)   How much the business's activities affects them

   (iii)   How much power and influence they have

   (iv)   How much they participate in the business's activities   **(10 marks)**

(b)   Demonstrate how Mendelow's system provides a means for showing the significance of different stakeholders.   **(5 marks)**

(c)   Assess the views expressed by the government minister on how businesses should respond to stakeholder concerns.   **(10 marks)**

(Total = 25 marks)

5 SPV   45 mins

SPV is listed on the stock exchange of a central European country. The company manufactures a wide range of pharmaceutical products including modern drugs used in preventing and treating cancer, AIDS and similar diseases. SPV has three factories where drugs are produced and one research and development facility.

The board of directors comprises the chairman/CEO, three executive and two non-executive directors (NEDs). Separate audit and remuneration committees are maintained, although the chairman has a seat on both of those committees. The NEDs are appointed for two and usually three 4-year terms of office before being required to resign. The internal auditor currently reports to the board (rather than the financial accountant) on a monthly basis, with internal audit reports normally being actioned by the board.

There have recently been problems with the development of a new research and development facility. On a number of occasions the project has fallen behind schedule and the costs have been much greater than expected. Because of developments that have taken place elsewhere in the pharmaceuticals industry while the project was being completed, concern has been expressed that the facility cannot now represent value for money. A couple of large institutional investors has raised concerns about this, and have indicated their intention to raise the issue at the annual general meeting and possibly vote against the accounts.

Throughout the project one of the non-executive directors criticised the way the project had been approved and monitored. She claimed that the board had been led by the senior managers in the Research and Development department and had acted as no more than a rubber stamp for what they wanted to do. She is threatening to resign at the annual general meeting on the grounds that the board is failing to function effectively and she does not wish to be held responsible for decisions on which she has had no effective input. As a result, the other non-executive director has also raised questions about the way the board is functioning.

Required

(a)   Explain the main responsibilities of the board, identifying the ways in which SPV's board appears to have failed to fulfil its responsibilities.   **(12 marks)**

(b)   Evaluate the structures for corporate governance within SPV, recommending any amendments you consider necessary to those structures.   **(13 marks)**

(Total marks = 25)

6 Sentosa House (Examiner question)   45 mins

Sonia Tan, a fund manager at institutional investor Sentosa House, was reviewing the annual report of one of the major companies in her portfolio. The company, Eastern Products, had recently undergone a number of board changes as a result of a lack of confidence in its management from its major institutional investors of which Sentosa House was one. The problems started two years ago when a new chairman at Eastern Products (Thomas Hoo) started to pursue what the institutional investors regarded as very risky strategies whilst at the same time failing to comply with a stock market requirement on the number of non-executive directors on the board.

Sonia rang Eastern's investor relations department to ask why it still was not in compliance with the requirements relating to non-executive directors. She was told that because Eastern was listed in a principles-based jurisdiction, the requirement was not compulsory. It was simply that Eastern chose not to comply with that particular requirement. When Sonia asked how its board committees could be made up with an insufficient number of non-executive directors, the investor relations manager said he didn't know and that Sonia should contact the chairman directly. She was also told that there was no longer a risk committee because the chairman saw no need for one.

Sonia telephoned Thomas Hoo, the chairman of Eastern Products. She began by reminding him that Sentosa House was one of Eastern's main shareholders and currently owned 13% of the company. She went on to explain that she had concerns over the governance of Eastern Products and that she would like Thomas to explain his non-compliance with some of the stock market's requirements and also why he was pursuing strategies viewed by many investors as very risky. Thomas reminded Sonia that Eastern had outperformed its sector in terms of earnings per share in both years since he had become chairman and that rather than question him, she should trust him to run the company as he saw fit. He thanked Sentosa House for its support and hung up the phone.

Required

(a)   Explain what an 'agency cost' is and discuss the problems that might increase agency costs for Sentosa House in the case of Eastern Products.   **(7 marks)**

(b)   Describe, with reference to the case, the conditions under which it might be appropriate for an institutional investor to intervene in a company whose shares it holds.   **(10 marks)**

(c)   Evaluate the contribution that a risk committee made up of non-executive directors could make to Sonia's confidence in the management of Eastern Products.   **(4 marks)**

(d)   Assess the opinion given to Sonia that because Eastern Products was listed in a principles-based jurisdiction, compliance with the stock market's rules was 'not compulsory'.   **(4 marks)**

(Total = 25 marks)

7 VSYS

45 mins

VSYS Inc manufactures a range of computer products including silicon chips, hard drives and advanced graphic cards from its single factory located in a medium-sized town in central USA. About 20% of the working population are employed at VSYS, and the company has a reputation for being a good employer with specific focus on maintaining and enhancing benefits for its employees. A local university runs courses specifically for potential employees of VSYS.

Although the company is profitable, the recent management accounts show falling margins with the possibility of a loss being made next year; the first in the 25 year history of the company. The main reasons for the falling profits have been identified as increasing competition from manufacturers in the Far East, and ongoing quality control issues with several key manufacturers. A recent feasibility study shows that moving production to a Far Eastern country would enable VSYS to take advantage of lower labour costs and proximity to suppliers of high quality components. The administration and marketing functions would remain at their current location. While a final decision has yet to be made, the Board is aware of the negative impact this could have on the image of the company and are therefore reluctant to make a firm commitment.

Movement of production systems to the Far East is seen as a particular problem for VSYS. Specific areas of concern include:

(i)   Obtaining and maintaining supplies from new suppliers
(ii)   Setting up production lines with new workforce and new machinery
(iii)   Maintaining sufficient inventory of materials to meet demand when the delivery times are uncertain
(iv)   Implementing any necessary revisions to the management accounting systems

However, the Board is confident that the move will be successful and looks forward to a positive response from workers and shareholders.

Required

(a)   (i)   Explain the main principles of corporate governance for listed companies, with specific reference to establishing and maintaining an internal control system and the role of internal audit.

        (ii)   Identify and assess any risks or potential problems with the internal control system in VSYS arising from the decision to outsource operations to the Far East, briefly describing methods of minimising those risks or problems.   **(16 marks)**

(b)   Analyse the extent to which VSYS's plans to outsource to the Far East represent a change in its social responsibility stance and evaluate the consequences of a change in stance.   **(9 marks)**

(Total = 25 marks)

8 Internal audit effectiveness   45 mins

As the newly-appointed finance director of a quoted company, you have just been asked by the chairman to advise him on the effectiveness of the existing internal audit department.

The chairman explained that internal audit has been established in the company for many years. The chief internal auditor, who has held this post for many years, has reported direct to the chairman. He has always had a right of access to the Board, and, since the establishment of an Audit Committee, has worked closely with that committee.

However, there had been increasing friction in recent years between the chief internal auditor and your predecessor as finance director. Internal audit was regarded by your predecessor as expensive, slow, cumbersome, and ineffective.

Required

Write a report to the chairman recommending how the effectiveness of the internal audit department should be assessed.

Your report should deal specifically with the following issues.

(a)   Recommendations of whether you should carry out the assessment yourself, or, if not, who should do so

(8 marks)

(b)   Recommendations of specific objectives for the internal audit department related to the aims of the department. You should explain how performance of the internal audit department against each of its objectives could be evaluated, and provide for each objective an example of a performance measure that could assist in this.   **(17 marks)**

(Total = 25 marks)

9 FAB   45 mins

Mr Parker is chairman and chief executive of FAB, a company which is likely to seek a listing on the local stock exchange within the next two years. The board currently consists of Mr Parker, three long-serving directors, and three directors who have been appointed to the board within the last year. All directors are executive directors.

Mr Parker is aware that the company's corporate governance arrangements may not fulfil the requirements of the local stock exchange. He is also concerned that the purposes of the internal control system are not fully understood by the board, especially the newer members. He has asked you, a business consultant, for advice.

Required

(a)   Identify the weaknesses in the current structure of the board and recommend what action the company should take to remedy these.   **(10 marks)**

(b)   Explain, in the context of an internal control system, the terms *'control environment'* and *'control procedures and policies'*, providing examples of the areas within a business where an internal control system is expected.   **(7 marks)**

(c)   Explain the need to review the effectiveness of the internal control system, making specific reference to the actions of management, the audit committee and the board in the monitoring process.   **(8 marks)**

(Total = 25 marks)

10 Audit committees

45 mins

KPN is a major hotel group that will shortly be seeking a flotation on the stock market. At present the company does not have any non-executive directors or an audit committee. One of KPN's most significant local competitors, NN has recently collapsed; certain of the competitor's shareholders have raised issues about the ineffectiveness of the non-executive directors and in particular the failure of the audit committee to deal with major accounting problems. As this news story is topical, the directors of KPN want to understand why NN's non-executive directors might have failed to exercise sufficient supervision, and how the audit committee that KPN will be required to establish can function effectively.

Required

(a)   (i)   Discuss the limitations of depending on non-executive directors to improve corporate governance.

      (ii)   Recommend how the effectiveness of audit committees can be enhanced.   **(17 marks)**

NN was also criticised for failing to respond adequately to customer complaints. The directors of KPN are therefore considering the introduction of formal arrangements for hearing and dealing with complaints.

Required

(b)   Explain what improvements will be needed in control systems if such formal arrangements were introduced and their impact on the role of the audit committee.   **(8 marks)**

      (Total = 25 marks)

11 Independence of internal audit

45 mins

The directors of GP are considering establishing an internal audit department and have raised a number of questions. One issue most of them are unsure of is how internal audit differs from external audit.

Required

(a)   Identify the principal differences between internal and external (registered) auditors, using the following criteria:

      (i)   Eligibility to act

      (ii)   Security of tenure

      (iii)   Primary objective and the limitations on the scope of the auditor's work in order to achieve this objective.   **(10 marks)**

One of the directors has quoted an article saying that the internal auditor should have independence in terms of organisational status and personal objectivity that permits the proper performance of his duties.

Required

(b)   (i)   Explain what is meant by independence in this context, listing and briefly explaining the freedoms and privileges needed for employees of an organisation to be able to act effectively as internal auditors.

      (ii)   Discuss the alternative organisational structures which can help to achieve this independence of internal audit, and the ways in which an audit committee can contribute to this.   **(11 marks)**

The chairman has raised the issue of how the chief internal auditor should be remunerated. In GP, bonus payments related to annual profits form a significant part of the total remuneration of all senior managers.

Required

(c)   Discuss whether it is appropriate for the chief internal auditor to receive a bonus based on the organisation's profit, or whether it could be seen to compromise his independence.   **(4 marks)**

      (Total = 25 marks)

12 PNY

45 mins

PNY is a book publisher. Each year, it publishes over 10,000 new book titles that range from popular fiction through to specialist guides on 120 different towns worldwide. Over 50,000 titles are stocked in its warehouse awaiting sale to book wholesalers, and recently individual consumers via its Internet site.

Over the last few years, significant amounts of new technology in the form of on-line trading with suppliers and use of the Internet as a selling medium have been implemented into PNY by outside contractors. However, no independent audit of the Internet trading site has been carried out and the site is left to run more as a marketing tool than selling media. There have been relatively few sales from the site since it started operating. No specific reasons have been put forward for lack of sales. A perpetual inventory system has also been in use for the last two years, providing real time information on inventory balances with the aim of reduction of inventory losses due to theft.

Four staff are employed in the internal audit department. The staff have worked in the company for 10 years. Important family and social commitments have meant they do not want to move location and they have little ambition for promotion. The chief internal auditor reports to the Financial Director, who also sets the remuneration levels of internal audit department staff. Training within internal audit is limited to one day's update on audit procedures each year, the lack of staff mobility being given as a reason not to provide detailed training schemes.

Internal audit testing methods focus on substantive testing of transactions, tracing those transactions through the accounting system as far as possible. Where there is a break in the audit trail, where possible, the transaction is located again after the break and testing continues. Testing of inventory takes place at the year end when a full inventory count is carried out in association with the external auditors.

Risk management policies in PNY are under the control of the Financial Director. The policy is written by the Head of Accounts and then agreed by the board. The Head of Accounts also acts as the whistle-blowing nominee to hear reports of potential whistle-blowing from employees. The company has not established an audit committee.

Required

(a)   Explain the contents of a risk management strategy for fraud. **(10 marks)**

(b)   Evaluate the risks inherent in PNY's systems and the internal audit department and recommend how those risks should be overcome. **(15 marks)**

(Total = 25 marks)

13 Franks & Fisher (Examiner question)

45 mins

The board of Franks & Fisher, a large manufacturing company, decided to set up an internal control and audit function. The proposal was to appoint an internal auditor at mid-management level and also to establish a board level internal audit committee made up mainly of non-executive directors.

The initiative to do so was driven by a recent period of rapid growth. The company had taken on many more activities as a result of growth in its product range. The board decided that the increased size and complexity of its operations created the need for greater control over internal activities and that an internal audit function was a good way forward. The need was highlighted by a recent event where internal quality standards were not enforced, resulting in the stoppage of a production line for several hours. The production director angrily described the stoppage as 'entirely avoidable' and the finance director, Jason Kumas, said that the stoppage had been very costly.

Mr Kumas said that there were problems with internal control in a number of areas of the company's operations and that there was a great need for internal audit. He said that as the head of the company's accounting and finance function, the new internal auditor should report to him. The reasons for this, he said, were because as an accountant, he was already familiar with auditing procedure and the fact that he already had information on budgets and other 'control' information that the internal auditor would need.

It was decided that the new internal auditor needed to be a person of some experience and with enough personality not to be intimidated nor diverted by other department heads who might find the internal audits an inconvenience. One debate the board had was whether it would be better to recruit to the position from inside or outside the company. A second argument was over the limits of authority that the internal auditor might be given. It was pointed out that while the board considered the role of internal audit to be very important, it didn't want it to interfere with the activities of other departments to the point where their operational effectiveness was reduced.

Required

(a) Explain, with reference to the case, the factors that are typically considered when deciding to establish internal audit in an organisation. **(10 marks)**

(b) Construct the argument in favour of appointing the new internal auditor from outside the company rather than promoting internally. **(6 marks)**

(c) Critically evaluate Mr Kumas's belief that the internal auditor should report to him as finance director. **(4 marks)**

(d) Define 'objectivity' and describe characteristics that might demonstrate an internal auditor's professional objectivity. **(5 marks)**

(Total = 25 marks)

IDENTIFYING, ASSESSING AND CONTROLLING RISKS

Questions 14 to 19 cover identifying, assessing and controlling risks, the subject of Parts C and D of the BPP Study Text for Paper P1.

14 LinesRUs
45 mins

The LinesRUs Company is responsible for maintaining the railway infrastructure for the rail network in a large European country. Main areas of responsibility for the company include:

- Ensuring that the railway tracks are safe
- Signalling equipment is installed correctly and works properly
- Maintenance of overhead power lines for electric trains

Income is fixed each year dependent on the number of train services being operated and is paid via a central rail authority. The company is granted a sole franchise each year to provide services on the rail network.

Work is scheduled in accordance with the amount of income, and to provide LinesRUs with an acceptable operating profit. Any additional work over and above standard maintenance (e.g. due to foreseen factors such as bridges being damaged by road vehicles and unforeseen factors such as car drivers falling asleep and driving their cars onto railway tracks) is negotiated separately and additional income obtained to repair the infrastructure in these situations.

A lot of maintenance work is relatively simple (e.g. tightening nuts and bolts holding railway tracks together) but is extremely important as an error may result in a train leaving the rails and crashing. The board of LinesRUs is aware of many of these risks and attempts to include them in a risk management policy.

However, recently a train was derailed causing the death of 27 passengers. Initial investigations show that faulty maintenance was the cause of the derailment. One of the unforeseen consequences of the crash has been a fall in the numbers of people using trains with a subsequent fall in income for train operators. LinesRUs are being sued by the train operators for loss of income, and the national press are suggesting LinesRUs must be incompetent and are calling for a re-evaluation of the method of providing maintenance on the rail network.

Required

(a) Discuss the stages of an appropriate risk analysis policy for LinesRUs. **(16 marks)**

(b) Discuss the options available to LinesRUs to deal with the risks arising from the rail crash mentioned above. **(9 marks)**

(Total = 25 marks)

15 Doctors' practice
45 mins

A large doctor's practice, with six partners and two practice nurses, has decided to increase its income by providing day surgery facilities. The existing building would be extended to provide room for the surgical unit and storage facilities for equipment and drugs. The aim is to offer patients the opportunity to have minor surgical procedures conducted by a doctor at their local practice, thus avoiding any unfamiliarity and possible delays to treatment that might result from referral to a hospital. Blood and samples taken during the surgery will be sent away to the local hospital for testing but the patient will get the results from their doctor at the practice. It is anticipated that the introduction of the day surgery facility will increase practice income by approximately 20 per cent.

Required

(a)   Evaluate the additional risks that the doctors' practice may expect to face as a consequence of the introduction of the new facility and explain how a risk management model might be used to understand and control such risks.

(14 marks)

(b)   Explain the meaning of the term 'risk appetite' and discuss who should take responsibility for defining that appetite in the context of the scenario outlined above.

(5 marks)

(c)   Analyse how an internal audit of the practice may contribute to an assessment of its risk management procedures.

(6 marks)

(Total = 25 marks)

16 Question with answer plan: ASG

45 mins

ASG is a UK-based company manufacturing high quality wood based products such as fences, gates, tables and chairs. The company imports wood from Norway and sells its products in the United Kingdom, United States and a number of North African countries. Although the products are relatively bulky to distribute, ASG has built up a well-known brand name over the last few years; its products are now normally regarded as high quality.

Purchases are made from Norwegian companies on the basis of confirming a contract for wood roughly four months before supply is available. This enables forestry managers to monitor demand, matching this with supply to ensure that overall the number of trees cut down does not exceed the capacity of each forest to grow new trees.

Sales in the USA and North African markets are made following the distribution of catalogues in major cities. The catalogue provides prices in local currencies inclusive of postage and packing and is valid for six months. ASG's competitors in France and Germany use the same sales method. Sales in North Africa have been hindered in recent years by growing political unrest caused by the perception that countries have been assisting known terrorists.

Required

Identify and evaluate the risks, financial and other, that may affect ASG, explaining what actions, if any, ASG can take to minimise those risks.

(25 marks)

17 IDAN

45 mins

Company overview

IDAN is a large banking and financial services group that is listed on both the London Stock Exchange and the New York Stock Exchange. The group has over 20 million customers throughout the world and operates in 35 countries on four continents. The IDAN Group is composed of a mix of retail and commercial businesses that include corporate and investment banking, private banking and commercial banking.

Trends within the Financial Services Sector

The Board of Directors of IDAN is aware that a number of trends within the sector will require the bank to substantially re-design a number of its operating and information systems and review the nature of the interface between the internal audit and risk management functions. Current issues that are having an impact on the financial services sector include:

*   A new European Union law requiring banks to provide details of interest paid on personal savings accounts held by non-residents. A withholding tax of 15% is to be imposed on such income and details must be sent by the bank to the tax authorities in the EU country where the recipient resides.

*   Forecast rises in interest rates over the next two years.

*   The elimination within the UK of the use of personal signatures as the authorisation for credit and debit card transactions and their replacement with personal identification (PIN) numbers.

- The increasing use, by personal customers, of both telephone and internet banking services. Over 40% of bill payments, standing order amendments and balance transfers by such customers were processed in this way during the last 12 months compared with 28% the previous year.

- A growth in the number of cases being sent to the financial ombudsman or the financial industry regulator relating to claims of mis-selling or incorrect advice on the part of financial services companies in the supply of a range of savings and investment products.

- As a result of threats of terrorist activity, money laundering legislation has been introduced or tightened in all of the countries in which IDAN has banking operations.

Required

(a)   Explain the main categories of risk that are faced by a bank such as IDAN and discuss the advantages of risk categorisation in the design of a risk management system.   **(10 marks)**

(b)   For every one of the six issues identified in the question, recommend the controls that might be introduced to minimise IDAN's exposure to such risks.   **(15 marks)**

(Total = 25 marks)

18 Cave Trust   45 mins

About 25 years ago, two people visiting a mountain range discovered a large underground cave. The find was considered to be 'exceptional' by the scientific community as the cave was the largest and best preserved example of a 'living cave', that is a cave where specific underground formations such as stalactites were still growing. Years of secret development, involving significant costs that frequently exceeded budget, meant that the cave was only opened for public view last year. The development was funded mainly by the national government of the country the cave was located in and a bank loan. The cave is now maintained as a non-profit making Trust, (The Cave Trust) controlled by a mixture of local people interested in maintaining the cave as well as experienced mountaineers, cave explorers and scientists.

Visitors to the cave now pay a fee of about €40 for access to the cave; the fee includes the services of an experienced tour guide. The fee of €40 was derived by the Trust as appearing to be good value for money for guests, as well as providing some income to pay for the new tour guides etc. Tickets for cave access are sold near the cave entrance, where a restaurant, museum and shop are also located. The restaurant, museum and shop are manned by paid employees, who mostly work part-time. Other income is available from government grants.

Other items of expenditure within the cave include air conditioning and humidity systems to maintain the cave environment, light, heat and power and computer based security systems. Additional expenditure will be required in the next 18 months for extensions to the museum, more space in the restaurant and research areas for school children as well as further development of access to the extensive cave system.

Unfortunately over the last few months, the Trust has suffered a loss of income and adverse press coverage due to embezzlement of monies received in the shop and various thefts in the restaurant. Although the perpetrators were caught, dismissed and successfully prosecuted, the Trustees are concerned that the frauds were not identified earlier because of a poor organisational culture. In particular there appears to be a lack at attention to the controls that should have been operating to prevent these frauds, and a willingness to trust colleagues rather than follow up suspicions.

The national government that provided part of the funding for development of the cave complex has recently indicated that funding will be withdrawn in six months. Unfortunately, the Trust does not have any contingency plan to overcome this loss of income.

Required

(a)   Explain how risks are identified and managed within a company, providing examples from the CAVE Trust where possible.   **(10 marks)**

(b)   Evaluate the risk management strategy for income generated by the Trust, suggesting how the Trustees should amend the strategy following the decision of the government to withdraw funding.   **(5 marks)**

(c)   Explain how the Board of Trustees should analyse the impact of threats to the Trust's reputation.   **(5 marks)**

(d)   Recommend measures that the Trust can implement in order to improve employee culture and reduce the risk of fraud in future.   **(5 marks)**

(Total = 25 marks)

19 Cerberus   45 mins

During the past three years, Cerberus, a large defence contractor in the UK and USA, has been adversely affected by a series of internal control failures. These incidents resulted in major losses being incurred and brought the company to the brink of collapse. Although the threat of company failure now appears to have receded, the shareholders, who have seen their investment in the company decrease dramatically, recently replaced the board of directors. The new board is determined to ensure that the company avoids any such problem in the future and believes that this has to be done by the board demonstrating greater concern about the operation of internal controls and fulfilling relevant corporate governance requirements.

Required

Write a report advising the Board of Directors of Cerberus on:

(a)   The key responsibilities of Board members in relation to ensuring the effectiveness of internal controls

(7 marks)

(b)   The methods used to assess such effectiveness   **(12 marks)**

(c)   The regulations that govern the reporting to the stock market of the results of internal control reviews

(6 marks)

(Total = 25 marks)

PROFESSIONAL VALUES AND ETHICS

Questions 20 to 26 cover professional values and ethics, the subject of Part E of the BPP Study Text for Paper P1.

20 Ethical considerations   45 mins

You were appointed Financial Controller of a firm of builders' merchants almost a year ago, with the prospect of becoming Finance Director if you performed well.

The problem customer

An old-established customer, a contractor, X Ltd, which has expanded to take on a very large contract, is causing problems with delayed payments. X Ltd is a family firm, largely owned by its Managing Director, Y.

Following a discussion at a management meeting, the Sales Director and a member of your staff visited the customer with instructions to 'try and resolve the matter of delayed payments'.

The meeting

At the meeting, the Sales Director took the lead, having known Y for many years. Y provided the last annual accounts and the latest management accounts and contract accounts. This one large contract that X Ltd had undertaken represents some 70% of its current activity.

If all, or almost all, suppliers allow additional credit for material, and X Ltd uses its very limited remaining bank facilities to pay the workforce, Y thinks the company should be able to complete the next stage of the contract, get the architect to certify the work has been completed, and obtain a progress payment. This would enable X Ltd to pay suppliers, get more materials, and finish the contract. However, Y considers the company will make a significant loss on the contract and will only be able to trade on a much reduced scale thereafter.

The Sales Director suggested, and Y agreed, an arrangement by which Y would make a payment from personal funds, against which your company would release materials to X Ltd. When it receives the progress payment X Ltd will pay your company from its company's funds and reduce the amount owing to well within normal terms. Your company will then repay Y the personal funds he has paid.

It was agreed that this arrangement should be discussed and agreed with your Managing Director in the morning.

After the meeting

On his return, the Sales Director commented that this sort of arrangement was probably the only way of getting any money back - if X Ltd went into liquidation nothing would be recovered.

Later you received a telephone message that Z, the Finance Director of another firm of builders' merchants and whom you know through local business group meetings, has asked you to telephone urgently regarding the credit status of X Ltd.

Required

Write a report to your Managing Director, evaluating the options available and recommending the action to be taken on the account and on the telephone message.

(25 marks)

21 Environmental and social issues   45 mins

Z plc is a publicly quoted company. Its products are based on raw materials grown in tropical countries and processed either in these countries or in the eventual sales markets. Processing is undertaken partly by Z plc and partly by sub-contractors. The products are branded and sold worldwide, but mainly in the United Kingdom and North America. They are sold to consumers through a very large number of outlets.

The non-executive directors have for some time expressed concern that the company has not developed any systems of environmental or social reporting to shareholders, although many comparable companies already publish such information as part of their Annual Report. A government minister has now stated that legislation will be considered if all companies do not make progress on reporting on social and environmental policies.

The chief executive has always regarded reporting as ideally never exceeding legal requirements.

As management accountant, you have been asked by the finance director to draft a report to the Board on the potential environmental and social issues on which reporting may be required.

Required

Discuss the reasons for, and the problems involved in, preparing this report, and explain how the following issues will impact upon this report:

(a)   The range of environmental and social issues to cover
(b)   The range of business activity to cover
(c)   The information requirements at board level as well as the information to be published

(25 marks)

22 Edted

45 mins

You are a consultant employed by Edted Plc. The directors have raised a number of concerns connected with corporate social responsibility and requested your guidance. You have been supplied with extracts from the discussion on social responsibility at the last board meeting.

Extracts from board meeting minutes

The chairman commented that he had read that companies were benefiting in terms of image and more sales from 'ethical' consumers if they were perceived as good corporate citizens. He was unclear of the exact meaning of the term corporate citizenship.

The sales director commented that a key element of good corporate citizenship was managing the company's relationship with the natural environment. He therefore regarded it as top priority for the company to introduce an effective environmental management system.

The finance director was more sceptical of the concept of corporate citizenship, claiming that staff co-operation would be necessary if the company was to act as, and be perceived as, a good corporate citizen. She suspected that this would depend on the factors in their background that determined their ethical approaches: 'We ourselves can't teach our employees to be good citizens'.

Required

Prepare a report for the directors that:

(a)   Explains the concept of corporate citizenship and identifies the main elements involved in being a good
       corporate citizen   **(5 marks)**

(b)   Assesses the main issues that Edted will face if it adheres to the European Union's Eco-Management and
       Audit Scheme (EMAS) and explains how requirements would differ if it adopted the ISO 14000 standards
                                                                                              (9 marks)

(c)   Discusses the finance director's viewpoint that Edted can have little influence over its employees' attitudes
       to ethics and how the employees view the board's wish for Edted to be seen as a good corporate citizen
                                                                                             (11 marks)

(Total = 25 marks)

23 Code of conduct

45 mins

The Managing Director of a company which makes and sells defence equipment worldwide has had a most unhappy meeting with his Chairman.

They have both just read a newspaper report of a statement made by a disgruntled ex-employee, after a court case for compensation for his dismissal.

In the statement, the ex-employee stated that the company had been selling equipment in breach of a United Nations embargo, and that such sales have been made on a number of occasions.

The Chairman is concerned because:

(i)   He did not anticipate such unfortunate public criticism of the company

(ii)   He was not aware of such irregular sales

(iii)   He thought all possible had been done, by establishing an audit committee in line with the Combined Code recommendations, to ensure that such problems would never arise

(iv)   He thought the internal audit department should have detected *all* actions contrary to the Company code of conduct and reported them to him immediately.

Required

(a)   Discuss the case for establishing an audit committee and demonstrate how it may contribute to the solution of problems such as those outlined above. **(13 marks)**

(b)   Discuss the extent to which the internal audit department may be involved in ensuring compliance with the Company code of conduct, and recommend the steps that may be required to ensure that decisions taken within a company are ethical. **(12 marks)**

(Total = 25 marks)

24 Drofdarb

45 mins

Drofdarb plc is a British publicly owned company, which competes mainly on the UK market for sporting goods: replica kits, training equipment, leisurewear and sporting accessories such as balls and pads. It has a Board of Directors that comprises the following:

Chairman	Mr S McNamara
Chief Executive	Mr I Harris
Finance Director	Mr C McKenna
Executive Director (Clothing)	Mr D Solomona
Executive Director (Equipment)	Mr J Langley
Non-Executive Director	Mr S Hape
Non-Executive Director	Mr A Lynch

The Chairman, Mr McNamara, is concerned that Drofdarb's previously good reputation as a good "corporate citizen" may have become tarnished after the following:

•   The introduction of a new computer system combining manufacturing, ordering and accounting procedures in the last 12 months

•   Press reports suggesting widespread non-compliance with the corporate governance regulations among FTSE 350 companies, especially in relation to non-executive directors

- Rumours of poor controls within the finance function at Drofdarb leading to allegations of financial irregularities.

The finance function is staffed mostly by ACCA members and students – any claims regarding the quality and integrity of his staff are hotly refuted by the FD Mr McKenna, who feels that the company already does enough to meet the requirements for good internal controls.

Mr McNamara has been assessed as independent in his role as Chairman, leaving a need for a third non-executive director (NED) to make the balance of independent to non-independent board members 50:50. A vacancy is to be advertised in the next month.

Mr McKenna has suggested that instead of repeating the lengthy and expensive recruitment process that preceded the appointment of both Mr Hape and Mr Lynch, the company should consider the appointment of Mr B McDermott. His credentials are as follows:

- Current executive director of Sdeel plc – a competitor of Drofdarb's

- Previously the external auditor of Drofdarb – he resigned his position as senior partner two years ago in favour of a more commercial role

- Mr McDermott was appointed by Sdeel because of his knowledge of the industry and his family's connections with Sdeel's historical owners, who had sold up and bought into Drofdarb some 20 years before – he currently owns a 2% shareholding in Drofdarb as well as "a few shares to balance his portfolio" in Sdeel plc.

Mr McNamara is keen for the board to be seen to be following good corporate governance practices. He is also mindful of the requirements of the Turnbull Committee in ensuring internal controls are sufficient and that no problems exist with trusting staff. Consequently he has contacted the current auditors to advise him on what he should do.

Required

You are the senior partner of the current auditors and have agreed to respond to Mr. McNamara. Draft notes for your discussions with him that aim to:

(a) Describe the fundamental ethical principles that should be present in all finance staff, and what needs to be done in the business to encourage staff to act ethically **(9 marks)**

(b) Explain the main elements of a risk-based approach by the board to internal controls, and discuss the limitations of a risk-based approach **(6 marks)**

(c) Describe the role of a non-executive director and discuss whether Mr B McDermott would be a suitable independent non-executive director of Drofdarb **(10 marks)**

(Total = 25 marks)

25 Purchasing and entertainment   45 mins

(a) Explain how a control system can help to minimise the risk of fraud in purchasing. **(11 marks)**

Some codes of conduct appear to have a double standard. One such is quoted below.

Customer and supplier relations

The company does not seek to gain any advantage through the improper use of business courtesies or other inducements. Good judgement and moderation must be exercised to avoid misinterpretation and adverse effect on the reputation of the company and its employees. Offering, giving, soliciting or receiving any form of bribe is prohibited.

Business courtesies

Gifts, favours and entertainment may be given in the following circumstances.

(i)   If they are consistent with customary business practices.
(ii)   If they are not excessive in value and cannot be construed as a bribe or payoff.
(iii)   If they are not in contravention of applicable law or ethical standards.
(iv)   If they will not embarrass the company or the employee if publicly disclosed.

Gifts, favours, entertainment or other inducements may not be accepted by employees from any person or organisation that does or seeks business with, or is a competitor of, the company, except as common courtesies usually associated with customary business practices. An especially strict standard applies when suppliers are involved. Favours or entertainment, appropriate in our sales programmes may not be appropriate or acceptable from suppliers. It is never acceptable to accept a gift in cash or cash equivalent.

Required

(b)   Discuss the acceptability of the above code of conduct. If you consider it appropriate, recommend any amendments you would wish to see in the code of conduct.   **(14 marks)**

(Total = 25 marks)

26 JH Graphics (Examiner question)   **45 mins**

The board of JH Graphics, a design and artwork company, was debating an agenda item on the possible adoption of a corporate code of ethics. Jenny Harris, the chief executive and majority shareholder, was a leading supporter of the idea. She said that many of the large companies in the industry had adopted codes of ethics and that she thought it would signal the importance that JH Graphics placed on ethics. She also said that she was personally driven by high ethical values and that she wanted to express these through her work and through the company's activities and policies.

Alan Leroy, the creative director, explained that he would support the adoption of the code of ethics as long as it helped to support the company's long-term strategic objectives. He said that he could see no other reason as the company was 'not a charity' and had to maximise shareholder value above all other objectives. In particular, he was keen, as a shareholder himself, to know what the code would cost to draw up and how much it would cost to comply with it over and above existing costs.

Jenny argued that having a code would help to resolve some ethical issues, one of which, she suggested, was a problem the company was having over a particular image it had recently produced for a newspaper advertisement. The image was produced for an advertising client and although the client was pleased, it had offended a particular religious group because of its content and design.

When it was discovered who had produced the 'offending' image, some religious leaders criticised JH Graphics for being insensitive and offensive to their religion. For a brief time, the events were a major news story. As politicians, journalists and others debated the issues in the media, the board of JH Graphics was involved in intense discussions and faced with a dilemma as to whether or not to issue a public apology for the offence caused by the image and to ask the client to withdraw it.

Alan argued that having a code of ethics would not have helped in that situation, as the issue was so complicated. His view was that the company should not apologise for the image and that he didn't care very much that the image offended people. He said it was bringing the company free publicity and that was good for the business. Jenny said that she had sympathy for the viewpoint of the offended religious leaders. Although she disagreed with them, she understood the importance to some people of firmly-held beliefs. The board agreed that as there seemed to be arguments both ways, the decision on how the company should deal with the image should be Jenny's as chief executive.

Required

(a)   Analyse Jenny's and Alan's motivations for adopting the code of ethics using the normative-instrumental forms of stakeholder theory.   **(8 marks)**

(b)   Assess Jenny's decision on the possible apology for the 'offending' image from conventional and pre-conventional moral development perspectives.   **(4 marks)**

(c)   Explain and assess the factors that the board of JH Graphics might consider in deciding how to respond to the controversy over the offending image.   **(10 marks)**

(d)   Comment on the legitimacy of the religious group's claims on JH Graphics's activities.   **(3 marks)**

(Total = 25 marks)

27 CER   90 mins

The Campaign for Economic Relief (CER) is a charity based in a European country. The charity was established 35 years ago by a rich philanthropist business person (Mr Smyth) and is now ranked amongst the 10 largest donors of charitable relief in Europe. Mr Smyth is now retired and at the age of 71 is still actively involved in the running of the charity where he chairs the board and provides daily input into where aid should be directed from the charity. He understands that he may appear to have too much power within CER, and accepts that corporate governance could be clearer. Advice will be obtained on this area in the near future.

Aid is created for projects in countries in Africa, India and Eastern Europe etc. Aid is provided either in terms of goods, like tents and food, seeds and equipment for drilling wells, or financially to be spent in target countries according to the specific requirements of recipients of aid in that country. Like many large international charities, CER derives its income from the following sources:

- Donations (68% of total)– from the general public either directly to CER's head office or via collections made in CER shops (see below) or via house-to-house using donation envelopes collected by volunteers. The amount of donations fluctuates throughout the year (less in winter but increase during the summer) and depending on the number of other charitable events taking place.

- Various fund raising activities (10%)– mainly a chain of shops but also includes sponsorship from events such as the "walk for water" campaign to raise funds for drilling wells in countries suffering from long term drought.

- Legacies (4%) – in wills – CER provides a free will writing service where it is named in the will as a beneficiary

- Tax relief on donations from private individuals (18%) – CER can claim basic rate income tax back from the government in its jurisdiction.

Main areas of expenditure include:

- Salaries (8% of total) – Board & finance department in home country as well as operations costs in donee countries

- Donations for aid packages (70%) (as outlined above). Donations are made on a needs basis where possible although lack of international co-operation between aid agencies can result in duplication of assistance. Distribution of aid is sometimes dependent on political will and can be interrupted by violence either within a country or specifically directed at aid workers.

- Grants for specific purposes (5%) (based on some legacies being given for specific purposes – that is, not general aid projects)

- Buildings and premises costs (10%) (CER runs 450 charity shops with approximately 2 paid (shop managers) and 25 volunteer staff per shop. Volunteers work on average 6 hours per week and are employed by the shop managers based on shop staffing requirements only).

- Advertising (7%)

Published financial information is limited, although CER's auditors are advising that CER follow recent charity reporting guidance issued by the International Federation of Accountants. Information for the board is also limited and produced normally 45 days after the end of each calendar month. Board members attempt to make appropriate decisions with the information available, although some lack of experience in charities and board work (many directors receive a minimal salary being effectively "volunteers") limits their decision making ability.

CER and its auditors have recently faced criticism from a charity watchdog pressure group. The body has used CER as an example to claim that trustees and auditors do not do enough to ensure that charity income is spent effectively and charity aid goes to the right people.

The board of CER believes that the income stream of CER must be placed on a sounder footing – that is becoming less reliant on donations. There is an opportunity to purchase a chain of 205 coffee shops and re-brand these using CER's logo and sell coffee under the "TradeForFree" banner. However, the purchase is outside CER's current financial means and the board are considering approaching the Intercontinental Bank to arrange suitable finance.

Required

(a) (i) Discuss the risks facing the charity in its home country and abroad in its aid work. Categorise those risks by those that affect only the home country, those affecting the overseas countries and those affecting both home and overseas countries.

(ii) Briefly discuss how each risk could be mitigated. **(20 marks)**
(including 2 professional marks)

(b) Explain how CER could start to implement appropriate corporate governance structures as a means of enhancing the status of the charity. **(8 marks)**

(c) Discuss the arguments for an extension of the work auditors carry out in relation to charities such as CER.
(12 marks)
(including 2 professional marks)

(d) Discuss how the InterContinental Bank can obtain assurance that CER will not default on the loan to purchase the coffee shops. **(10 marks)**

(Total = 50 marks)

28 VCF

90 mins

VCF is a small listed company that designs and installs high technology computer numerical control capital equipment used by multinational manufacturing companies. VCF is located in one Pacific country, but almost 90% of its sales are exported. VCF has sales offices in Europe, Asia, the Pacific, Africa, and North and South America and employs about 300 staff around the world.

VCF has annual sales of $200 million but the sales value of each piece of equipment sold is about $3 million so that sales volume is relatively low. Sales are always invoiced in the currency of the country where the equipment is being installed. The time between the order being taken and the final installation is usually several months. However a deposit is taken when the order is placed and progress payments are made by the customer before shipment and upon delivery, with the final payment being made after installation of the equipment.

The company has international patents covering its technology and invests heavily in research and development (R&D about 15% of sale) and marketing costs to develop export markets (about 25% of sales). VCF's manufacturing operations are completely outsourced in its home country and the cost of sales is about 20%. The balance of costs is for installation, servicing and administration, amounting to about 15% of sales. Within each of the cost classifications the major expenses (other than direct costs) are salaries for staff, all of whom are paid well above the industry average, rental of premises in each location and travel costs. Area managers are located in each sales office and have responsibility for achieving sales, installing equipment and maintaining high levels of after-sales service and customer satisfaction.

Although the head office is very small, most of the R&D staff are located in the home country along with purchasing and logistics staff responsible for liaising with the outsource suppliers and a small accounting team that is primarily concerned with monthly management accounts and end of year financial statements.

VCF has a 40% shareholding held by Jack Viktor, an entrepreneur who admits to taking high risks, both personally and in business. The Board of four is effectively controlled by Viktor who is both Chairman and Chief Executive. The three other directors were appointed by Viktor. They are his wife, who has a marketing role in the business, and two non-executive directors, one an occasional consultant to VCF and the other a long-term family friend. Board meetings are held quarterly and are informal affairs, largely led by Viktor's verbal review of sales activity.

Viktor is a dominating individual who exercises a high degree of personal control often by-passing his area managers. Because the company is controlled by him Viktor is not especially concerned with short-term profits but with the long-term. He emphasises two objectives: sales growth to generate increased market share and cash flow; and investment in R&D to ensure the long-term survival of VCF by maintaining patent protection and a technological lead over its competitors.

Viktor is in daily contact with all his offices by telephone. He travels extensively around the world and has an excellent knowledge of VCF's competitors and customers. He uses a limited number of non-financial performance measures, primarily concerned with sales, market share, quality and customer satisfaction. Through his personal contact and his twin objectives, Viktor encourages a culture committed to growth, continual innovation, and high levels of customer satisfaction. This is reinforced by high salary levels, but Viktor readily dismisses those staff not committed to this objectives.

The company has experienced rapid growth over the last 10 years and is very profitable although cash flow is often tight. A high margin is achieved because VCF is able to charge its customers premium prices. The equipment sold by VCF enables faster production and better quality than its competitors can offer.

Viktor has little time for traditional accounting. Product costing is not seen as valuable because the cost of sales is relatively low and most costs incurred by VCF, particularly R&D and export marketing costs, are incurred a long time in advance of sales being made. R&D costs are not capitalised in VCF's balance sheet.

Although budgets are used for expense control and monthly management accounts are produced, they have little relevance to Viktor who recognises the fluctuations in profit caused by the timing of sales of low volume but high value capital equipment. Viktor sees little value in comparing monthly profit figures against budgets because sales are erratic. However Viktor depends heavily on a spreadsheet to manage VCF's cash flow by using sensitivity analysis against his sales and cash flow projects. Cash flow is a major business driver and is controlled tightly using the spreadsheet model.

The major risks facing VCF have been identified by Viktor as:

- Competitor infringement of patents, which VCF always meets by instituting legal actions

- Adverse movements in the exchange rate between the home country and VCF's export markets, which VCF treats as an acceptable risk given that historically, gains and losses have balanced each other out.

- The reduction in demand for the equipment due to economic reasons

- A failure of continued R&D investment to maintain technological leadership; and

- A failure to control costs.

Viktor considers that the last three of these risks are addressed by his policy of outsourcing manufacture and continuous personal contact with staff, customers and competitors.

When VCF became listed, the board appointed an external non-executive director, a senior partner from a local firm of lawyers. However she only served as a non-executive director for a few months before resigning, as she had reservations about the way the board ran the company and the role of Viktor. In particular she objected to Viktor's references to corporate governance codes as 'irrelevant to real-world business'.

Required

(a) Identify and evaluate the existing controls within VCF (including those applied by Viktor). **(14 marks)**

(b) Write a report to the Board of VCF recommending improvements to the company's corporate governance, risk management strategy, and internal controls. **(20 marks)**
(including 4 professional marks)

(c)   Discuss the relevance of the basic ethical concepts underpinning corporate governance to VCF and infer the ethical viewpoint that treats implementation of corporate governance recommendations as the best means of maximising the value of VCF.   **(16 marks)**

(Total = 50 marks)

29 Ronald Co

Ronald Co is based in one country but trades in many different jurisdictions. Its main business is the import of clothes and other textiles from Far Eastern countries for resale, either in its own country or neighbouring jurisdictions. Ronald Co is owned by a parent company listed in the USA. The parent company receives dividends from Ronald but does not provide any financial support. Ronald Co is a material subsidiary of the parent.

In recent years, sales and profits have fallen for Ronald, partly as a result of increased competition in the clothing market and partly as a result of adverse movements in exchange rates. While some of Ronald's competitors have also been affected by this fall, some companies that simply purchased fabric and then made garments in their home country have had less exposure to this problem.

As a result of falling sales, the board of Ronald decided to arrange some medium term loans, using as security Ronald's main warehouse. Ronald's parent company was unwilling to provide support; however, the suggestion that Ronald established a subsidiary to finance the debt was taken seriously by the board of Ronald at the time. An investigation of the feasibility of raising finance, including the preparation of a cash flow forecast, was undertaken by Ronald's auditors, ARC & Co. Additional control systems to manage the debt and monitor cash flows (including recording receipts from customers) to limit overdraft exposure were also designed at the same time by ARC & Co.

However, during the audit of Ronald, ARC & Co identified significant weaknesses in the cash management systems, which indicated cash collections were less than actually indicated by the system; in effect Ronald had understated receivables and overstated cash. The senior audit partner considered this a reason for qualification of the audit report. The Board of Ronald tended to disagree, because in their view the weakness was in control design, not control implementation and use. This weakness had already been reported to the chief financial officer by a junior clerk in the accounts department. The clerk was told to "mind his own business" because the issue was under control. The clerk was subsequently concerned that the directors were attempting to manipulate the financial statements.

Without involving the audit committee, the Board of Ronald threatened to remove the auditors if the financial statements were qualified on this matter. Subsequent discussions also indicated that the Board would also ignore another issue if the report was not qualified. An audit senior in ARC & Co had been entertaining a senior member of the finance department on a regular basis, possibly in an attempt to obtain inside information on any control weaknesses at Ronald. It was later determined that the senior held 5% of the share capital of Ronald's parent company and was attempting to obtain inside information.

Required

(a)   Categorise and evaluate the business risks facing the Ronald Company.   **(12 marks)**
(including 2 professional marks)

(b)   Explain the main provisions of the Sarbanes-Oxley Act that affect Ronald and discuss whether Ronald meets those provisions.   **(14 marks)**

(c)   Explain the ethical conflicts in the provision of audit services to Ronald and discuss how each of those conflicts can be resolved.   **(12 marks)**
(including 2 professional marks)

(d)   Explain the purpose of an internal audit committee and evaluate the extent to which a committee should have resolved the problems outlined in Ronald.   **(12 marks)**

(Total = 50 marks)

Answers

1 Remuneration

Text references. Chapters 1 and 3.

Top tips. The answer to (a) required appreciation of the reasons for the recommendations made by the corporate governance reports. We have quoted from the Combined Code, but it would certainly be acceptable to quote from other reports.

In (b) the kind of complex remuneration package described would be applicable only to a small number of Chief Executives. At first sight you might feel that you need specialised knowledge to deal with the scenario. However if you absorbed the detail, explained the effects of each element of the package in turn, and made a sensible conclusion dealing with the overall effect of the package you would have earned good marks. In particular you needed to identify the separate effects of the share option scheme and the conditional allocation of shares.

Possible traps/things not to do in (b) included generally discussing motivational theories without referring to the specific case details and implying all elements of the package were equally important. You also shouldn't have discussed possible manipulation of profits; this was not required by the question and is improbable over a longer time scale.

Easy marks. If you had good knowledge of relevant corporate governance provisions, you should not have found (a) too difficult, as the question covers various important issues.

(a) **The two non-executive directors constitute the remuneration committee**

Membership of remuneration committee

The recommendations fulfil the requirement in many governance reports that the **remuneration committee** should consist **wholly of non-executive directors**. The main purpose of the committee should be to recommend the remuneration of executive directors. Having the committee staffed by non-executive directors means that executive directors do **not decide their own remuneration**.

Numbers of non-executive directors

Most reports also recommend that the board should include a **significant number of non-executive directors** in order that their views should carry sufficient weight. The UK Combined Code for example recommends that at least half the board should be non-executive directors. It may be that the board of this company is small, and non-executive directors are two out of four, although for a listed company this is unlikely.

Reliance on directors

The Combined Code also identifies the issue of not placing **undue reliance on certain directors**. It is possible that the company will be relying too much on its non-executive directors if there are only two of them, as they will be required to attend board meetings, carry out various duties as full board members and staff various board committees. If they have limited time available because of commitments elsewhere, they may not be able to pay sufficient attention to all their duties. For this reason the **minimum number of non-executive directors** that the Cadbury report recommended was **three**.

Personal financial interests

Independence

The **Combined Code** stresses that a key role of non-executive directors is to bring an independent judgement to the board's decision-making. Hence most or all **non-executive directors should be independent** of the company; this means that apart from their shareholdings and fees as directors, they should have no financial interests. This includes **participation in the company's share option or performance-related pay scheme**, or being a member of the company's pension scheme.

Cross-directorships

The Combined Code also states that **non-executive directors should not have cross-directorships with executive directors**. This means that executive directors of Company A should not be non-executive directors of Company B if non-executive directors of Company A are executive directors of Company B. Cross-directorships could result in agreements to set each others' remuneration at a higher level than what is considered desirable.

Chairman's service contract

Problems of lengthy service contracts

This statement highlights the potential problem a remuneration committee faces when determining the length of a service contract. A **long service contract** may help retain a key member of the management team. However a long notice period means that there are **financial disincentives to remove the director** – the compensation for loss of office is likely to be high. This may in practice mean that a **fundamental shareholder right**, to remove a director, is **undermined**.

Limiting service contracts

The Combined Code recommends that **service contracts** should normally be for **one year**, although a longer period may be acceptable if the director has been appointed from outside, on **initial appointment**. Exceptional circumstances may have existed when the chairman was given his original contract but would not apply long-term, and hence his service contract should now be for a shorter period.

(b) **Salary**

The basic salary of £516,000 is substantial, suggesting that the Chief Executive is one of the small number of highly-paid and highly sought-after directors able to effectively and profitably steer a large public company. Although not directly performance related, his salary can be expected to increase in line with the fortunes of the company. Its size has probably affected his decision to stay with the company.

Bonus

The size of bonus is more under the control of the Chief Executive since it is **related to the performance of the company** (which is, after all, his primary concern). The maximum bonus of 25% of salary is considerable (a possible £129,000 based on last year's salary). There are no specific criteria for its achievement, however. It is based on the Remuneration Committee's *assessment*. This may mean that the level of the bonus is **susceptible to company politics**, which **may reduce its motivational effect**.

Since it is based on annual performance it may **encourage a short-term view**, but that will depend on how the Remuneration Committee carry out their brief.

Employee profit-sharing scheme

Although this is linked to the performance of the company, the £8,000 maximum payment means that it is **insignificant** in comparison to the rest of the package. If the Chief Executive performs adequately this payment is almost certain to be made.

Other benefits, including pension contribution

As with the salary, these are **substantial** (particularly the £85,000 pension contribution). It is unlikely that these are performance related and so will have **limited motivational effect**.

Conditional allocations of shares

At an initial value of 50% of salary, these shares could represent a **significant part** of the package and thus have a **large motivational impact**. Such an incentive is **good from the shareholders' point of view** since not only is it directly related to TSR but the three-year time scale discourages short-term thinking.

An **area of concern for the Chief Executive** may be the **volatility of share values**. If the stock market falls, his shares' value may be diminished even if the company's relative performance is good. Alternatively, the group could perform well in its market sector but if the sector has not performed well in relation to the FT-SE 100, the bonus could be reduced (even to nothing).

Share options

These could also be very **lucrative** and so provide a **strong motivational force**. Their **value is dependent on the state of the stock market**, however, which is **out of the Chief Executive's control**.

From the shareholder point of view, this is a **sensible form of remuneration** for the Chief Executive as the focus is on shareholder return over three years. Whether the target of above average FT-SE 100 performance is fair depends on the company. If it is an average FT-SE company the Chief Executive will consider the target reasonable. Shareholders may consider that an above average performance is needed, however.

A **sliding scale such** as that used with the share allocations would **have a better motivational impact** than an 'all or nothing' target.

Overall effect of the total package

The motivational effect of the package is linked to how easily the Chief Executive can control the internal and external environment of the group and therefore its fortunes.

Both the share schemes are potentially very valuable to the Chief Executive and are **linked to long-term success**. They are therefore an appropriate financial motivator for the group to use since they are directly related to shareholder return.

There is a relatively large fixed element to the package. Although the Chief Executive may not feel the need to increase his earnings beyond this fixed level, his personal ambitions should be considered. **People are usually motivated by success itself** as well as the financial rewards that accompany it.

2 Nerium Engineering

Text references. Chapter 3 on remuneration, Chapter 5 on the role of the audit committee.

Top tips. (a) is a good summary of the role of the audit committee; as well as the review functions, note the importance of the audit committee as a point of contact for staff. To answer the second part of (a) you need to go a bit beyond what the codes say and consider the knowledge that committee members need to have to carry out their scrutiny role effectively.

(b) can largely be answered on the basis of management accounting knowledge, particularly the key points about links with strategy, responsibility accounting and the need for a variety of performance measures.

Note that the answer to (c) has to have more depth than the other parts, because the question verb, discuss, is a higher level verb. Therefore you must ensure that you make some points for or against each measure. The criteria listed in (b) should obviously be used as means of judging each measure.

Easy marks. The main tasks carried out by the audit committee should represent about 8 easy marks in part (a), so revise this area if you struggled with it.

REPORT

To: Non-executive director
From: Accountant
Date: 24 December 20X3
Subject: Audit and remuneration committee

You have written to me for advice about various questions relating to audit and remuneration committees. The views below summarise the main points of corporate governance best practice in a number of regimes.

(a)   (i)   **Role and responsibilities**

Monitoring accounts

One of the main roles of the audit committee is to **monitor the integrity of the financial statements** of the company. This will mean that the audit committee should **review the significant financial reporting issues and judgements** made in connection with the preparation of the financial statements that are prepared by the company. The audit committee should also review the **clarity and completeness of disclosures** in the financial statements. Where the audit committee is not satisfied with any aspect of the financial reporting by the company, this should be reported to the board of directors.

Review of control systems

The audit committee should **review the company's internal financial control system** and, unless addressed by a separate risk committee or by the board itself, **risk management systems**. The audit committee should **assess the scope and effectiveness of the systems** established by management to identify, assess, manage and monitor financial and non financial risks.

Whistleblowing arrangements

The audit committee should **review arrangements** by which staff of the company may, in confidence, raise concerns about possible improprieties in matters of financial reporting, financial control or any other matters. This is commonly known as **whistleblowing**.

Monitoring internal audit

The audit committee also has responsibilities for the **internal audit** function and should monitor and **review the effectiveness of the company's internal audit function**. If there is no internal audit function, the audit committee should consider whether there is a need for one each year and make recommendations to the board.

Maintaining relations with external auditors

In general terms the audit committee is responsible for overseeing the company's **relations with the external auditor**. The audit committee has primary responsibility for making recommendations on the **appointment, reappointment and removal** of the external auditors. The audit committee should assess the **qualification, expertise, resources, effectiveness and independence** of the external auditors annually. The audit committee should approve the **terms of engagement and the remuneration** to be paid to the external auditor in respect of audit services provided. The audit committee should also develop and **recommend to the board the company's policy** in relation to the provision of **non-audit services** by the external auditor. The objective here should be to ensure that the provision of such services does not impair the external auditor's independence or objectivity.

Dealing with concerns

Wherever the audit committee's monitoring and review activities reveal cause for concern or scope for improvement, it should make recommendations to the board of directors on action needed to address the issue or to make improvements.

(ii) **Main qualities that a member of the audit committee should possess**

The main qualities that a member of the audit committee should possess will differ for different types of organisation but I can give you some general guidance. All new audit committee members should be given an **induction programme** and all members should receive **training** on an ongoing basis.

Independence

At least **three members of the committee** should be **independent non-executive directors**. Independence means having no financial or other connection with the company other than receiving directors' fees and possibly owning shares. Independent non-executive directors should not receive performance-related bonuses, or payment by shares or share options for example.

Financial experience

At least **one** member of the audit committee should have significant, recent and relevant **financial experience** for example as an auditor or finance director of a listed company. Ideally this person should have a relevant **professional qualification**.

Financial literacy

In general given the role and responsibilities of the audit committee there is a need for some degree of **financial literacy** amongst the other members of the audit committee. This will vary according to the nature of the company, but experience of corporate financial matters will normally be required.

Overview of business

Individual members of the audit committee should have an **overview of the company's business** and be able to identify the main business and financial dynamics and risks.

(b) **Performance measures**

A performance measure should follow a number of basic principles.

Link with strategy

The measure should be **clearly linked** to the **strategic goals** of the company.

Individual performance

A performance measure for an individual should, as far as possible, **reflect the contribution** of that individual to achieving the performance.

Interests of shareholders

The performance measure should be **identifiable with the interests of shareholders** and the wider stakeholder community.

Flexibility

The measure should **require the minimum of adjustment** to ensure consistency in the light of any strategic and operational changes that occur.

Difficult to distort

The measure should not be able to be manipulated easily, nor should there be **incentive or opportunity** to manipulate it. Possibly manipulation is less likely if the performance measure is one of a number of different **qualitive and quantitative, financial and non-financial measures**, a sort of **balanced scorecard.**

(c) **Types of measure**

Measures for monitoring the performance of a company, and individuals, can be grouped into three categories, market-based measures, earnings-based measures and internal performance measures.

(i) **Market-based measures of performance**

These are based on the **movement in the market price of the company's shares** over a given time period. An advantage of this method of performance measure is that it is **aligned closely** to the **creation of shareholder value**, which is generally assumed to be the prime objective of a company. A widely-used market-based measure is **Total Shareholder Return** (TSR) which is a measure of the return earned by shareholders over a given period, in terms of dividends received and movements in the share price. The return is expressed as a percentage of the share price at the start of the period.

A drawback to market-based measures is that share price movements **fluctuate continually with supply and demand**, and the prices that are used to measure the rise or fall in the share price over a period might not be properly representative of their true market worth. A further limitation of market-based measures is that although they can measure company performance, they **cannot identify which individuals contributed** to the achievement of the return.

(ii) **Earnings-based measures of performance**

These are based on **profit-related measures of performance**, such as EPS, growth in EPS and return on investment. Again these measures are linked to shareholder interests, the key financial objective of maximising profit. They provide a definite indicator of what has happened, and it is easy to view trends.

Although widely used in incentive packages, earnings-based measures have several weaknesses. They are **short-term measures of profit,** and ignore the longer term, ie what an individual has achieved that will affect future results rather than historical results. Accounting profit can be **prone to manipulation**, unlike share price movements and dividend payments. A further criticism is that an earnings-based measure **ignores risk:** if a company increases profits by investing in high-risk projects, profits might go up but shareholder value could fall.

(iii) **Internal performance measures**

These are measures of performance derived from **internal reporting systems**, but that are of significance to shareholders. Internal measures can be both **financial and non-financial**. Financial measures include cash flow return on investment or shareholder value added. Non-financial measures can relate to any key performance objective, such as customer satisfaction (however measured) or the creation of intellectual capital. With the growth in the use of the balanced scorecard approach to setting performance targets, it seems likely that many incentive schemes will be based on internal measures.

The main problems with internal measures include the difficulty of **benchmarking certain performance indicators** against what is achieved in other companies. Other companies may not publish the data required, particularly as regards non-financial measures. In addition when a number of different measures is used, it can be difficult to **assess the relative importance** of each.

3 MegaMart

Text references. Chapters 1-3.

Top tips. The scenario gives a pretty clear account of several very significant failures of corporate governance. It's worth starting your answer by stating the problem in terms of corporate governance theory, that is the agency problem. Not only are there inadequate opportunities for the shareholders to challenge the behaviour of Rex Lord, but the mechanisms that could be used (remuneration arrangements) have been subverted for Rex's benefits.

Careful planning is also necessary; it's possible to say a lot about non-executive directors in (a) and hence leave yourself with nothing to say in (b). The framework suggested in the Higgs report (strategy, scrutiny, risk and people) is a useful one to use as a basis for an answer on the contribution of NEDs.

Easy marks. Rex Lord's transgressions of governance best practice are quite blatant, so you should have no difficulty in securing one or two marks at least for each of the main issues we deal with in our answer.

(a) **MegaMart situation**

Rex Lord has been using MegaMart plc as a vehicle to **pursue his own ends**, thus depriving the shareholders and other stakeholders of their legitimate expectations. There appears to be a serious **agency problem** within the company with the shareholders (the principals) being unable to exercise control over Rex Lord, their agent/manager. Rex has been maximising his personal rewards, and appears also to have been pursuing his own objective of growth (and hence personal glory) rather than profit and share price maximisation.

In order to do this he has contravened several well-established **rules of corporate governance** that are incorporated in, for example, the London Stock Exchange Combined Code.

Leading management roles

There are **two leading management roles:** running the Board and running the company. There should be a clear division of responsibilities so that there is a balance of power and no single person has unfettered powers of decision-making. Rex Lord's clear **exploitation of his power** illustrates why this is a good rule. The board cannot make a Chief Executive truly accountable for management if it is itself led by the Chief Executive. A further reason for splitting the job is that **the two roles of Chairman and Chief Executive** are demanding roles, and it is difficult for the same person to have the time or ability to do both jobs well.

Non-executive directors

Governance reports state that there should be a **strong and independent** body of NEDs with a recognised senior member other than the Chairman. The Combined Code states that at least half the board should be **independent non-executive directors**. This is to ensure that their views carry sufficient weight and that power and information is not concentrated in the hands of one or two individuals. MegaMart does not have the non-executive presence to provide this assurance.

Directors' remuneration

Governance reports acknowledge that remuneration levels should be **enough to attract directors of sufficient calibre**, but companies should not pay more than is necessary. Directors should not be involved in setting their own remuneration. A **remuneration committee**, staffed by independent NEDs, should determine specific remuneration packages. Quite clearly, MegaMart has failed to conform with these requirements as far as Rex Lord's remuneration is concerned, with the result that there appears to have been no adequate scrutiny of his complex and possibly excessive remuneration arrangements.

Communication with shareholders

Rex Lord appears to have failed to abide by the guidance that companies should communicate directly with **institutional shareholders** and use the AGM as a constructive means of communication with **private investors**. The Hermes Principles, for example, state that companies should seek an honest, open and ongoing dialogue with shareholders. They should clearly communicate the plans that they are pursuing and the likely **financial and wider consequences of those plans**.

Auditors

There are two significant threats to the **independence of the auditors** that should be reviewed both by them and by MegaMart's audit committee (which should be made up of NEDs). The first is that having been in post for 20 years, there is a danger that the auditors have become **complacent and even acquiescent** in their relationship with Rex Lord. In any event, governance codes suggest that the partner in charge of the audit should change after a maximum of five years.

The second threat is associated with the provision of services other than audit. There is a risk that the auditors effectively act in a management role, doing things that should be reserved to the directors and managers of the company. The Sarbanes-Oxley legislation prohibits auditors providing **appraisal or valuation services**, or **management functions**.

Compliance with the Stock Exchange Combined Code

As a quoted company, MegaMart should include in its financial statements a narrative report of how it applied the **principles** of the Combined Code and a statement as to whether it complied with its **specific provisions**. We are not told whether or not this was done. There is also a danger that the board may regard disclosure of non-compliance as by itself an acceptable alternative to compliance. Non-compliance is only justified if there are good reasons, and these should be disclosed in the accounts.

(b)   **Position of NEDs**

As discussed above, quoted companies such as MegaMart should have an influential and numerically significant body of NEDs. As already mentioned, these directors should form both the **audit** and **remuneration committees**. All members of the remuneration committee and a majority of the audit committee should be independent NEDs.

Contribution of NEDs

Strategic experience of business

NEDs should bring to their role **wide experience of business** and possibly of organisations in other spheres. This should enable them to give **good strategic advice** to the board as a whole and to individual directors, possibly in a mentoring role. They should also be prepared to challenge the strategic decisions of the executive directors. The recent performance of MegaMart suggests that strategy should have been more robustly discussed than it seems to have been.

Scrutiny

NEDs should **scrutinise the performance of executive management** in meeting goals and objectives. This would be particularly important for MegaMart given recent poor performance linked with the high rewards given to Rex Lord. In their role as members of the audit committee, they should also **scrutinise the performance of the auditors** and question whether there are conflicts of interest.

Risk management

Non-executive directors should satisfy themselves that **financial information** is **accurate** and that financial controls and **systems of risk management** are **robust**. Given MegaMart's acquisition of smaller retail groups, the group's risk management systems should have evolved to meet changing demands, and NEDs would need to monitor whether this was happening.

Ethical problems

NEDs should be alert for the emergence of problems with an **ethical dimension** or issues of **corporate social responsibility**. Independent NEDs, in particular, should be able to act as a kind of **conscience** for the board as a whole. Strong NEDs may have raised questions over issues such as **premature disclosure** of information; NEDs on the audit committee might have taken the responsibility to investigate the insider dealing allegations.

Advice on appointments

NEDs may have a valuable role to play in the **selection and appointment of new board members**. They should be alert for issues such as board succession and bringing in directors with external experience, which appear to have been neglected at MegaMart.

4 Stakeholders

Text references. Chapter 1.

Top tips. Starting (a) with a definition of stakeholders is good technique. The primary/secondary and active/passive methods of classification link in with Mendelow's matrix in (b).

(c) starts with a statement of what appears to be the managers' view and then discusses the criticisms of it. Using clear criteria is designed to counter the problem of management not setting priorities, but this then leads to the complication of how to keep some stakeholders satisfied whilst pursuing the interests of others. It's important also to consider the moral and ethical normative viewpoints (acting towards stakeholders in a certain way because it's morally right rather than it's in a business's best interests). Enlightened self-interest is suggested as possibly the best way of dealing with the conflicting viewpoints and complications.

Easy marks. You must be aware of the different ways of classifying stakeholders in (a), although the usefulness of these methods may have been difficult to discuss. Mendelow's matrix in (b) also represents fundamental knowledge.

(a)   **Definition of stakeholders**

A stakeholder in an organisation is any person or group with an **interest in what the organisation does**.

Internal, connected and external stakeholders

One commonly used way of classifying stakeholders is by their **level of involvement with the business**. **Internal stakeholders** are the insiders, the managers and employees, whose objectives are likely to have a strong and immediate influence on how the business is run. **Connected stakeholders** include **shareholders**, whose prime interest is a return on their investment, **bankers** (interested in the security of any loan they make), **customers** (products and services) and **suppliers** (payment and future business). **External stakeholders** include the government, local authorities, pressure groups, the community at large, professional bodies. They are likely to have quite diverse objectives and have varying abilities to ensure that the company meets them.

This method of classification is useful for analysing what the **objectives of stakeholders** are likely to be and how the stakeholders are **likely to apply pressure**.

Narrow and wide stakeholders

This classification groups stakeholders by how much they are affected by the **activities** of the business. **Narrow stakeholders** are those **most affected** by the organisation's strategy – shareholders, managers, employees, suppliers, dependent customers. **Wide stakeholders** are those **less affected** by the organisation's strategy – government, less dependent customers and the wider community.

This way can help businesses decide which stakeholders are likely to be **most interested** in their activities. In addition, if the stance the government minister is taking is felt to be valid, this method helps businesses decide to which stakeholders' interests it should pay most attention.

Primary and secondary stakeholders

This method classifies stakeholders by **how much power and influence** they could potentially exercise over the business. **Primary stakeholders** are those without whose support (or lack of opposition) the business will have difficulty continuing. These include major customers and suppliers, also the government and regulators. **Secondary stakeholders** are those whose loss of support won't affect continuation, such as members of the local community.

This classification is a good way of emphasising **power** over the business and whose support managers must retain.

Active and passive stakeholders

This method groups stakeholders by **how much they participate in a business's activities and particularly influence decision-making**. **Active stakeholders** include managers and shareholders and also others who seek to exert an influence such as regulators or pressure groups. **Passive stakeholders** are those who do not normally seek to influence strategy such as many shareholders, local communities and government.

This classification is most useful as an indicator of **how much time and effort** directors and managers will need to spend dealing with the interests of stakeholders. It is less effective as an indicator of potential shareholder power and influence. Some passive stakeholders, for example shareholders holding a significant % of shares, may intervene effectively if they feel that there is a fundamental threat to their interests.

(b)   **Use of stakeholder theory**

Stakeholder theory provides a **framework** for mapping the **differing concerns of stakeholders**, focusing on **interest in activities and power held**.

Mendelow classifies stakeholders on a matrix whose axes are **power held and likelihood of showing an interest** in the organisation's activities. These factors will help define the type of relationship the organisation should seek with its stakeholders, and how it should view their concerns. Stakeholders in the bottom right of the matrix are more significant because they combine the highest power and influence.

Level of interest

	Low	High
Low	A	B
High	C	D

Power

(i)   **Key players** are found in segment D: the organisation's strategy must be **acceptable** to them, at least. An example would be a major customer.

(ii)   Stakeholders in segment C must be treated **with care**. While often passive, they are capable of moving to segment D. Large institutional shareholders might fall into segment C.

(iii)   Stakeholders in segment B do not have great ability to influence strategy, but their views can be important in **influencing more powerful stakeholders**, perhaps by lobbying. Community representatives and charities might fall into segment B.

(iv)   **Minimal effort** is expended on segment A.

(c)   **Fundamental stakeholder view**

The **fundamental stakeholder view**, which the government minister may be implying, asserts that a commercial organisation must aim to satisfy all its stakeholders, and that it is the job of management to **balance somehow** the interests of the different stakeholders.

Accountability to shareholders

Many would take issue with this view. Critics such as Milton Friedman have suggested that **managers are employed to serve the owners of the business**, that is shareholders. The main interest of the owners of a business is **long term increase in the value of their wealth**. Managers are accountable to shareholders for that wealth. If managers are argued to have wider social responsibilities towards stakeholders, then they have to act in some ways that are not in the interest of the owners, **their principals**. They will be spending money for purposes other than which they are authorised. They therefore are not acting properly as agents, but making decisions about **social responsibility** that are the responsibility of government.

Accountability to whom

If it is accepted that businesses have responsibilities to stakeholders other than shareholders, there is then the problem of the **limits of accountability** to each group. Ultimately it is argued that managers who are accountable to **everyone are effectively accountable to no one**. Managers have **unfettered power** to determine organisational priorities, and the balance between different stakeholders will be achieved by managerial discretion. The problem with this is that they will favour their own interests, and the organisation's system goals over other ones. The balance might be heavily loaded in their favour.

Criteria to use to determine priorities

Managers thus need to **prioritise rationally the interest of certain stakeholders**. The classification of stakeholders described above provides a method, with managers spending most time on stakeholders whose **interest and power** over the business is greatest. However critics would claim that the narrow and wide stakeholder classification is most significant and businesses need to pay most attention to those whose who are most affected by businesses' activities – their **narrow stakeholders**.

Satisficing

There is also the issue of how much the business needs to satisfice the concerns of certain stakeholders, to do enough to keep them happy even if they are not primarily pursuing their interests. Some of these stakeholders' interests are clearcut and businesses will have to work within the framework of keeping them happy. Businesses will need to **fulfil regulations** to avoid the attention of legal authorities and fulfil lending terms if they are to continue to receive loan finance. Other stakeholders' positions are less clear. Even If it is acknowledged that shareholders are not the only significant stakeholders, **what levels of return** should businesses regard as a minimum to meet the interests of shareholders.

In addition what is the extent to which businesses must operate within a **framework of moral laws**. Some critics emphasise that business managers cannot **avoid their normal moral obligations**, particularly **avoiding harm to others, respecting the autonomy of others, telling the truth and honouring agreements**. Only after fulfilling these can they maximise shareholder wealth and fulfil other stakeholder interests.

Enlightened self-interest

Enlightened self-interest can be seen as the stakeholder argument in weaker form, that **economic success is most easily achieved** by keeping all significant stakeholders happy. **Employees, customers and suppliers** are clearly key stakeholders; without them a business could not exist at all. Keeping stakeholders such as regulatory authorities, pressure groups and the local community happy can be seen as ensuring that **management time** is not diverted into combating them, and hence managers can concentrate on achieving economic success.

5 SPV

Text references. Chapter 3.

Top tips. There are various ways of grouping the responsibilities of the board, so your answer to (a) may not have followed the same structure, although it should have brought out much the same points. You would only have received limited credit if you failed to discuss the weaknesses with SPV's board. Note that (a) includes control system issues as well as corporate governance, since the board is responsible for ensuring control systems are adequate and identifying major weaknesses.

(b) is designed to allow you to identify the weaknesses in the corporate governance of an organisation. The weaknesses are mainly directed around the composition of the board and its major sub-committees.

Easy marks. If you have a good understanding of the corporate governance requirements, there is enough material in the scenario to enable you to score well on (b).

(a)   **Role of board**

Each individual board of directors will take on particular tasks peculiar to their own company and these will be different from company to company. However there are three key tasks that will be addressed by all boards of directors to one degree or another.

Strategic management

The development of the strategy of the company will almost certainly be led by the board of directors. At the very least they will be responsible for **setting the context for the development of strategy**, defining the nature and focus of the operations of the business and determining the mission statement and values of the business.

Strategic development will also consist of **assessing the opportunities and threats** facing the business, **considering, developing and screening the strategic proposals and selecting and implementing appropriate strategies**. Some or all of this more detailed strategic development may be carried out by the board, but also may be delegated to senior management with board supervision.

In the case of SPV the board appears to have had inadequate involvement in the development of strategy. Whilst the board may use advice from expert managers, the board should also have challenged what they provided and carried out its own analysis; possible **threats from rivals** appear to have been inadequately considered.

Control

The board of directors is ultimately responsible for the **monitoring and control** of the activities of the company. They are responsible for the financial records of the company and that the financial statements are drawn up using appropriate accounting policies and show a true and fair view. They are also responsible for the **internal checks and controls in the business** that ensure the financial information is accurate and the assets are safeguarded.

The board will also be responsible for the direction of the company and ensuring that the managers and employees work towards the **strategic objectives** that have been set. This can be done by the use of plans, budgets, quality and performance indicators and benchmarking.

Again what has happened with the projects appear to indicate board failings. It seems that the board failed to spot **inadequacies in the accounting information** that managers were receiving about the new project, and did not ensure that **action was taken by managers to control** the overruns in time and the excessive costs that possibly the accounting information may have identified. The board also seems to failed to identify inadequacies in the information that it was receiving itself.

Shareholder and market relations

The board of directors also has an important role externally to the company. The board are responsible for **raising the profile of the company and promoting the company's interests** in its own and possibly other market places.

The board has an important role in managing its relationships with its shareholders. The board is responsible for **maintaining relationships and dialogue** with the shareholders, in particular the institutional shareholders. As well as the formal dialogue at the annual general meeting many boards of directors have a **variety of informal methods** of keeping shareholders informed of developments and proposals for the company. Methods include informal meetings, company websites, social reports, environmental reports etc.

The institutional shareholders' intention to vote against the accounts is normally seen as a **last resort** measure, if other methods of exercising their influence and communicating their concerns have failed. This indicates that the board has **failed to communicate effectively** with the institutional shareholders.

(b) **Suggestions for corporate governance**

Composition of the board

Corporate governance requirements normally indicate that the board of directors should comprise **equal numbers of executive and non-executive directors**. By having only two non-executive directors, SPV may not be following requirements. SPV needs to appoint at least one more non-executive director to the board.

There is also a **lack of any relevant financial experience** amongst the non-executive directors. Again, corporate governance regulations normally suggest that at least one NED has **financial experience** so they can monitor effectively the financial information that the board is reviewing. Making the new appointee an accountant would also help to fulfil this requirement.

Role of chairman/CEO

Corporate governance regulations normally require that the roles of the **chairman** (the person running the board) and the **CEO** (the person running the company) are split. The reason for this is to ensure that no one person has too much influence over the running of the company. The only exception to this rule is that the roles can be combined for a short period of time where the company faces significant difficulties and giving more power to one person will assist in overcoming those difficulties (eg Marks & Spencer in 2003). As SPV does not appear to have any significant difficulties at present, then the roles of chairman and CEO should be split at the earliest opportunity.

Appointment and nomination committees

The chairman of the board is normally allowed to sit on the audit and remuneration committees to ensure that decisions made are in agreement with the overall objectives. Issues that are not clear with the current structures relate to the **composition of those committees**. Corporate governance requirements indicate **these committees** will **normally comprise NEDs**, including the senior NED. This is to limit the extent of power of the executive directors. SPV needs to ensure that this requirement is being followed.

Service contracts

Service contracts for NEDs normally last for a **maximum of 3 years**, with appointment for a **third term** being classed as **unusual**. The duration of contracts is limited to ensure **payments for early termination of contracts** are **not excessive**. The re-appointment provisions apply to ensure that new NED's are being appointed as directors on a regular basis. NEDs who have been on the board for a few years may become **too familiar with the operations** of the company and therefore not provide the necessary external independent check that they are supposed to do.

Service contracts need to be **limited to 3 years**, with re-appointment for a third term being exceptional rather than the norm.

Internal audit

The internal audit department usually reports to the financial accountant as that person may have a **vested interest** in not taking any action on the reports, especially where reports are critical of the accountant. In that sense, reporting to the board is acceptable.

However, the board as a whole may **not have the time** to **review internal audit reports** and again may be tempted to ignore them if they are critical of the board itself. Corporate governance regulations indicate that the internal audit department **should report to the audit committee** with reports being forwarded to the board. This ensures that the report is heard by the NEDs, who can then ensure that internal audit recommendations are implemented where appropriate, by the board.

In SPV, the internal auditor needs to report to the audit committee, for reasons already mentioned above.

6 Sentosa House

Text references. Chapters 1, 2 and 8.

Top tips. In (a) the key elements that incur agency costs are means of obtaining information and controls established over the agent.

In (b) you need to think about threats to value and the various problems associated with a cavalier attitude towards control – including risks to your own reputation for being associated with it.

(c) sees the risk committee as having a similar monitoring remit to the audit committee, and hence needing to be composed of non-executive directors. This is not necessarily the case under many corporate governance regimes, and companies may have more flexibility in the role they give to risk committees and staffing risk committees with executive directors. However you have to focus here on the circumstances described in the question.

(d) represents a core point in relation to principles-based regimes. It illustrates the significance of listing rules and investor reaction. Remember also that a principles based-regime implies companies comply or explain why not – and stating that the company hasn't complied because compliance isn't compulsory is never an adequate explanation.

Easy marks. All question parts appear to be of roughly equal difficulty, and this may be a common feature on this paper.

ACCA examiner's answer. The examiner's answer to this question is included at the back of this kit.

Marking scheme

			Marks
(a)	2 marks for definition of agency costs	2	
	1 mark for each problem identified and briefly discussed	5	
			7
(b)	1 mark for each relevant point identified and briefly described on conditions for intervention	7	
	1 mark for each relevant point made on Eastern Products	3	
			10
(c)	1 mark for each relevant point made		4
(d)	1 mark for each relevant point made		4
			25

(a) **Definition of agency costs**

Agency costs arise from the need of **principals** (here shareholders) to monitor the activities of agents (here the board, particularly the chairman). This means that principals need to **find out what the agent is doing**, which may be difficult because they may not have as much information about what is going on as the agent does. Principals also need to **introduce mechanisms to control the agent** over and above normal analysis. Both finding out and introducing mechanisms will incur costs that can be viewed in terms of money spent, resources consumed or time taken.

Problems with agency costs in Eastern Products

Attitudes to risk

The first reason for increased agency costs is that the company's attitude to risk is a major area of concern on which Sentosa requires more information, since the **risk appetite** appears significantly greater than what would normally be expected in this sector.

Unwillingness of chairman to be monitored

Agency problems will certainly increase because Thomas Hoo is **unwilling to supply any information about the reasons for his policies**, certainly indicating arrogance and also a **lack of willingness to accept accountability**. This means that Sentosa will have to find out from other sources, for example any non-executive directors who are on the board. Alternatively they may contact other investors and take steps to put more pressure on Thomas Hoo, for example by threatening to requisition an extraordinary general meeting.

Inadequacy of existing mechanisms

Existing mechanisms for communicating concerns appear to be **inadequate**. There are **insufficient non-executive directors** on the board to exert pressure on Thomas Hoo. There is **no risk management committee** to monitor risks. The investor relations department is **insufficiently informed and unhelpful**. Thomas Hoo has abruptly dismissed the one-off phone call. Because of the seriousness of the concerns, ideally there should be **regular meetings** between Thomas Hoo and the major shareholders, **requiring preparation** from both parties.

Combining shareholder concerns

Thomas Hoo may be able to ignore shareholder concerns, because of the **shareholding patterns**. Although institutional shareholders are concerned, those who want to take action may not together hold a sufficiently large shareholding to enforce their views.

(b) **Active intervention**

Active intervention by an institutional shareholder by making an attempt, for example, to change the board is regarded as a serious step, and may result in a **significant increase in agency costs**. However there are a number of reasons why it might happen.

Threats to value of shareholding

Institutional shareholders may intervene if they perceive that management's policies could lead to a fall in the value of the company and hence the **value of their shares**. There could be concerns over strategic decisions over products, markets or investments or over **operational performance**. Although they can in theory sell their shares, in practice it may be difficult to offload a significant shareholding without its value falling. Here although Eastern Products is currently making high returns, Sentosa may judge that the **risk of a major strategy** going wrong is **too high**.

Lack of confidence in management integrity

Institutional investors may intervene because they feel management cannot be trusted. At worst they may fear **management fraud**; this could be a worry in this scenario given that Thomas Hoo has done away with a key component of the control system (the risk committee) without good reason.

Failure to control management

Institutional investors may take steps if they feel that there is **insufficient influence** being **exercised by non-executive directors** over executive management. The disappearance of the risk committee is also a symptom of this problem.

Lack of control systems

Intervention would be justified if there were **serious concerns about control systems**. Thomas Hoo's actions may indicate a fundamental flaw in control arrangements with management able to bypass whatever systems are in place.

Failure to address shareholder concerns

Even if there is no question of dishonesty, there may be intervention if institutional investors feel that management is **failing to address their legitimate viewpoints**. Thomas Hoo is solely focused on returns whilst **failing to address the issue of risk**.

Failure to comply with stock market requirements

Eastern Products' failure to comply with corporate governance concerns appear to be quite blatant. The institutional investors may be concerned that they will **suffer criticism** if they are perceived as conniving in these breaches because they have not taken action. It may also **threaten the value of their shareholding** if the stock market turns against Eastern Products.

Pressure from their own investors

Institutional investors' own investors may exert pressure on them **not to invest in high-risk companies**, or **companies with a poor ethical reputation**.

(c) **Importance of risk committees**

Risk committees are considered to be **good practice in most worldwide governance regimes**, particularly in situations like this where there are doubts about the attitudes of executive management. A risk committee staffed by non-executive directors can provide an **independent viewpoint** on Eastern Products' overall response to risk; a significant presence of non-executive directors, as required by governance guidelines, would be able to **challenge Thomas's attitudes**.

Determining overall exposure to risk

The first contribution the committee can make is to pressure the board to determine what constitutes **acceptable levels of risk**, bearing in mind the likelihood of the risks materialising and Eastern Products' ability to reduce the **incidence and impact** on the business.

Monitoring overall exposure to risk

Once the board has **defined acceptable risk levels**, the committee should monitor whether Eastern Products is remaining within those levels, and whether **earnings are sufficient** given the levels of risks that are being borne.

Reviewing reports on key risks

There should be a regular system of reports the risk management committee covering areas known to be of **high risk**, also **one-off reports** covering conditions and events likely to arise in the near future. This should facilitate the monitoring of risk.

Monitoring the effectiveness of the risk management systems

The committee should **monitor the effectiveness of the risk management systems**, focusing particularly on **executive management attitudes towards risk** and the **overall control environment and culture**. A risk management committee can judge whether there is an emphasis on effective management or whether **insufficient attention** is being **given to risk management** due to the pursuit of high returns.

(d) **Significance of principles**

In a principles-based jurisdiction, corporate governance is underpinned by certain basic ethical concepts such as **integrity and accountability**. These should be applied willingly and clearly are not designed as an excuse for non-compliance.

Principles and requirements

In most principles-based jurisdictions, the general guidance is often combined with specific stock market requirements as here with the **number of non-executive directors**. Companies have to comply with requirements if they are to continue to enjoy a stock market listing.

Comply or explain

Other, less specific, requirements are based on what would normally be regarded as **best practice** and thus investors would expect companies to comply with them. If companies don't, they should supply good and clear reasons for non-compliance. This Eastern Products has failed to do.

Investor reaction

Even if reasons are supplied, investors can challenge them. Ultimately, if not satisfied, they **can put pressure on Eastern Products'** share price by selling their shares.

7 VSYS

Text references. Chapters 2, 4 and 5.

Top tips. (a) (i) is mainly theory based, although you will need to read carefully the requirement to ensure that the correct sections of corporate governance are discussed in the answer. Mention can be made of the Turnbull report or similar country specific guidance, although this is not essential to obtain a pass.

Having defined what an internal control system should do in (i), you may have a better idea of the points that can be made in (a) (ii) of the answer. For example, recognising that the board should be making decisions to overcome operational risks in the company may help identify the problem of not taking an appropriate decision from the company's benefit concerning movement of production to the Far East.

The obvious points to make in (b) are that the decision to take jobs overseas appears to indicate a change in attitude towards employee stakeholders and a change in ethical stance. However the point that some see acting in economic self-interest as ethical is also an important one to make even if you don't agree with it. In addition this is a good example of a business decision that affects a number of different stakeholders, some for better, some for worse. How to decide between them? One way is to consider the consequences to the company of stakeholder responses (an instrumental position).

Easy marks. The discussion on corporate governance in (a)(i) doesn't need to be tied into VSYS's circumstances; you should score most of the marks available for this part.

(a) (i) **Aim of corporate governance**

Corporate governance **refers to the way in which companies are governed** with the overall aim of implementing practices and procedures to ensure that a company is run in accordance with its objectives. The overriding principle of governance relates to the **split between ownership and**

control of a company. The **shareholders own a company** as they purchase shares and as a result of this risk of investment, share in the rewards of ownership, that is dividends received. However, the **directors are in charge of and run the company on a day-to-day basis**. As the directors are effectively **agents** of the shareholders, they must ensure that the company is run for the shareholders' benefit; corporate governance provides a control and reporting function to show that the shareholders' interests are being met.

There may be other interests that the board of directors must also take account of in running the company such as employees.

Internal control system

Part of their **overall duty of running the company** will also result in the directors **setting up an internal control system** to help ensure that transactions are recorded and the assets of the company are protected. The main elements of an internal control system were summarised in the UK by the Turnbull report, with other countries having similar guidance.

The internal control system should:

(1) **Facilitate the effective and efficient operation of a company**, by enabling it to respond to specific risks that may hinder it from achieving the company's objectives. The risks faced may be operational, financial or compliance, for example, with the objectives relating to minimising loss of assets or ensuring that liabilities are understood and managed.

(2) **Ensure the quality of internal (management) and external reporting**.

(3) **Ensure compliance with laws and regulations** and also with the company's internal policies regarding the overall conduct of the business.

However, while a sound system of internal control does not provide complete assurance that situations above will not occur, it does help to ensure that the likelihood of their occurrence is minimised.

Internal audit

One of the key features of an internal control system is the establishment and maintenance of an internal audit department; in fact this is normally a stock exchange requirement for larger listed companies. Internal audit is normally defined as 'an **independent appraisal activity** established within an organisation as a service to it. It is a control which functions by examining and evaluating the adequacy and effectiveness of other controls'. The internal audit department therefore assists other members of the organisation in discharging their responsibilities, from the board in reviewing the internal control system to more junior managers in monitoring systems.

Internal audit will therefore **review the internal control system** over the management and financial accounting systems to identify potential and actual weaknesses. Reports will be made to management on these weaknesses with recommendations for amendment to systems.

(ii) **Potential problems with the internal control systems in VSYS**

Lack of appropriate action

It appears that the board of VSYS have noted the problem of retaining productive capacity in the USA and at least one possible action of moving that capacity to a Far East country. However, it is not clear whether **the board appreciates the seriousness of the situation** or whether any other options, such as cutting the cost base in the USA, have been evaluated. What is clear is that some action is needed to **ensure that the company remains in existence**. Failing to take action may result in the board **failing in their fiduciary duty** to the shareholders causing loss of their investment and future earning stream.

Possible lack of appropriate management experience

The lack of board action leads to another possible internal control weakness; possible lack of appropriate managerial talent and control at board level. The **internal control system should ensure the overall quality of management**. Lack of decision on relocating to the Far East could be caused simply by lack of **managerial ability** or **will** to take that difficult decision. Internal audit may need to report in confidence to the audit committee on this matter and recommend that directors with appropriate decision-making ability are appointed.

Possible non-compliance with laws – USA

The possible reduction in the workforce in the USA will mean that many employees **will be entitled to some redundancy pay**. There is the possibility of breach of employment law, whether deliberate or not, in processing and payment of pay. Internal audit will need to review any redundancy calculations on a test basis to ensure that employment law has been complied with.

Possible non-compliance with laws – Far East

Establishing a factory in the Far East will mean that VSYS will have to **comply with the laws and regulations of a foreign country**. The directors must ensure that the law in the country is understood, possibly by hiring local solicitors. Otherwise, there is a risk that VSYS will break a law inadvertently leading to poor publicity and, at the extreme, closure of the new factory.

Overall risks from new systems

Setting up a new factory in the Far East will also mean **establishing new management and financial accounting systems** in that country. Risks inherent in establishing those systems may be minimised by **exporting the systems currently** being **used in the USA**. However, it is unlikely that no modifications will be necessary, as new systems will be necessary to meet the specific situation in the new location. New systems always provide a risk of failure or incorrect reporting due to lack of adequate testing or implementation problems. Internal audit will need to review the systems in detail to try to minimise the errors that occur.

Communication risks – Far East to USA

Establishing a **new production location** will mean that **regular management and other reports** will be sent between **two geographically diverse locations**. This new communication system will run risks such as **communications being lost or intercepted** en route. The board will need to ensure that **appropriate encryption systems** are introduced across the communication system to minimise these risks. Renting time on a virtual private network will help to decrease communication risk where a dedicated link is too expensive to maintain.

Board control

Geographical distance from the USA to the Far East may **limit the board's ability to maintain appropriate control of the new production location**. The risk is that the new factory may manufacture the computer components correctly, but meeting its own constraints regarding mix of components produced or timescales for production. To maintain adequate control, a director may have to be appointed to be in residence at the new factory to ensure both locations are attempting to meet the objectives of VSYS.

(b) **Change in social responsibility viewpoint**

VSYS appears to be considering changing its viewpoint in response to economic pressures. Previously it looks as if it was treating its employees in a **normative** way, providing benefits because it was the right thing to do. The switch to the Far East would appear to taking an **instrumental approach,** using the opportunity to employ workers at lower wages as a chance to increase its own profits. It appears to be narrowing its focus from taking a wider **ethical/philanthropic** view of its responsibilities to taking an **economic/legal line**.

However there are a number of complicating factors.

Pristine capitalist

Those holding the pristine capitalist, economic liberal view would argue that taking the profit-maximising decision will lead to the **best social consequences** as well. The view is that taking the decision on grounds of economic self-interest and improved efficiency will promote **maximum economic growth** and hence **maximum social welfare.**

Differing stakeholder interests

There is also the issue of how to judge between the **conflicting claims of different stakeholders.** Undoubtedly **current employees** are significant stakeholders and they will lose out. In addition the community around VSYS is heavily dependent on the company for employment. Decreasing the number of employees will also **decrease the amount of disposable income** in the town. Knock-on effects could include **closure of suppliers and retail businesses** used by the local population.

However **customers'** viewpoints are also important, and they presumably would welcome the improved quality that a move to the Far East would mean. However if they consider themselves to be ethical consumers they may also be concerned with the loss of American employment. **Suppliers** currently located in the Far East would welcome the increased business and improved relationship that a move would bring.

Providing Far Eastern employment

The decision to take employment away from America to the Far East could also be justified on the ethical grounds of **providing increased employment opportunities** in the Far East. Although the wages paid may not be as high as in America, VSYS could **justify its position** by claiming that it is paying higher wages and also providing better benefits and opportunities than other companies operating in the area.

Consequences of change in stance

Legal issues

It can probably be assumed that VSYS will **fulfil all its legal responsibilities** so that there will be no legal issues arising from the move in production.

Employee redundancy – morale

However moving production to another country would have a **significant negative impact** on the morale, both of production staff prior to relocation of the facility, and the administration and marketing staff left in the company. Remaining staff would tend to **fear for their own jobs**, while staff being made redundant would normally have **lower productivity**, and could provide **additional quality control problems**. Some form of incentive in the form of enhanced working conditions or reassurance for remaining staff would help alleviate the negative impact of the move.

Bad publicity – nationwide when many jobs being outsourced

Given that VSYS has a reputation for being a good employer and appears to produce high quality products, moving production with the associated loss of jobs could result in **adverse publicity** for the company. Possible actions against the company could include **boycott** of the company's products by consumers and possible **picketing** of the company to disrupt supplies. There may be little VSYS can do to retain confidence, although some form of publicity marketing exercise focusing on the number of jobs remaining in the USA could be carried out.

Inability to return to the USA

Given the significance of the move, VSYS may find it very difficult to return to the USA. **Skills** would be **lost** in its local town (the university course is almost certain to close as demand for workers falls) and employees would relocate to find other jobs.

8 Internal audit effectiveness

Text references. Chapter 5.

Top tips. (a) brings in the issue of independence, which is likely to be a feature of most questions on internal audit, given the stress on independence in the syllabus. The question takes a different angle to the issue of who internal audit **reports to,** although the issue of internal audit-finance director relations is still very relevant.

(b) may appear to cover issues that you encountered in 2.6 or F8. However evaluation of the effectiveness of internal control systems is an important requirement. You may well have to consider the role of internal audit when a question scenario presents you with internal control systems that you have to assess.

One problem is measuring internal audit's work in terms of it being a prevent control or detect control. Clearly internal audit is at least partly a deterrent, designed to prevent carelessness or fraud. But how much can the absence of fraud be used to judge internal audit (does the apparent absence of fraud mean that internal audit have failed to detect it?). Performance may be easier to measure in other areas, where internal audit recommendations can be assessed in terms of whether recommended improvements in value for money or behaviour have been implemented.

Easy marks. Based on your previous experience of auditing, you may have found the first section, dealing with accounting controls, to be the easiest part. However note the majority of (b) deals with other areas of the control systems, and effective internal audit often needs to be an integral part of those systems.

REPORT

To: Chairman
From: Finance Director
Date: 1 December 20X7
Subject: Effectiveness of the Internal Audit Department (IAD)

Internal audit is an **independent appraisal function** established by the management of an organisation for the **review** of the **internal control system** as a service to the organisation. It objectively examines, evaluates and reports on the adequacy of internal control as a contribution to the **proper, economic, efficient** and **effective use of resources.**

It is an internal control therefore and, like all internal controls, it should be assessed for effectiveness. This appears to be a suitable time for such an investigation.

(a)   **Who should carry out the assessment?**

        Need for independence of reviewer

        The IAD must **maintain** its **independence** from those parts of the organisation which it audits (ie most of the operations of the business). This independence must be maintained when the IAD is itself the subject of the audit for the sake of future IAD audits, and to obtain an objective result in this case. This criteria would exclude me as Finance Director.

        Use of audit committee

        Other members of the board might be appropriate investigators, but the prime candidate would be a member of the **Audit Committee** (AC) as the IAD acts as almost an executive arm of the committee. A member of the AC with appropriate knowledge and experience would be required.

        Another company's internal audit department

        Alternatives to the AC that we might consider include the **IAD** of **another company**, which might be approached through contacts of our executive directors. **Confidentiality** might be an issue here; we would need to make sure that the other company was not a competitor etc.

External auditors

Another option would be to use our own **external auditors**. If they were happy with our IAD, then future co-operation between the two sets of auditors might produce a saving in the external audit fee. However, if they were unhappy with the work of our IAD, then the external auditors may decide that they need to perform extra audit work in future, and **fees might** then **rise.**

Conclusion

I do not feel it is appropriate for me to decide who should carry out the investigation of IAD: this is a decision that should be made by the **board.**

(b)   **Objectives and performance measurement of internal audit**

(i)   **Accounting controls**

Objectives

The main objectives are to obtain evidence of whether the business has **appropriate controls** in place that are operating effectively, and to **recommend improvements in control** that may be required. Internal audit's work would cover reviewing the design of internal control systems, detailed testing of controls and recommendation of improvements.

Performance measures

Specific performance measures would depend on the reports made by internal audit. A satisfactory report in a particular area could be measured against the **problems** that arise in that area. Thus for example a satisfactory report on controls over the security of inventory could be measured against the level of inventory loss.

If internal audit recommend improvements in an area, evaluating these recommendations is more difficult. Internal audit's recommendations may make no apparent difference to the problems occurring in a particular accounting area. However their work may act to **prevent more serious problems**, in which case an appropriate measure of success would be the **non-occurrence of fraud.** In addition internal audit's recommendations may not be implemented. This may be due to other failings in the organisation's system or **shortcomings** in the **reports** given by internal audit, something considered below.

(ii)   **Non-financial controls**

Objectives

Again the objectives will be checking whether **appropriate controls** are in place that are **operating effectively**, in areas such as responses to customers. However what is appropriate is likely to be determined by management. The audit committee may require that internal audit **concentrate** on **certain important controls** within an area rather than reviewing the whole range of controls. In particular auditors will wish to see that control systems have changed in accordance with **changes in important variables**, for example changes in the requirements of customers.

Performance measures

It is also likely that internal audit's role will be **more proactive** than for accounting controls; recommendations will be expected for improvements to be made in the matters reviewed.

(iii)   **Compliance with laws and regulations**

Objectives

The objectives here are similar to those for work on accounting controls, except that internal audit is seeking to **prevent non-compliance** with relevant laws and regulations. These laws and regulations may also demand that certain **specific controls** must be **operating effectively**, and so internal audit must check those controls are working.

Performance measures

The performance measures would be whether **breaches** that were not identified by internal audit have **occurred,** and the consequences of those breaches; payments of fines or penalties or time spent dealing with communications with regulatory authorities.

(iv)   **Internal practices**

Objectives

The areas of internal practices that internal audit may seek to consider include policies for **compliance with codes of best practice** such as the corporate governance reports. They also include **general business practices** such as planning, internal communication and staff problems.

Performance measures

Performance of internal audits will be judged by the activity being reviewed. Compliance with codes of best practice may be **reported** on by **external auditors** or **commented** on by **shareholders** or the **media,** and avoidance of adverse comments from these sources will be a measure of success. The results of review of staff policies can be measured by the rate of **staff turnover** or the number of staff grievances. Internal audit's comments on **planning** could be judged by the **quality of plans** produced, and improvements in adherence to those plans.

Improvements in information systems

Internal audit's recommendations in this area relate very strongly to the general aims described above, of making sure that management are furnished with the **information necessary** to do their job effectively.

Important measures are **management reaction** to recommendations made and whether the improvements **change management behaviour** (for example management modify plans because the information system identifies the probability of an overspend on budget). Recommendations for improvements in information systems should also lead to **improvements** in the **quality and timing of external reporting.**

Utilisation of resources

A major part of internal audit's activities may well be a review of **value for money,** the economic, efficient and effective use of resources.

Performance measures should focus on **recommendations** on **each of the elements** of value for money, whether costs have been reduced, better use made of available resources and the desired results achieved. Excessive emphasis by internal audit on cost control for example may mean that costs fall, but sales fall as well because of reduced levels of customer service.

Internal audit reports

The quality of internal audit reports has obvious relevance to all the other objectives, since it will influence the response to recommendations. Criteria that would be used to judge reports include the **speed of issue**, whether **presentation** is clear, whether **sufficient prominence** is given to the **most important points** in the report, and whether **recommendations** are **specific** and **practical**.

In addition internal audit's role will assume enhanced importance if, as well as issuing reports, internal audit is allowed to follow up its reports by **seeking and obtaining action** by operational departments on recommendations included in the reports. Over time there should be a **reduction** in the **number of reports**, as improvements are implemented and weaknesses are corrected.

9 FAB

Text references. Chapters 3 and 4.

Top tips. In (a) the best way to structure an answer to questions like this is to focus firstly on a narrow solution (separation of the roles of chair and chief executive), then widen the scope to consider the functioning of the board as a whole and the role of NEDs, and then to consider the relevance of general relevant corporate governance measures such as disclosure.

(b) clearly requires definitions of the concepts mentioned, so these need to be provided in the answer. In the UK, the Turnbull guidance provides specific areas for internal controls; however thinking of the company, the management and the external environment provides some guidance to the areas where controls are required.

(c) provides the overall framework for the answer with the four key areas being mentioned. These areas therefore need to be stated clearly in the answer. Additional detail from relevant guidance such as Turnbull could again be provided.

Easy marks. Generally a very reasonable question, with not much difference in terms of difficulty between each part.

Report to the Board of FAB

To: Board members
From: Management accountant
Date: 23 July 20X0
Subject: Internal control systems

(a) **Separation of roles**

The main recommendation of most reports is that the roles of chair and chief executive should be held by **two different people**. This is to avoid any one individual having unfettered powers of decision; the chair would also take the lead in reviewing and if necessary replacing the chief executive. However the effectiveness of the split may be limited if the chair is a '**company person**', someone who has been linked maybe as a director to the company for a long time.

Lead director

If the two roles are combined, some governance reports recommend the need for a **recognised lead director representing an independent element on the board**. However the effectiveness of this individual may be limited by not having the means of control that a chairman has.

Board

Most reports also suggest that the board as a whole acting effectively **is a necessary control**. This means that no one group of directors should **dominate decision-making** since that group may have the same interests as the chair or chief executive.

To safeguard against domination by a small group, **effective nomination procedures** for the board are required. Most reports recommend companies establish a **nomination committee**, staffed by independent non-executive directors, to control director recruitment. The committee should look to **recruit directors with sufficient calibre** and credibility. In addition the board must also ensure that it operates well **by holding regular meetings** and **systematically considering the organisation's controls and risks**.

Non-executive directors

A further counter to the excessive power of the chief executive is the existence of a strong group of non-executive directors (NEDs). The reports aim to ensure that NEDs are **well represented numerically** by requiring that at least a third or half of the board are NEDs, and that the majority of NEDs should be **independent**, having no connection with the company other than their fees and shareholdings.

Independent non-executive directors

Independent NEDs are an important presence not just on the main board, but also staff key **board committees**, particularly the remuneration and audit committees. They thus play a key role in major decisions of interest to the shareholders, such as director remuneration, and also provide a contact point for external auditors, concerned shareholders or employees who wish to raise issues of malpractice.

Disclosure

The reports require that departures from the codes are disclosed and the reasons given specified. A failure to split the role of chair and chief executive would require disclosure, and then arguably it is up to shareholders to **voice their disquiet** if they do not agree with this. However as the company will be seeking a listing shortly, it may lessen the appeal of the company's shares if it is seen to be flouting the corporate governance guidelines.

(b) **Control environment**

The overall **control environment** within a company provides the **framework within which the detailed internal control system within a company operates**. It includes the **overall corporate culture** and **attitude of directors and employees** to internal control. A positive attitude to controls indicates that the internal control system is likely to be effective.

Control procedures and policies

The actual **control procedures and policies** within an organisation provide the **actual internal controls being used**. The control system will therefore help to ensure the orderly and efficient running of the business. The corporate governance systems in individual countries provide examples of the areas where internal controls are expected. In the UK, the Turnbull report identifies three specific areas for internal controls.

(i) **Business operations**

Specific internal controls to maintain business operations relate to:

- Safeguarding the assets of the business
- Preventing and detecting fraud and error
- Ensuring the completeness and accuracy of the accounting records
- Ensuring the timely preparation of reliable financial information

(ii) **Management**

Controls are required to ensure the **quality** of **internal management and external reporting**. The board is charged with ensuring that management of appropriate quality is available to ensure that appropriate and correct decisions are made in the organisation. Similarly, systems and controls must be in place to ensure the financial statements, interim accounts etc. are produced on time.

(iii) **Compliance with laws and regulations**

Controls are required to ensure **compliance with the different laws and regulations affecting the business**, as well as the **company's internal policies and procedures** concerning the conduct of the business. Appropriate external monitoring will be necessary to detect changes in legislation, and ensure that the company complies with those changes.

(c) **Reviewing internal control systems**

Overview of review

Reviewing the effectiveness of internal control is one of the **primary responsibilities of the directors of a company**. The actual authority to conduct the review may be delegated to the **audit committee**; however, the board will still be responsible for the statements on internal control in the company's annual report and accounts. It is generally expected that the review of internal control will be carried out annually.

The actual control system in a company consists of many different control, communication and monitoring procedures, so it is impossible for any one committee or board to conduct detailed investigations. However, some review is appropriate and will normally include the following features.

Management responsibility

Apart from internal audit, the **main source of monitoring will be reports from management**. UK guidance from the Turnbull report, for example, notes that reports from the management to the board should provide a **balanced assessment** of the **significant risks** and the **effectiveness of the control system** in managing those risks. As managers are the agents of the board, this assessment should provide an honest opinion of the internal control systems and make recommendations for detailed amendments where necessary.

Audit committee responsibility

An essential part of reviewing internal controls is the **ongoing monitoring of the control systems**. Regular reports will be expected on the **department's operation of controls**, possibly from the Internal Audit department, or from other internal and external monitoring. These will be provided to the audit committee for their consideration. Summaries of these reports will then be forwarded to the board to assist in their overall monitoring function.

Board responsibility

The board is ultimately responsible for the ongoing monitoring of internal controls. It must therefore be confident in its own ability to carry out this task and ability to make a decision on the **effectiveness of internal control**. Reports from other sources including the internal and external auditors will be required where additional assurance is required.

10 Audit committees

Text references. Chapter 5.

Top tips. Although (a) requires you to apply your knowledge of the corporate governance codes, it does not require a general discussion of corporate governance principles. Your answer to (a) instead needed to focus on general areas of control within an organisation.

In (b) you would have gained marks for discussing focusing on the needs of customers and obtaining feedback from customers. Your answer also needed to discuss how the audit committee members could be involved, by reviewing the reliability of measurement of customer feedback and in their role as directors advising on strategic issues.

Our answer also discusses how the operation of audit committees may have to change as a result of expansion of its responsibilities. It may be valuable for the audit committee to be given extra responsibilities, but the audit committee should, under the corporate governance codes, be staffed by non-executive directors with limited time.

Easy marks. If you had good knowledge of the work of audit committees, the second part of (a) should have been straightforward.

(a)   (i)   The effectiveness of non-executive directors may be limited by the following factors.

Having the same perspective as executive directors

The corporate governance reports stress the importance of non-executive directors possessing independent judgement and being appointed by a nomination committee. However the nomination committee may restrict its search to **directors** who will 'fit in' with the rest of the board, and may be **unwilling to recruit** from a **diversity of backgrounds,** for example stakeholders such as employees.

In addition many non-executive directors will only agree to serve on the boards of companies if they admire the company's chairman or its way of operating.

Lack of independence

In many companies non-executive directors have been appointed through business or social contacts with directors. It may be difficult to find **non-executive directors** who **fulfil the independence requirements** of the corporate governance reports or freedom from any relationship that compromises independence.

Lack of business knowledge

This can be the other side to the problem of lack of independence. Potential non-executive directors who have good knowledge of the business and industry may have gained that knowledge through links with the company in the past.

Lack of human resource management

Limited time may mean that non-executive directors do not have proper **induction** into the company, nor **proper updating and refreshment** of their skills and knowledge of the company. Their **performance may not be appraised** regularly; it should form part of an **annual appraisal** of the **board's activities**.

Limited time

The most knowledgeable and effective non-executive directors are likely to have other significant demands on their time. As directors they have to fulfil **certain legal requirements.** Apart from their contributions to the main board, they will also probably spend time at **meetings of board committees** such as the audit and remuneration committees. The limited involvement resulting from the lack of time may limit their ability to contribute to board meetings since they are **unable to obtain** a **broad enough picture** of what is happening throughout the organisation.

Information available

Non-executive directors' contribution will also depend on the information that is readily available to them as directors. This will be influenced by the quality of the **organisation's information systems**, and also the **willingness** of **executive directors** to supply information about their activities.

Role of board

The corporate governance reports stress the importance of non-executive directors being involved in **strategic decisions.** If non-executive directors are involved in formulating strategy, they can fulfil what Sir John Harvey-Jones sees as their key role, of **warning of potential problems** and hence **preventing trouble**. However board meetings may focus almost entirely on **current operational matters** and **short-term operational results**. In addition a focus at board meetings on short-term results may mean that non-executive directors **assess** the **performance** of the organisation using short-term indicators and its management, and do not focus on **longer-term issues** such as changes in product mix or re-engineering of the organisation's processes.

Inability to resist pressures

Non-executive directors have limited options when faced with a **united group** of **executive directors** who are determined to push through a policy with which the non-executive directors disagree. Their ultimate weapon is **resignation**, but if all or a number of non-executive directors resign, they may precipitate a **crisis of confidence** in the company. Alternatively they can **remain in office,** but then if serious problems arise, the executive directors may have to depart from the board, leaving the non-executive directors with the responsibility for **'picking up the pieces'**.

(ii) The effectiveness of audit committees could be improved in the following ways.

Appointment requirements

Appointments could be **recommended** by the **annual general meeting**. Alternatively certain stakeholders, for example employees could have the right to appoint a member. These measures might improve the independence of committee members. The **term of office** of committee members could also be **limited** to ensure the committee retained a fresh perspective.

When nominating potential members, the selection process could be biased towards **recruiting members** with **financial accounting experience** or **experience of large control systems**. Members who have accountancy experience will be able to question the judgements management make when preparing accountancy information.

Expansion of responsibilities

There are various ways in which the committee's remit might be expanded. They could have responsibility for **reviewing compliance** with **laws and regulations** such as environmental legislation or ethical codes. Certain **transactions** could also be **referred automatically** to them for review.

Internal audit

As a major function of many audit committees is to oversee the role of internal audit, it follows that a **more effective internal audit function** will lead to more effective operation of the audit committee by improving the quality of information that the audit committee review.

Statutory backing

Audit committees may become more effective if their establishment by certain organisations is made **compulsory.** The recommendations of internal audit will also be **reinforced by stricter accounting and auditing standards.**

Improvement in operations

Changes that might improve the way audit committees operate include the following.

(1) Having **clear terms of reference** agreed by the board

(2) Establishment of an **annual plan** giving details of the areas on which the committee will focus

(3) Establishment of **standards** for the **frequency** of, and **form of reporting** to, the main board

(4) Regular **review** of the **effectiveness** of the audit committee including whether its recent work has been correctly focused.

(b) **Dealing with complaints**

One aspect of control systems improvement will be **dealing with complaints** from customers. However the control systems cannot just concentrate on dealing with complaints as even resolved complaints may lead to regulatory action, and poor experiences may influence the subsequent purchasing decisions of customers.

Customer feedback

Controls must also be implemented to obtain **customer feedback** on an ongoing basis. These may enable management to obtain a more representative view of customer reaction; those who complain may not be typical, and the regulatory body may take into account overall customer reaction. A variety of methods will be necessary as individual means may be unrepresentative (because for example only a small minority return customer service questionnaires).

Customer charter

The results of complaints and surveys must influence the controls that **prevent problems**. An enhanced regulatory regime means that this type of control is likely to be more important. A **customer charter** should be introduced. Other prevention controls may have to be better directed than they have previously; **training** may have to be focused more on staff in direct contact with the customer, and address specifically the issues that can cause problems with customers.

Change in audit committee role

Audit committees may have to spend more time on **reviewing compliance** with the **regulations** set down by the regulatory bodies, and also on compliance with the organisation's own customer charter. In their role as supervisors of internal audit, the committee should **check** that **internal audit** adequately **consider** the **procedures** designed to **prevent problems** and to **obtain evidence** of **customer views**.

Because audit committees are reviewing these matters, they may be able to **anticipate future developments** such as increased regulation or changes in customer demands. This intelligence will affect the discussions on strategy of the main board.

Membership of audit committees

If audit committees responsibilities are to increase in this way, there will be certain implications for the way they operate. Their **membership** is likely to be **expanded,** with the addition of members with the necessary knowledge of customer requirements and industry regulations. Audit committees may no longer be able to consider all matters as one body, and may split into **sub-committees** with one concentrating on financial controls and another on responses to industry pressure.

11 Independence of internal audit

Text references. Chapter 5.

Top tips. You needed to understand the **uncertainties** surrounding internal audit. In theory anyone can act as an internal auditor and internal auditors have no statutory security of tenure. Importantly also internal auditors' work may stretch significantly beyond the areas of accounting records and controls in which the external auditors are primarily interested.

(b)-(c) discuss the practical aspects of independence and you should be able to describe the meaning of the term in that context. A good way to approach (b)(i) is to think of the ways in which operational departments can have contact with or influence internal audit. (b)(ii) brings out the important links between internal audit and the audit committee. The threat to independence is fundamental in (c).

Easy marks. Internal-external audit differences are basic knowledge for this area so (a) should have been straightforward.

(a) (i) **Eligibility to act**

Under the law in most countries, a person is generally **ineligible** to act as **external** auditor if he is an **officer** or **employee** of the company, a **partner** or **employee** of such a person or a **partnership** in which such a person is a partner. An internal auditor is an employee of the company. External auditors must usually also belong to a **recognised supervisory body**, and this means they must hold an appropriate qualification, follow technical standards and maintain competence.

By contrast **anyone** can act as an **internal** auditor even if they do not have a formal accounting qualification. It is up to the company's **management** who they appoint.

(ii) **Security of tenure**

External auditors are **appointed** to hold office until the conclusion of the **next general meeting**. They can be **dismissed** by an **ordinary resolution** of **shareholders with special notice** in general meeting, and have the right to make **representations**. External auditors **cannot** be **dismissed** by **individual directors** or by a vote of the **board**. The only influence directors can have on the removal of external auditors is through their votes as shareholders. The rules on security of tenure are there because of the need for external auditors to protect the interests of shareholders by reporting on directors' stewardship of the business.

By contrast, as **internal** auditors are employees of the company, they can be dismissed by the directors or lower level of **management**, subject only to their normal employment rights. The company may have **corporate governance** measures in place to improve the security of internal auditors (discussed further below).

(iii) **Primary objective and limitation on the scope of the audit work**

The primary objective of **external** auditors is laid down by statute, to report on whether the company's accounts **show a true and fair view of the state of the company's affairs** at the period-end, and of its **profit or loss** for the period. External auditors are also required to report if certain other criteria have not been met, for example the company **fails** to **keep proper accounting records** or fails to make **proper disclosure** of **transactions** with directors. **Statutory rules** mean that management **cannot limit** the **scope of external auditors' work**. External auditors have the right of access to all a company's books and records, and can demand all the information and explanations they deem necessary.

Internal auditors' objectives are **whatever** the company's **management decide** they should be. Some of the objectives may be similar to those of external audit, for example to confirm the quality of accounting systems. Other objectives might be in areas which have little or no significance to the external auditor, for example recommending improvements in economy, efficiency and effectiveness. As the objectives of **internal** audit's work are decided by management, **management** can also decide to **place limitations** on the scope of that work.

(b) (i) **Access and situation**

An internal auditor cannot have the same amount of independence as an external auditor. However, internal audit can be given various **powers and access** to senior managers which allow independent comment, in a free and professional manner, about the internal control of the business (or any matter under investigation). In particular, the following points will ensure a satisfactory level of independence within the organisation.

(1) Internal auditors should **not act** in any **operational capacity**, particularly at managerial level. They should be concerned *only* with the functioning and management of the internal audit department.

(2) The internal audit department should **not** be **controlled** by any **operational managers.** It should be **controlled directly** by the **board** of directors or **audit committee**.

(3) **No area** of records, personnel or assets should be **closed** to the internal auditor. Any such restrictions would invalidate internal audit's full power of investigation.

(4) **Recruitment, training** and other personnel matters within the internal audit department should be **dealt** with only by the **Chief Internal Auditor,** not by outside managers or the board.

(ii) There are two structures in which the internal audit department may operate.

(1) **Reporting to the board**

Even though not a voting board member, the internal auditor will report directly to the full board. This is far superior to reporting directly to line management or to the finance director or managing director, as it does not allow an individual manager or director to suppress or neglect an internal audit report.

(2) **Reporting to the audit committee**

The audit committee will consist mainly or entirely of non-executive directors, and thus internal audit will maintain the independence of his or her report.

This method is advantageous as it brings together people with great expertise in such control matters who have the **time** to **discuss** them without bias and outside any operating considerations. The committee will also be able to **advise internal audit** on procedures and further action and, because of its seniority, be able to persuade the board to **take action** on any matters raised by internal audit.

A further advantage of an audit committee is that it can act as a **forum** for **communication** between the various parties involved in financial control. The Cadbury report recommended that audit committees should be attended by the finance director, the head of internal audit and a representative of the external auditors.

(c) **Independence**

In external auditing it is considered to be a **compromise** of **independence** to accept presents, discounts, bonuses or commissions from audit clients. In many ways this will also apply to the chief internal auditor, as an 'officer' of the board.

Reward

Conversely, the chief internal auditor is an employee of the company, which pays a salary to him or her already. As part of the internal control function, helping to **keep down costs** and **increase profitability**, surely the chief internal auditor should have a reward for adding to the profit of the business.

Conclusion

The problem remains that, if the chief internal auditor receives a bonus based on results, he or she may be tempted to allow **certain actions, practices or transactions** which should be stopped, but which are increasing the profit of the business, and therefore the bonus. The chief internal auditor's remuneration should not therefore be related to the company's profits; instead any bonus should be related to the performance of the internal audit department.

12 PNY

Text references. Chapters 5 and 8.

Top tips. In answering (a), you need to identify the three key elements of an anti-fraud strategy. These are:

- Fraud prevention
- Identifying fraud
- Responding to fraud

You will need to provide 2 or 3 good points on each part of the strategy to obtain a good pass standard.

For (b) it is critical to review the information being provided in the scenario to identify risks in internal audit and the processes in the company. The scenario does provide plenty of clues, so identify these and then be sure to finish the point with recommendations for changes within the internal audit department.

Easy marks. The fraud discussion in (a) is fairly general, and the elements should hopefully be familiar.

(a) A **risk management strategy** for fraud will contain three elements:

- Fraud prevention
- Identifying fraud, and
- Responding to fraud

Fraud prevention

The fact that a risk management strategy for fraud is in place within an organisation will itself act as a **deterrent against fraud**. Fraud is less likely to be attempted if the potential perpetrators of that fraud know they are more likely to be caught.

Key methods of preventing fraud

(i) **Having an anti-fraud culture in the organisation**

This means that all **staff are encouraged to treat each other and external parties** such as customers and suppliers **with respect** and that reasons for decisions are transparent. The policy will be enforced partly by **contracts of employment** that will indicate actions that employees must take, eg ensuring security of client data, and partly by the **overall culture**. The latter point could be directors providing an example to staff in their dealings with customers.

(ii) **Risk awareness**

There should be **awareness amongst staff that fraud could be taking place**, which will be reinforced by **appropriate training programmes** within the entity. In some situations, such as anti-money laundering regulations, annual refresher training on money laundering is necessary simply to maintain awareness of this issue. Where fraud has been identified, appropriate publicity could be given to this, again to maintain awareness of the issue.

(iii) **Whistle blowing**

This relates to **disclosing information on possible frauds** by people not involved in that fraud and where the fraud does not appear to have been identified and acted on by normal channels such as internal audit. **Maintaining an anti-fraud culture** may help whistle-blowers come forward with information, although fear of reprisals by management including inappropriate dismissal may limit the number of disclosures. The Public Interest Disclosure Act of 1999 may provide some benefit to whistle-blowers in the United Kingdom, although dismissals by the government itself in recent years (eg in the context of immigration fraud) indicate that the Act may not be fully effective.

(iv) **Internal control systems**

Appropriate internal control systems will also help to prevent and detect fraud. The **use of controls** such as **segregation of duties** and **authorisation** controls ensure that fraud can only take place by collusion between staff. This will help to minimise the incidence of fraud.

Identifying fraud

As noted above, good internal control systems will assist in preventing and detecting fraud. Fraud identification normally results from the **work of internal audit** and internal investigation, rather than the **work of external auditors**. External auditors in their engagement letter recommend that their work cannot be relied upon to detect fraud.

Specific tasks of internal audit which will help to detect fraud include:

(i) **Performing regular checks** to ensure that assets are accounted for – eg inventory counts and cash counts.

(ii) **Monitoring key ratios** and other accounting indicators and transactions for unusual or unexplained movements eg receivable days increasing, payments made to an overseas subsidiary without justification.

(iii) **Receiving information from whistle-blowers**. The audit committee or the chief internal auditor is normally nominated as the person to receive whistle blowing reports from employees.

Responding to fraud

Where fraud is suspected, then an **appropriate investigation** should be carried out into those suspicions. Actions to be taken will depend on the outcome of the investigation, but could include internal disciplinary and/or legal proceedings.

(b) **Inherent risks and internal audit**

Independence of audit reports

There is **no audit committee** in PNY – **so all internal audit reports are directed to the financial accountant**. This procedure raises **two specific risks** regarding the contents of internal audit reports:

(i) Firstly, as the Finance Director is directly responsible for employing the internal auditors, the internal auditors may feel **uncomfortable** about writing reports that are critical of the financial accountant. There is the possibility, real or not, that an adverse report could adversely affect promotion or remuneration prospects of the internal auditors.

(ii) Secondly, there is **no guarantee** that the Finance Director will **take action** on the reports. Again, the Finance Director may have a **vested interest** not to make amendments to the control systems and could block or amend any report prior to it being presented to the board.

These problems could be avoided by **establishing an audit committee** or, if this is not feasible within PNY, **by sending internal audit reports to another board director**, possibly the Chief Executive Officer to maintain a division between the person employing internal auditors and the person reviewing their reports.

Ability and independence of staff in internal audit

The internal audit department employs four staff. As noted in the scenario same staff have been working in the department for the last 10 years as they value the stability of the job and due to family and social commitments have no desire to move or seek promotion to move demanding roles. This implies two risks with the work of the internal audit department:

(i) Staff may **not have kept-up-date** with the latest technology and therefore be unable to perform audits sufficiently well to test the newer systems in PNY. This comment is borne out by the lack of training within internal audit.

(ii) The internal audit staff may **no longer** be **sufficiently independent** of PNY or its staff to be able to produce a completely objective report. Internal audit may be too familiar with some systems to notice mistakes, and certainly too friendly with staff in PNY to want to criticise them too much in internal audit reports.

These problems could be avoided by **introducing new staff** into the internal audit department and possibly by providing internal audit staff with **secondments** into other areas of the company (eg the management accounting department) to ensure that they have an appropriate break from internal audit.

Weaknesses in audit testing

The process of testing in the internal audit department focuses on **substantive testing of transactions**. While this does provide **appropriate evidence** that transactions are being recorded correctly in the books and records of PNY, there are other concerns.

The accounting systems in PNY have been **upgraded** in recent years, while internal audit staff have received only limited training. This indicates a risk that internal audit staff may **not have the skills or abilities** to **audit the new online systems in PNY**. The fact that audit trails are lost and may not be located again tends to confirm this view.

Audit testing in the department needs to be upgraded to include **computer assisted audit techniques** to ensure that the new computer systems are audited appropriately. This may mean **employing new staff** in internal audit, **training existing staff** and certainly **purchasing new computers and audit software** to be able to carry out internal audits effectively.

Physical inspection of assets

Even with a perpetual inventory system, audit testing of inventory appears to be **limited to the end of the year**. There is a risk that **inventory is misappropriated** during the year and this would not be identified until the year end.

The perpetual inventory system does allow **physical inventory to be checked** to the book inventory on a regular basis throughout the year. Internal audit procedures should be amended to take account of this change.

Whistleblowing

The Head of Accounts sets the **risk management policy** in the company and also hears reports from potential whistle blowers. This in itself is **not necessarily a risk** within the systems of **PNY** as long as the Head of Accounts is seen to be **sufficiently independent** to be able to hear reports and take appropriate action.

However, given that whistleblowing is not discussed with an audit committee, an independent body in a company, the Head of Accounts may appear to have a vested interest in **not taking action on reports**, especially if this adversely affects **PNY**. The **chief internal auditor**, being **independent of the board**, may be a more appropriate person to hear reports.

Focus on substantive testing

The **focus on substantive testing** by the internal audit department implies that there is **limited, or even no control testing being carried out**. This is a **weakness with audit testing** because the control systems within PNY, that are specifically designed to ensure that transactions are **appropriate**, **authorised** and **help prevent fraud**, are not being tested. Control weaknesses could be occurring without the internal auditors knowing about them.

Using substantive testing also implies that **audit testing** will be **time consuming** – it takes a lot longer to substantively test one invoice by tracing it back to source documentation, than it does to check that the appropriate signature has been placed on the document.

To ensure that the internal control **systems in PNY** are working correctly, the internal auditor must **focus audit testing on control tests**. This will provide appropriate audit evidence that controls are working as well as being more time efficient.

13 Franks & Fisher

Text references. Chapter 5.

Top tips. There are a number of clear hints in the scenario directing you towards using the Turnbull list in (a). The marking scheme is quite generous in terms of rewarding basic knowledge as opposed to application to Franks and Fisher.

You need to read questions like (b) carefully; you are only being asked to make the case for appointing externally, not for appointing internally. However part of the case for appointing externally is a negative one; it's not a good idea to appoint internally because of failure to be objective/independent.

(c) illustrates that you need to look out for words such as critically in question requirements. They will generally mean that the bulk of your answer to that part will discuss problems with the views. The issue of internal audit reporting relationships is likely to feature in many exams, so you must have the arguments clear in your mind.

(d) Illustrates the importance of being able to define certain terms. If you couldn't think of any factors, think what could lead to auditors not judging situations fairly.

Easy marks. If you had good knowledge of the Turnbull report, you should have been able to generate ideas for (a) quite easily.

ACCA examiner's answer. The examiner's answer to this question is included at the back of this kit.

Marking scheme

		Marks
(a)	1 mark for each factor identified and briefly discussed	7
	1 mark for each factor applicable to Franks & Fisher	3
		10
(b)	1 mark for each relevant point identified and briefly described	6
(c)	1 marks for each relevant point made	4
(d)	2 marks for definition of objectivity	2
	1 mark per relevant characteristic identified and briefly described	3
		5
		25

(a) **Turnbull report**

The UK Turnbull report lists a number of considerations which will be taken into account when deciding whether to establish an internal audit department; most are relevant here.

Scale and complexity of operations

This has clearly increased recently with **rapid growth** meaning more products and activities being taken on, and possibly more that can go wrong. Internal audit review can act as a check on the decision-making processes, that all the **implications of the change in business** have been **fully considered**.

Number of employees

Increases in employee numbers are an indication of changes in size and the need for **development of human resource systems**, which internal audit would wish to evaluate.

Changes in organisational systems

Overall control systems will have to develop, and **internal audit** will be an important part of this change. Internal audit may be particularly needed as a check on the development of other parts of the system; with rapid growth, there is a danger that information systems for example may not develop in a way that is best for the company.

Changes in key risks

Changes in products and activities will bring changes in risks. There will be **risks associated with the production and sales of the new products**, such as production stoppages, health and safety considerations and distribution difficulties. There may also be **changes in the general risks** that Franks and Fisher faces, with possibly the **increased risk of inefficiencies and diseconomies of scale**. Internal audit can **review the adequacy** of the **overall risk management systems for** coping with these changes and carry out work on specific areas of high areas.

Problems with internal systems

The breakdown has highlighted possible problems with **quality standards**. The recent changes may mean that they would be **inadequate anyway even if rigorously enforced**. However they have not been employed conscientiously, and this calls into question whether other parts of the control systems are working as effectively as they should be. Internal audit should definitely investigate this.

Unacceptable events

Clearly the production breakdown was an unacceptable event because of its **consequences and its avoidibility**. Franks and Fisher is trying to establish itself in various product markets and therefore disruption in supply could have particularly serious consequences. If internal audit recommendations can reduce the chances of this happening in future, clearly this will be a major benefit.

Cost-benefit considerations

The fact that the board are talking about limiting internal audit's work may indicate that cost-benefit considerations are significant. Fears that internal audit will interfere with operational departments may well be exaggerated, and well-directed internal audit work should **bring benefits**. However if internal audit's work is going to be seriously limited, it may not be worthwhile employing an internal auditor.

(b) ### Arguments in favour of external recruitment

Other experience

An external recruit can bring **fresh perspectives** gained from working elsewhere. He can use his experience of other organisations' problems to **identify likely risk areas** and **recommend practical solutions** and **best practice from elsewhere**.

Independence of operational departments

An internal recruit is likely to have built up **relationships and loyalties** with people whom he has already worked, perhaps owing people favours. Equally he could have **grievances or have come into conflict with other staff**. These could compromise his independence when he comes to audit their departments.

Prejudices and biases

An internal recruit is likely to have **absorbed the perspectives and biases** of the organisation. He thus may be more inclined to treat certain individuals or departments strictly, whilst giving others the benefit of the doubt when maybe that is not warranted.

Auditing own work

Recruiting internally could mean that the internal auditor has to **audit the department** for which he worked, or **even his own work**. These would mean that he **lacked the detachment** necessary **to be objective**. This would not be a danger with an external recruit not previously involved with operations.

(c) ### Inappropriateness of reporting to Mr Kumas

There are a number of reasons why internal audit should not report to Mr Kumas

Independence of internal audit

Internal audit's **independence** as a check on internal controls will be compromised by having to report to Mr Kumas, because he has **responsibility for operations** as an **executive director**. Instead internal audit should report to the chair of the audit committee, on the grounds he is, or should be, an **independent non-executive director** with no operational responsibilities. The corporate governance codes emphasise the importance of this.

Employment of internal audit

If internal auditors report to Mr Kumas, he will have **responsibility for establishing their pay and conditions**. Thus they will have a significant personal interest in not producing adverse findings and hence antagonising him.

Work of internal audit

Part of internal audit's work will be on the **finance function** for which Mr Kumas is responsible. If Mr Kumas is in charge of internal audit as well, he may be able to ensure that internal audit coverage of the finance function and his own work is **not as rigorous** as it should be, and may be able to **water down or suppress adverse audit findings.**

Using Mr Kumas' help

Even if internal audit did not report to Mr Kumas, he would **still have to supply them with the budgets and other control information** he has and generally provide assistance. However internal auditors should not rely on him for audit knowledge as they should themselves possess **sufficient knowledge and experience** to carry out their responsibilities effectively.

(d) **Definition of objectivity**

Objectivity means **not letting bias, conflict or undue influence of others** to override professional or business judgements. It implies detachment and not letting personal feelings intrude into professional judgements.

Demonstrating objectivity

Lack of favouritism

Internal auditors should **not accept gifts nor undue favours** from the departments that they are auditing.

Fairness

Internal auditors should avoid the perception that they are out to **'hit' certain individuals or departments**. They should **not take sides**, not being influenced by office politics in determining the work carried out and the reports given.

Not responding to intimidation

Internal auditors should choose which areas to audit based on their objectives and risk analysis, **and not be kept away** from certain areas by aggressive managers. Internal audit should also **cover the whole management process** and **not just audit the operational areas**.

Valid opinion

Internal auditors should aim to deliver a report that satisfies the needs of their principal (the audit committee).This means **producing a report based on all relevant factors** rather than one **designed to please operational departments**.

14 LinesRUs

Text references. Chapters 7 and 8.

Top tips. This question should be easy to structure if you remembered the stages of the risk analysis process and the ways in which risk is managed. You then need to use imagination to apply it to LinesRUs; there is plenty to prompt your thoughts in the question. The risk quantification section makes the important point that past experience may not always be a reliable guide to the level of future losses.

In (b) LinesRUs is seeking risk minimisation (ultimately as near zero as possible) rather than risk avoidance. Remember also that transfer of risk may not be possible, even if LinesRUs had a better safety record.

Easy marks. Both (a) and (b) follow a framework which you should know.

			Marks
(a)	Risk identification	4	
	Risk assessment	4	
	Risk profiling	4	
	Risk quantification	4	
	Risk consolidation	4	
	Give full credit for other similar frameworks	max	16
(b)	Risk responses. Up to 3 marks per response. To gain high marks, reference must be made to company circumstances	max	9
			25

(a) Risk identification

Risks cannot be managed without first realising that they exist. Managers need to maintain a **list of known or familiar risks** and the extent to which they can harm the organisation or people within it. Managers also need to be aware that unfamiliar risks may exist and maintain vigilance in case these risks occur.

Risk identification is an **ongoing process** so that new risks and changes affecting existing risks may be identified quickly and dealt with appropriately before they result in unacceptable losses.

LinesRUs appear to have **identified some risks** in their risk management policy. However, other risks do occur and managers within LinesRUs must be able to responsd to those risks quickly. One key factor appears to be whether LinesRUs is to "**blame**" for the risk situation crystallising. Situations with no blame appear not to affect LinesRUs (eg the driver falling asleep) whereas situations where negligence is implied are potentially damaging. One factor in the risk identification plan will be to have **lawyers ready** to defend LinesRUs in the case of potential blame situations.

Risk assessment

It may be difficult to forecast the financial affects of a risk until after a disaster has occurred. Areas such as **extra expenses, inconvenience and loss of time** can then be recognised, even if they were not thought of in initial risk analysis. In a severe situation, damage to the company's reputation could result in LinesRUs becoming bankrupt.

In this situation, there has been a loss of confidence in the company, the extent of which may not have been foreseen. This has resulted in:

(i) **Additional expense in terms of lost passengers** – legal advice will be needed to determine whether LinesRUs is liable and whether the company's insurance meets this liability.

(ii) What the **additional time and cost of repairing the track** will be and whether LinesRUs can claim additional income for this work.

Sources of information to ensure that the risk can be minimised may include:

- **Obtaining regular reports** from train operators on the state of the rail infrastructure.

- **Monitoring news feeds** such as Reuters for early indication of potential disasters.

- **Filing appropriate reports** of physical inspection of track as evidence of maintenance work carried out.

Risk profiling

This stage involves using the results of risk assessment to group risks into families. A consequence matrix is one method of doing this.

Likelihood	Consequences	
	Low	High
High	Loss of lower level staff	Loss of senior staff
Low	Loss of suppliers Major rail disaster not the company's fault	Major rail disaster affecting reputation of company. Loss of computer data on maintenance work. Loss of franchise

The analysis will be incomplete for LinesRUs because not all risks can be identified.

Risk quantification

Risks that require more detailed analysis can be quantified and where possible results and probabilities calculated. The result of calculations will show:

- Average or expected result or loss
- Frequency of losses
- Chances of losses
- Largest predictable loss

to which LinesRUs could be exposed by a particular risk.

The **likely frequency of losses** from a particular cause can be **predicted** with some degree of confidence from studying available records. The **confidence margin** can be improved by including the likely effects of changed circumstances in the calculation.

Unfortunately, **many of the risks facing LinesRUs** are **significant**. So while quantification can be enhanced by past events such as drivers falling asleep, they appear to be one-off situations meaning that the actual event may not occur again. However, the adverse effects of the risk in terms of costs necessary to repair the rail infrastructure will be helpful enabling LinesRUs to ensure that appropriate insurance is available – effectively guarding against loss by transferring the risk.

Risk consolidation and review

Risks analysed at the divisional or subsidiary level need to be **aggregated at the corporate level**. This aggregation will be required as part of the overall review of risk that the board needs to undertake. **Systems will be placed to identify changes in risks as soon as they occur**, enabling management to monitor risks regularly and undertake annual reviews of the way that organisation deals with risk.

There is no information on the **organisational structure** of LinesRUs. Given the risky nature of the company's business, LinesRUs is likely to be an independent legal entity to ensure that no other companies are adversely affected should LinesRUs go out of business.

(b) **Risk responses to train crash**

Avoidance of risk

LinesRUs may consider whether the risk can be **avoided**. However, given that maintenance work must continue and that errors are always possible, then the risk may **crystallise**. Avoidance is not possible.

The only method of avoidance would appear to be **termination of operations**. This again may not be appropriate given this would close LinesRU's business.

Reduction of risk

The risk can be **reduced by taking appropriate measures**. In the case of LinesRUs these will include:

- Ensuring that maintenance receives **appropriate training** and that the training is repeated on a regular basis.

- **Raising awareness** of the importance of work being carried out and the potential consequences of error.

- **Maintenance and enforcement of appropriate disciplinary procedures** where breaches of work practices have been identified.

LinesRUs may also consider loss control options. These may include:

- **Hiring of lawyers** to defend LinesRUs.

- **Release of publicity material** on the work of LinesRUs showing extent of maintenance normally carried out.

Retaining risk

This is where the organisation retains the risk and if an unfavourable outcome occurs it will suffer the full loss. In the case of the rail crash, LinesRUs may have to **retain the risk** if **suitable insurance cannot be found**. Given the uncertainties regarding the costs resulting from the unfavourable outcome, insurers may be unwilling to insure for this type of event.

Transfer of risk

The risk is transferred to a third party. As noted above, this may not be possible if insurers are **not willing to accept the risk**. Alternative methods of risk transfer may have to be considered including asking the state for some form of insurance.

15 Doctors' practice

> **Text references.** Chapter 5, 6 and 8.
>
> **Top tips.** (a) requires imagination, but the way to think is simply to ask what could go wrong. As with any business embarking on a new venture, there may be problems with anticipating demand and obtaining finance. Note that the second part of (a) does **not** ask you to describe a risk management model in detail, rather to discuss the uses of it or any other similar model.
>
> In (b) the risks are such that a risk manager needs to be appointed, although the practice is small enough for everyone to be involved in the decision to define risk appetite. The most important point in (c) is that systems auditing may focus on systems, not the risks that drive those systems.
>
> In (c) you don't need to go into detail about whether the practice should employ an internal auditor or who it should be. The question is based on the assumption that internal audit work will be performed.
>
> **Easy marks.** Quite a tough question with no particularly easy parts.

(a) (i) **Additional risks**

A number of additional risks arise from the introduction of the new facility, including the following.

Operational risks

(1) **Surgical equipment failure**

The practice may face threats to its income through **failures of its surgical equipment**, meaning that it cannot provide surgical procedures whilst the equipment is unavailable.

(2) **Storage facilities failure**

Environmental failures in the storage facilities for equipment and drugs may also lead to a **loss of income** if surgical procedures cannot be provided. The practice may also face the **costs** of **replacing the equipment** and drugs that have been contaminated.

(3) **Security**

The additional equipment and drugs stored may make the practice **more vulnerable** to **theft**.

(4) **Transportation risks**

The blood and samples taken may be contaminated by storage facilities problems at the surgery, and also by deterioration during transportation. This may result in **misdiagnosis** of illness and hence the **costs of giving patients** the **wrong treatment.**

(5) **High demand**

High demand at **certain times of the year** may mean that the practice **loses income** through being **unable to meet the demand**, or **incurs increased costs** through having to pay for **extra medical and nursing care**.

(6) **Hospital delays**

The practice may **lose income** through not being able to provide care because of **delays in testing** blood and samples at the local hospital.

(7) **Staff**

Existing staff **may not have** the **collective skills** necessary to operate the new unit. If new staff are employed, there may be a risk of **staff dissatisfaction** and hence **retention problems** with existing staff if new staff are employed on better terms.

(8) **Effect on existing care**

The resources required by the new facilities may mean **less resources are available** for existing work; hence the **areas of care** currently provided may suffer and **income** from these be **threatened.**

Legal risks

Providing more procedures may increase the risk of problems arising during treatment, and hence losses through the **costs of fighting or settling negligence claims**.

Regulatory risks

If shortcomings arise in the treatment provided, the practice's **regulatory body** may **intervene** and prevent the practice providing the surgical procedures it currently wishes to offer.

Financial risks

The new **facilities** will have to be **financed**. The practice may face problems in **meeting any finance costs** that it has to incur, particularly if the return on investment is not as good as forecast. Financing the investment may mean funds are lacking when required for other purposes, such as buying out a retiring partner.

Reputation risks

The practice may not achieve the income growth expected if the **standard of treatment** is believed to be lower than would be available in the hospital, or if because of operational difficulties **patients** were **forced to wait longer** for treatment than they would in a hospital.

(ii)   **Uses of risk management model**

Iterative model

The most important feature of models is that they demonstrate how risk management is a **continual process** and experience gained from carrying out all stages can impact upon all other stages of the cycle. Review by the **risk manager** or all of the doctors of the **effectiveness of risk management** needs to be built into the process.

Organisation– wide application

Models are used to assess **organisation-wide** risks and also **specific process or unit risks**. They also are used to assess the **interaction** between risks.

Logical process

Models show that risk management is a logical process, taking the organisation through **initial risk identification,** then **identification of events** that may cause **risks to crystallise, assessment** of **how great losses** might be and in the light of these how best to **respond to risks**. This will help identify who should be responsible for which aspects of the risk management cycle.

Role of monitoring and feedback

Models emphasise the importance of **monitoring risk management procedures** and controls once they are in place. The feedback from this monitoring will **impact upon future risk assessments** and also lead to **continuous improvements in processes**, following the **principles of feedforward control**.

Decision-making

Models emphasise that the results of all stages of the risk management process should impact upon **the organisation's decision-making process** and consequently **affect strategy** and also **the appetite the organisation has for risk.** The decisions taken as a result of this will in turn feed through to the risk assessment and management processes, modifying the views taken on **key risks** and the best ways to **respond to them.**

(b)   **Risk appetite**

Risk appetite is the amount of risk that the practice is prepared to **accept in exchange for returns** (the clientele effect). The new arrangements here are expected to increase income, and the risk appetite defines what risk levels will be **acceptable in exchange** for the increased income. Risk appetite also infers that the practice is willing to accept that risk has a downside as well as an upside, and the consequences of both are culturally acceptable.

Risk appetite decisions

In this situation, one of the senior partners in the practice would act as the risk manager and be responsible for analysing risk and recommending what **acceptable risk levels** might be in the **changed circumstances** for each of the major risks. However as the decision results from a major change in practices, the recommendations should certainly be approved by a majority of the doctors, and preferably be unanimous. The practice may also have to act within **constraints** imposed by government or regulator, which effectively limit the maximum amount of risk the practice can bear.

(c)   **Contribution of internal audit**

Internal audit could be used to add value by operating a **risk-based approach to auditing the practice's systems.** Although the practice would not be able to employ a full-time internal auditor, it could maybe employ experienced staff from elsewhere in the health service to perform the work.

Benefits of a risk-based approach

A risk-based approach would assess whether the risk management systems are sufficient to **assess and manage risk.** A risk-based audit would question the **appropriateness of risk management systems** as a means of managing risk and would question whether the **assessment of operational systems' risk** was fair. A risk-based approach therefore combines audit of operational systems with an audit of the risk management systems.

Usefulness of systems-based auditing

Systems-based auditing would focus on the overall functioning of the practice's operational systems. Systems-based auditing concentrates on:

(i)   The **procedures** in place to **achieve the practice's objectives**

(ii)   The **controls** that are in place to **manage the risks** that threaten the achievement of objectives

The systems-based audit will assess whether the **controls and procedures** in place are **appropriate** in the light of the **objectives management has decided** and the **risk management systems** that managers have adopted. It then tests whether procedures and controls are operating effectively.

16 Question with answer plan: ASG

Text references. Chapters 6 to 8.

Top tips. Identification and evaluation of the risks implies being selective in your answer and only discussing those risks that are relevant to ASG, as well as showing how likely they are to occur. Various 'clues' are provided in the scenario to help you focus on the specific area of risk, and you should use these to ensure that your answer is as relevant as possible to the scenario.

Any difference in the transaction and settlement date will lay a company open to exchange risk so watch out for that. Remember not hedging is always an option, although the company should make a conscious decision not to hedge. The hedging methods mentioned are forward and money market hedging. Remember economic risks are often more fundamental and longer-term as here. The company may also face the economic risk of foreign competition even if it doesn't trade abroad. Translation risk is of more limited importance, and will only affect very big individual transactions

Easy marks. Probably the discussion on transaction risks and on political risks. However the political risks must be relevant to the countries with which the business is trading. Some political risk is relevant here, but don't spend too much time discussing political risk if the business is trading with countries that are politically well settled.

Answer plan

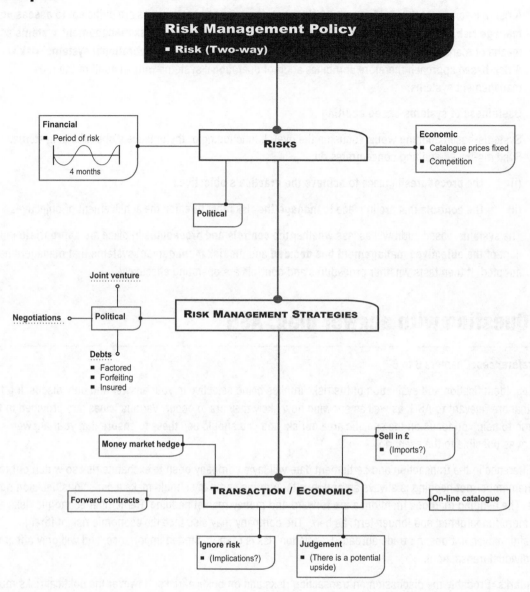

Transaction risk

ASG purchases wood by agreeing a fixed price for a given quantity of wood in one month in Norwegian Kroner, but paying for the wood four months later. This leaves ASG open to **transaction risk**, which is the risk that the **exchange rate will be different when paying for the wood compared to the exchange rate when the sale was agreed**.

There are two possibilities:

(i) **Sterling may weaken relative to the Norwegian Kroner**. This will have the effect of increasing the purchase price as it will cost more to purchase the Norwegian currency to fulfil the sale.

(ii) **Sterling may strengthen against the Norwegian Kroner**. This will have the effect of decreasing the purchase price because it will cost less to purchase the Norwegian currency.

The Norwegian supplier will be indifferent to the exchange rate movement because it will still receive the amount of money contracted for.

The risk that ASG needs to guard against is sterling becoming weaker compared to the Kroner.

Dealing with transaction risk

(i) **Ignoring the risk** and hoping that the exchange rate does not move significantly. This strategy will only be effective if, in retrospect, the exchange rate does not become worse.

(ii) **Actively deciding to do nothing** because the financial outlook indicates that the exchange rate will improve against the Kroner. Adopting this strategy depends partly on the financial forecast and partly on the perceived reliability of that forecast. There is still risk in doing nothing because the future may be worse than expected.

(iii) **Contracting to purchase the Kroner in the future** for a **fixed amount of sterling**, and paying a commission to a third party for this contract. The amount of commission payable will depend on the outlook for exchange rate changes. A small commission indicates that exchange rates are unlikely to change significantly and so the self-insurance option above may be more attractive. This option minimises risk because the actual amount of expenditure is known.

(iv) **Purchasing the Kroner now** and depositing them in a Norwegian currency account to pay the supplier when the debt becomes due. This option also minimises risk as the amount of expenditure is fixed. However, the option does assume that ASG has sufficient funds to place in a different currency denominated bank account for four months.

Economic risk

Economic risk refers **to the degree to which the value of the firm's future cash flows can be influenced by exchange rate fluctuations**. These risks normally occur before transaction risks simply because the actual transactions to purchase or sell goods or products have not yet occurred. Any gains and losses from economic risks tend not to appear in the financial statements of a company because they are subjective and difficult to measure.

Examples of economic risk for ASG

(i) **Sending out catalogues to the USA and North African markets with prices fixed for a number of months**. If sterling was to strengthen against the dollar or North African countries then ASG would receive relatively less income for each item sold. Depending on the profit margins built into the pricing structure, sterling income could fall to an extent that ASG would be making a loss on each item sold.

(ii) **ASG could also be under competition from companies in other countries selling into the same market**, for example France and Germany in the Euro zone. Favourable exchange rate movements could provide these countries with increased income. This increase could be used to **reduce selling prices** or **offer special discounts** in the USA, under cutting ASG's prices.

Dealing with economic risks

(i) **Denominating sales in sterling in the overseas catalogue**. This would remove completely the economic risk of the exchange rate fluctuating. However, most citizens prefer to order goods in their own currency, so this strategy may well result in decreased sales for ASG.

(ii) **Providing a catalogue with no prices** – effectively asking customers to telephone for prices or check an Internet site. Telephoning may not be an option due to cost and different time zones. Use of an Internet site is possible, as long as customers do not mind using two media to make their purchase. However, the Internet site could be updated regularly with new prices and amended to take orders, which may increase sales for ASG with the use of a new or different sales medium.

Political risk

Political risk is the **unwanted consequence of political activities**, which will have some effect of the value of the firm. It is normally detrimental effects that a most concerning.

Political risks could affect ASG in the following ways:

(i) Possible **discrimination against foreign businesses**, especially where those businesses are located in countries which appear to be putting pressure on North African countries, for example, to declare any terrorist links.

(ii) **Expropriation of assets already in that country**. ASG could lose title to inventory already despatched to North Africa.

(iii) **Exchange control mechanisms** affecting ASG unfavourably by limiting the amount of money that can be remitted abroad.

(iv) **Trade tariffs restricting trade in some goods**. This is unlikely to follow any action by ASG itself; for example the USA may ban imports of UK furniture if exports of US steel are not accepted in the UK.

Dealing with political risk

(i) **Negotiations with the foreign government** by some form of concession agreement to allow continued trade.

(ii) **Arranging a joint venture with a national company** to organise the sale of its products rather than retaining control from the UK.

(iii) **Taking out insurance** under government operated insurance schemes.

(iv) **Customer management** such as factoring or forfaiting debts.

17 IDAN

Text references. Chapter 6 broadly on risks, Chapter 5 deals with the role of internal audit.

Top tips. In (a) don't worry too much if your classification of risks differed from ours. A possible alternative is credit, market, operational, reputation, compliance and business risk. It's important to link your discussion into the scenario; it's evident for example that IDAN faces a number of legal/compliance risks. You might also have considered the logo framework.

(b) is an interesting mix of a number of controls; you need to give specific examples and also give some consideration to the risks of introducing new systems in response to changes. Note that IT controls are a significant element. You don't need a detailed knowledge of the money laundering regulations to answer that part; a systematic approach to risk management (establishing policies, staffing, training and management review) will get you the majority of marks. You can also use your own experience of dealing with banks when discussing opening an account with a new bank or using pin numbers.

Easy marks. Categorisation of risks in (a) should have provided a gentle start to the question as most of the 'normal' major risks apply. In (b), provided you make clear by using headers which risk you're discussing, you don't have to discuss the risks in the order given in the question, and can start with those you find easiest first.

(a) **Main categories of risk**

Business risk

Business risk is the potential volatility of profits caused by the **nature and type** of **operations** in which the company is involved. **Strategic risk**, the consequences of making the wrong strategic decisions, is an important element of business risk, since IDAN is faced with choosing in which areas of business to carry out further investment. IDAN also faces business risk through **failing to respond** as quickly as its competitors do to the **current changes in the business environment**. Deregulation means the group faces competition in some areas from outside the banking sector, such as entities other than banks offering more flexible or informal loan arrangements.

Credit risk

Credit risk is the risk of losses through the **bank's customers failing to meet their payment obligations**. This is a major source of risk for a bank, since much business will be loans on which interest and capital repayments have to be made. The risk of losses will depend on whether loans are secured on assets, or have no security backing.

Financial market risk

Financial market risk is the risk of losses through adverse movements in financial markets. This includes **changes in the foreign currency markets** (exchange risk), **changes in interest rates as expected here** (interest rate risk) and **other changes** in securities or derivatives markets.

Legal risks

Legal risks are the risk of losses resulting from IDAN **incurring legal penalties**, or having its **operations disrupted by legal action**. IDAN faces several risks in this area, including legal penalties for failure to supply details to the tax authorities or to implement money laundering requirements effectively, and successful claims against the group for incorrect financial services advice. Because IDAN operates in a number of different countries and has to comply with many different sets of laws and regulations, the risk of breaches somewhere may be increased.

Operational risks

Operational risks are the risks of losses caused by operational failures. This risk may be significant for IDAN since it is faced with having to **re-design its operational and information systems**. Problems with the design or implementation of new systems may lead to failure to provide a **proper service to customers** or **failure to supply managers** with the information they need to **supervise the business effectively**. Another significant risk is a **breakdown in the computer systems** resulting in customers being unable to use their credit or debit cards.

Fraud risks

IDAN may be vulnerable to **losses through fraud**, for example use by **unauthorised persons of PIN numbers**, or **fraudulent transactions over the telephone**.

Reputational risks

Reputation risk is the risk of adverse financial consequences such as lost business caused by failures resulting from another risk. This could arise through customers receiving a **poor service** through operational failures, **concerns** over the **security** of systems, and **imposition of legal penalties** because poor financial services advice was given.

Advantages of categorisation of risks

Event identification

Sorting risks into different categories enables the business to **identify situations or events** that will cause loss.

Risk response

Categorising risks should ensure they are dealt with in the most appropriate manner, for example developing systems to eliminate the risk of non-compliance with regulations or transfer of risk by insurance. Even when the same broad method is used for different risks, there may be variations, for example using **different insurers** to cover **operational and credit risks**.

Responsibility

Grouping risks enables the business to assess who will be responsible for dealing with them. Risks in **specialist areas** of the business may require internal or external risk management input, whereas **'mainstream' operational risks** can be dealt with by operational managers.

Monitoring

Categorisation of risks makes its easier for the directors to **fulfil their responsibilities** to ensure that the risks the business faces are managed to an acceptable level. Not only will it make risk monitoring easier, but the initial process of risk categorisation will require directors to respond to the results by ensuring appropriate systems are developed. Directors will also be able to fulfil their legal obligations to report on risk.

(b) **EU law**

To counter the risks of non-compliance, information systems will have to be amended to:

(i) **Identify accounts** held by **non-residents**; and also **separately identify accounts held** in each European country

(ii) **Automatically generate a 15% deduction** of **withholding tax when interest is paid** on these accounts

(iii) **Show details** grouped by each EU country of the account of the interest paid and the tax due

The listing of accounts held by non-residents should be checked independently of the processing function. The checker should:

(i) Confirm that **interest is shown** as **paid** on the due dates.

(ii) **Reconcile the list** with the **previous list sent to the tax authorities**. Any changes should be confirmed to listings of accounts transferred or closed, and any other changes investigated.

Internal audit should confirm that these checks are being carried out, and also check a **sample of accounts themselves**.

Forecast rises in interest rates

Interest rate risk is fundamental to the group's operations, as it may arise through trading activities or traditional banking work. The board therefore needs to consider the **desirable appetite** for this risk. The directors should also regularly review **IDAN's lending patterns**. Excessive concentration on long-term fixed interest lending will leave IDAN vulnerable to **not benefiting from interest rate increases**.

IDAN's treasury department should be looking to **hedge any of IDAN's own borrowing** that may become **more expensive** by using appropriate instruments such as interest rate caps.

IDAN should also have procedures in place for **monitoring the likely effects of interest rate changes** on each country or group of countries.

Elimination of personal signatures

Transition to new arrangements will require controls to ensure that all customers are notified of their PIN numbers by whatever methods are most appropriate. IDAN must also respond to the use of PIN numbers by appropriate security measures to combat the **risk of fraud**:

(i) The identification numbers supplied by IDAN to its customers should be reasonably **easy for the customer to remember**, but should **avoid combinations** that can easily be guessed. A four digit number avoiding such combinations as 1234 or 9999 might well be used.

(ii) Customers should be instructed to destroy **IDAN's notification** of their pin number.

(iii)   IDAN should make clear to customers what they should do if their cards are lost or stolen. If customers **report cards** to be **missing**, those cards should be instantly cancelled.

(iv)   If customers contact IDAN **claiming to have forgotten their pin numbers**, **IDAN staff** should ask for evidence of identification such as personal details before supplying their pin numbers.

In addition, IDAN will need to ensure that its own credit and debit cards function properly when used for payment by **pre-testing** the new arrangements. Once operational, there should be alternative **back-up facilities in place** to ensure operations can continue in the event of a major systems breakdown.

Increasing use of telephone and Internet banking services

Developments in new types of business carry the risk that the company's systems will not be able to cope with **increased demand**. Management therefore **need to monitor call waiting times against targets**, and **Internet response times**. Internal audit may need to carry out **detailed testing of transactions** to ensure that they have been processed accurately. **Extra training** may be required to combat problems.

Verification of identity controls will also be required to counter the risk of security breaches. This can be achieved by requiring a passcard or PIN number to be entered or quoted over the phone, along with an item of personal data such as **date of birth** or **mother's maiden name**. There should also be controls over the **security of the telephone system** and **encryption and firewall controls** to protect data transmitted by computer.

Misselling claims

Human resource controls are an important element of avoiding the **legal risk** of successful claims:

(i)   Recruitment processes should ensure the employment of **properly-qualified staff** and **obtaining references** on their experience.

(ii)   Staff should be trained in **appropriate selling techniques and ethical behaviour**. Staff should also be trained and continually updated in legal requirements

(iii)   **Staff remuneration schemes** should be carefully reviewed to ensure that they do not encourage inappropriate selling.

(iv)   If staff are found to have fallen below standard, they should incur **remedial training** or **dismissal** as appropriate.

IDAN should also have controls in place to ensure **staff behaviour is monitored**, for example requiring recording of all phone calls, and written records of all meetings which the customer confirms. Compliance checks should also be carried out on all written material that **IDAN issues**.

It should also implement a formal **complaints procedure**, which deals with **customer complaints speedily** and **actions findings**. This should not only ensure customers are compensated, but reduce the risk of complaints to legal authorities and highlight actions required to avoid recurrence of problems.

Money laundering

The key elements of a money laundering policy are:

(i)   Appointing a director or senior manager as **money laundering compliance officer**, backed by clear support from other directors for anti-money laundering requirements

(ii)   **Establishing written policies and procedures** which cover the money laundering regulations, detail the records to be kept and periods of retention and specify when the authorities should be notified

(iii)   **Verifying the identity of new customers**. This can be done for personal customers by a passport or identity card including a photograph, identifying the customer's name and permanent address. Similar confirmation of details should be obtained for companies, preferably from official bodies such as the UK registrar of companies

(iv)   **Training** all staff so that they are aware of the **signs of money laundering** and know that they are **legally required** to **report their suspicions**

(v)   **Tracking large or unusual transactions**, especially those taking place over more than one country. Accounts with unusual transactions may require continual monitoring

(vi)   **Regular review of policies** to ensure that they are effective and comply with any changes in regulations

18 Cave Trust

Text references. Chapters 6 and 8.

Top tips. In (a) it is important to identify the two key words of *identified* and *managed* in the scenario, as this provides the basic format for the answer. The management of risk implies looking at the various strategies in this area – the link to the scenario being that the Trust appears to have effectively ignored risk and that this is inappropriate.

(b) builds on (a) by checking what remedial action is now required to overcome the weakness of lack of risk analysis in the Trust. The focus of the answer must be on the loss of income with additional relevant and realistic comment on whether other income sources can be found.

(c) stresses the key point about reputation risk, that a loss of reputation can only occur if stakeholders react badly. Hence assessing the magnitude of reputation risk is linked to the evaluation of stakeholder interest and power. (d) combines positive measures with a necessary strengthening of the ethical and control framework. The Trustees have to take into account the fact that they are dealing with employees rather than volunteers; however you would have gained credit for pointing out how financial restrictions limit what they can do to address apparent employee grievances.

Easy marks. Identifying threats and risks is generally the easiest part of a question like this, and forms the basis of the rest of your answer. So be very alert for risks when you are reading through question scenarios.

(a)   **Identify the sources of risk**

A business review will be carried out by appropriately trained staff or external consultants to determine the business risks facing the company, or in this case the Trust. Specific risks that could affect the Trust could include:

Financial risk

An example would be **loss of key income or unidentified or unbudgeted expenditure being incurred**. The Trust is currently facing loss of key income as noted in the scenario, although unbudgeted expenditure in terms of collapsing roofs in the caves would also fall into this category.

Fraud risk

Employee fraud has happened in the Trust, with consequent damage to its reputation.

Technological risk

This results from **new or improved technology** that the company does not have access to or chooses not to use. While the Trust appears to lack some management information systems, there does not appear to be lack of any specific technology that would cause the risk of the company ceasing operations.

Reputation risk

In the case of the Trust there is the possible risk that the cave becomes **contaminated in some way**, thus losing its unique selling point of being the largest living cave open to the public. There is also a risk of loss of reputation through visitors being injured in the cave. Reputation has suffered because of media coverage of the fraud (discussed in (c) below).

Determine how the risks can be managed

There are four basic strategies for managing risks:

Avoidance

That is **removing the factors** that give rise to a risk. In the case of the Trust the risk of income sources could not be removed so this is not a viable option.

Reduction

The reason for the risk cannot be removed, but methods are identified to **reduce the risk to acceptable levels**. In the case of the Trust, this should have meant that alternative sources of income were identified prior to the situation becoming critical.

Transference

In this option, the risk is **transferred to a third party**, normally by the taking out of a suitable insurance policy. While the Trust could obtain insurance for business being affected by factors such as poor weather or strikes, it is less likely that insurance against sources of income not being available could be obtained.

Acceptance

The **risk is accepted** in the hope that it will not occur or that the consequences of the risk can be coped with if it does occur. This appears to have been the policy adopted by the Trust, given the problem that removal of the government funding is now causing.

Prepare an action plan for risk

For each identified risk, an **appropriate action plan** needs to be **determined**, based on the strategy adopted for that risk. Initial focus will be on those risks that have the **most adverse business impact** for the company, such as the **loss of income**. However, no action plan has been produced by the Trust, at least for the loss of income.

Appropriate actions for other risks identified would include:

(i)　　**Implementing appropriate internal controls** to limit employee fraud and ensure the cave system is maintained safely

(ii)　　**Obtaining public liability insurance** against **risks of the public** suffering injury while visiting the caves

The overall lack of risk management is worrying and needs to be addressed urgently by the Trustees.

(b)　　**Risk management of income in the Trust**

The risk management strategy for income in the Trust does not appear to be fully developed. It would appear the Trustees have become **complacent** in their **management of income** and the withdrawal of funding from the government was therefore a surprise.

Actions to be taken by the Trustees

Determine the effect of the loss of income on the Trust

No information is provided regarding the **extent of income** provided by the **government**, but it would appear to be important given that the cave system was partly developed using that income. Amendments will have to be made to the management accounts to show the effect of losing this income, and to identify whether this will result in a negative contribution.

Depending on the result of these amendments, a decision may have to be taken regarding the **viability of the Trust** to continue to operate the cave. Expenditure appears to be high and relatively fixed, in terms of the air conditioning system for the cave, staffing, etc. If fixed costs cannot be covered in the medium term, then the cave will have to close.

Investigate other income sources

Other sources of income should be investigated as a matter of urgency.

(i) **Charging a fee** to schools for the use of the research area

(ii) **Approaching universities** for grants to develop the cave system or to allow students of mineralogy to work in the caves

(iii) **Approaching the public** for donations to maintain the cave

(iv) **Obtaining additional bank finance**

(v) **Increasing entry fees**

An alternative may be to **reschedule the repayment of the bank loans** to decrease current expenditure.

For the future, the Trustees must also **undertake a full risk review** for the Trust, identifying other sources of risk and providing contingencies to overcome those risks.

(c) **Level of reputation risk**

The level of risk to reputation depends on two things:

- The **probability of events** occurring that will threaten the organisation's reputation
- The **responses of stakeholders** if these events occur

Probability of events

The probability can be reduced by **appropriate control systems operating effectively**. Control systems however at best can **reduce** rather than **eliminate risks**, and the extent to which they can reduce risks will depend on the nature of the risks. The Trust should be able to minimise the risk of defalcations by introducing appropriate controls such as **reconciliations** and **improving Trust culture.** The measures the Trust can take will have less impact on other risks, for example not being able to prevent the cave from flooding (though the Trust clearly should have appropriate evacuation procedures in place).

Responses of stakeholders

If events do occur, the impact will depend upon the reaction of key stakeholders in the Trust. **Visitors** are obviously important stakeholders. If for example they believe that there is a risk that the cave will flood, visitor numbers are likely to fall even if the Trust does have effective evacuation procedures in place.

Government has also been a key stakeholder, given the Trust's reliance on grant income. Government's priorities may be determined by events beyond the Trust's control (eg in Britain recent allegations that lots of organisations are suffering because of funds being diverted towards building facilities for the Olympics). However government funding may also be conditional on the Trust being well-run and having appropriate control systems in place.

Dealing with stakeholder concerns

If the Trust's reputation does appear to be threatened, it should attempt to take **effective action** as soon as possible. If for example there are safety concerns, if necessary the cave should be shut on days where it is felt to be too damp for visitors. In addition the Trust's **communications with its stakeholders** should emphasise the measures it has taken to try to address their concerns.

(d) **Stressing ideals of Trust**

It seems clear that employees are not as committed to the Trust's ideals as they should be, and perhaps the **Trustees' most important task** is trying to strengthen employees' commitment to the Trust. This can be done by regular communications such as **staff bulletins** and also **training/information days.** Possibly the trustees who are **cave explorers or scientists** can give regular talks to staff on the scientific importance of the cave.

Rewarding staff

The thefts, although wrong, may have been prompted by poor wages or working conditions. Unfortunately the **financial constraints** that the Trust faces means that Trustees are unlikely to be able to increase employee wages, or introduce bonuses if the Trust does make more income. The Trustees should nevertheless consider whether there are other ways in which **employees** can be **rewarded**.

Building integrity into systems

However as well as encouraging greater staff commitment, the Trustees also need to make clear to staff the importance of **integrity** and of adopting **zero tolerance** towards theft or fraud. The Trustees need to review human resource procedures. References should be **obtained** for **new staff members**; there should be **regular appraisals** for all staff and commitment to the controls that the Trust operates should be part of the appraisal process. The Trustees may also consider introducing a **code of conduct** to which all staff need to sign their commitment.

Communication channels

One specific way in which the Trustees can demonstrate their response to employee concerns is by clear communication channels. One of the **Trustees** could be nominated as the person to whom staff could communicate concerns about **possible risks,** not just of fraud, but in other areas. It should be stressed that staff members will not be penalised for reporting issues.

19 Cerberus

Text references. Chapters 4 and 9.

Top tips. You might have had problems deciding what should go into (a) and what into (b). Our answer to (a) is based on what boards must consider carefully when the system of controls is being established, and a brief note that the board is also responsible for monitoring.

(b) then goes into detail about the two key elements of the monitoring process, the ongoing review by the board and the wider (more strategic) annual review. Because 12 marks are available you can go into some detail about what the reviews should cover and how management should use different information sources to carry out an effective review.

The reference in (c) to reporting to the stock market just means what corporate governance reports need to say about internal controls. Mentioning the Sarbanes-Oxley requirements should gain marks, as these are stricter than most other countries, but have application to companies that trade in America.

Easy marks. If you have good knowledge of the Turnbull recommendations that represent best practice in this area of corporate governance, you should have found most of this question reasonably straightforward.

REPORT

To: The Board of Directors
From: Accountant
Date: 1 December 20X6
Subject: Board's responsibility for internal control

I am writing to set out what the board should do to fulfil its responsibilities to maintain an appropriate internal control system.

(a)   **Key responsibilities of board members**

Sound system of control

Corporate governance guidelines require the board to **maintain a sound system of internal control** to **safeguard shareholders' investments** and the **company's assets**. A sound system should aid operations by **responding to risks**, should **ensure the quality of reporting**, and help ensure **compliance with laws and regulations**.

Risks

In order to determine what constitutes a sound system, the board should consider the major risks the company faces, concentrating on

*   The **identification, evaluation and management** of all **key risks** affecting the organisation
*   The **effectiveness of internal control (see below)**
*   **Communication** to employees of risk objectives with targets and indicators
*   The **action that needs to be taken** if any **weaknesses** are found

Effectiveness of internal control

The board should consider the effectiveness of all internal controls, not financial controls but also operational, compliance and risk management controls. Board members need to consider:

(i)   The **nature** and **extent** of the **risks** which face the company and which it regards as **acceptable** for the company to bear within its particular business

(ii)   The **threat** of such **risks becoming** a **reality**

(iii)   If that happened, the company's ability to **reduce** the **incidence** and **impact** on the business and to adapt to changing risks or operational deficiencies

(iv)   The **costs and benefits** related to operating relevant controls

Feedback

The board must not regard establishing a good control system as a one-off exercise. The **risks** that drive the development of the internal control systems will **change** as the company's **strategy** and **business environment changes.** In addition **feedback** on how the controls have been operating is an essential part of a business's control systems; the feedback the board obtains should lead to modifications and improvements.

(b)   **Methods used to assess effectiveness of internal control**

Consideration of internal controls should be a regular part of the board's agenda and the board should also conduct a higher level annual review of internal control.

Regular review

The board should regularly consider the effectiveness of strategies for **identifying**, **evaluating** and **managing** the major risks, the **strength** of the **management and internal control environment and systems,** the **actions** being taken to **reduce the risks** found, and whether the results indicate that **internal control** should be **monitored more extensively.**

Annual review

When the board is considering annually the disclosures about internal controls in the accounts, it should conduct an **annual review** of internal control. This should be wider-ranging than the regular review; in particular it should cover:

(i)   The **changes** since the last **assessment** in **risks** faced, the company's **ability** to **respond** to **changes** in its business environment and whether the company's **objectives** and **risk appetite** should be **re-assessed**

(ii)   The **scope** and **quality** of management's **monitoring** of risk and internal control, and how well the **information systems** fulfil the board and management's **information needs**

(iii)   The **extent** and **frequency** of reports to the board and **communication with employees**

(iv)   **Significant controls**, **failings** and **weaknesses** which have or might have **material impacts** upon the accounts

(v)   The **effectiveness** of the **public reporting** processes in communicating a **balanced and understandable account** of the company's position and prospects

Information for review

To carry out effective reviews, the board needs to use a number of different sources of information. Part of the review of controls should be the quality of the reports the board is receiving.

(i)   **Performance measurement and indicators**

         Regular reporting of these measures should be built into the control systems. They should include not just **financial data** but also **qualitative measures** such as customer satisfaction.

(ii)   **Senior management monitoring**

         The board should consider reports on the **monitoring activities** undertaken by senior management below board level, such as control self-assessment and confirmation by employees of compliance with policies and codes of conduct. Management reports should highlight the impact of, and actions taken to remedy, **significant control failings and weaknesses.** Management should also report to the board risk any risk and control matters of particular importance, such as fraud, illegal acts or matters significantly affecting the company's reputation or financial position.

(iii)   **Audit committee and internal audit**

         The board should review regular reports from the audit committee and internal audit. The issues covered should include the committee's own activities in reviewing **control and risk management systems**, and also the **results of internal and external audit**, in particular the **control weaknesses identified.** The audit committee should also assess the **effectiveness of internal audit.**

(iv)   **Staff communications**

         The board should consider information communicated to them by staff on risk and control weaknesses. There should be channels of communication for staff to use to report **suspected breaches of laws, regulations or other improprieties.**

(v)   **Follow-up on problems**

         As part of the cycle of continual feedback, the board should review whether **changes or actions have occurred** in response to changes in risk assessment or weaknesses identified in previous reports.

(c) **Reporting on internal control**

The reports the board provides will depend on the stock exchange rules. Two major jurisdictions with differing requirements reflecting a differing approach to corporate governance are the UK and the USA.

UK requirements

The board should disclose, as a minimum, in the accounts the existence of a **process** for **managing risks**, how the board has **reviewed** the **effectiveness** of the process and that the **process accords** with **UK guidance**. The board should also include:

(i) An **acknowledgement** that they are **responsible for the company's system of internal financial control** and **reviewing its effectiveness**

(ii) An **explanation** that such a system is designed to **manage** rather than eliminate the risk of **failure** to **achieve business objectives**, and can only provide **reasonable,** and not absolute, **assurance** against material misstatement or **loss**

(iii) A **summary** of the process that the **directors** (or a board committee) have **used to review the effectiveness** of the **system of internal financial control** and consider the need for an **internal audit** function if the company does not have one. There should also be disclosure of the process the board has used to deal with **material internal control aspects** of **any significant problems** disclosed in the annual accounts

(iv) **Information** about those **weaknesses** in internal financial control that have resulted in material losses, contingencies or uncertainties that require disclosure in the financial statements or the auditor's report on the financial statements.

USA requirements

Under the Sarbanes-Oxley requirements, annual reports should contain **internal control reports** that state the responsibility of management for establishing and maintaining an **adequate internal control structure** and **procedures for financial reporting.** Annual reports should also contain an **assessment** of the **effectiveness** of the **internal control structure** and **procedures** for **financial reporting,** additionally disclosures of any **material weaknesses** in internal control. Auditors should report on this assessment.

If you have any further questions on these issues, please do not hesitate to get in touch.

20 Ethical considerations

Text references. Chapter 11.

Top tips. The single 25 mark requirement makes this question a tough one.

The way to approach this question is to remember that you are looking to generate a dozen or so discussion points, each worth 2 marks or so. Under each of the possible options you will need to examine the consequences, both the financial consequences and any other consequences that may seem ethically relevant. You are also looking for threats to integrity that will apply whatever the situation and should try to make as much use of the information in the scenario as possible. For example the information may cast doubt on the proposed action and indicate that alternative action is better.

Although it's not specifically stated as professional marks in the question, you would probably gain some credit for using a memo format, including an introduction summarising the problem. You'd also gain marks for thinking more widely and addressing at the end of your answer other issues the situation raises.

Easy marks. Because of the nature of the question, the easiest marks are those for using the right answer format.

REPORT

To: The Managing Director
From: The Financial Controller
Date: 1 November 20X6
Subject: Issues arising from the meeting with X Ltd regarding payment of their debt

Introduction

We are being asked to supply further materials on credit to X Ltd on the understanding that this offers our best chance of being paid both for long-outstanding existing debts and the further debts that will arise.

Firstly I need to point out that our **Sales Director** feels that we should accept what has been informally agreed but she has **openly admitted that she has difficulty in taking an objective view of the situation**, having done business with Y for many years.

However, the agreement that is being proposed leaves me with **grave doubts**, both on ethical grounds and from the point of view of the business.

Our options are:

(a)   Accept the agreement as proposed;
(b)   Sue for payment or simply write off the debt;
(c)   Refuse the payment from Y but supply further materials in any case.

(a)   **Accepting the agreement**

       Consequences of acceptance

       This option puts us in a position where we are owed (and are at risk of losing) not only our existing debt of £A but also a further amount (say £B, based on past trading experience).

       Significance of personal payment

       I am not sure what the **role of the personal payment** is meant to be. It is not a bribe, although seems doubtful, since the intention is that it would be repaid. Presumably it is a sign of good faith, but why not inject the funds directly into the company and pay off some debts now? If Y is not willing to risk loaning the funds to his company, why should we be any more willing to take the risk of supplying further goods?

       Reaction of other suppliers

       In any case, recovery of our debt depends not only on our support but also that of all or almost all of **X Ltd's other suppliers**. We have no guarantee that this support will be forthcoming. (Indeed, I have just received a telephone message from another supplier indicating that they too are worried about X Ltd's position, and asking for our view (see below).)

       Implications of liquidation

       If the company is forced into liquidation by other creditors (or if X Ltd cannot complete the next stage of the work) what are we expected to do about the **personal payment**? I am not sure how it would be viewed by the law. It would put us in a more advantageous position than other creditors, but unfairly so.

       Other issues

       There are other matters that cause me to have doubts.

       •   Why can X Ltd not obtain an **advance from their bank** against the promise of the next progress payment? Has this option been attempted? If not, are the bank fully aware of the difficulties of X Ltd?

       •   Are X Ltd already **'trading wrongfully'**, which is illegal? To knowingly enter into an agreement that allows this to continue calls our own integrity into question.

(b) **Suing for payment or writing off the debt**

Financial implications

Since we are unlikely to recover our debt this option will simply **increase our loss** because we will have to pay legal costs. X Ltd may be counting on the fact that we know this.

Consequences of this option

One possible virtue of this option is that the threat of liquidation, or liquidation itself, may force Y to come to an **arrangement with all creditors** if we are unable to persuade him to try this by other means.

Impact on reputation

Writing off the debt now has the virtue that we do **not risk losing a further amount** by supplying more materials. On the down side, it could make us **look 'soft'** to other customers, and it is possibly unduly harsh not to give X Ltd a chance to recover the situation. It is not in our long-term interests for our customers to go out of business.

I cannot recommend either of these options except in the very last resort.

(c) **Refuse the payment but supply the materials**

Implications of this option

This is a better option because it leaves us with a clear conscience **regarding the payment, and does not compromise Y in any way**. The **other problems remain**, however.

Requirements of situation

We need to be assured that:

(i) X Ltd really can **complete the next stage of the contract**

(ii) X Ltd can **secure the support of its other creditors.**

If we are satisfied on point (i), we could encourage X Ltd to **enter into negotiations** with all of its suppliers. We can let it be known that we will be willing to help if others are: this will put X Ltd in a stronger position.

If X Ltd is able to get the level of support needed, this option is the one that I recommend.

Enlisting other suppliers

If both you and Y agree to this I may have an immediate opportunity to help out, since (as I mentioned) I have already had an enquiry from an acquaintance working for another supplier who will also, I think, be keen to **salvage something** from the situation if at all possible.

Confidentiality is an issue at present, so for the time being I have sent a fax explaining that we are currently negotiating with X Ltd and that I will be in touch once I know the outcome of our talks. (You will realise that my own professional integrity could be compromised if I supply information that could be considered misleading. I cannot simply ignore the enquiry or be cagey about it since this could itself be construed as a 'bad' reference.)

(d) **Wider issues**

Credit control problems

We need to consider whether this situation has arisen due to problems with **credit control** on our part. It could perhaps be argued that we should have worked more closely with X Ltd to prevent the problem arising in the first place. We should have been aware that X Ltd was taking on a much larger contract than it has previously been used to dealing with and we should have anticipated problems.

Credit control improvements

Over the next few days I shall be looking into ways in which our credit control systems can be adapted to ensure that external matters such as this are taken into account.

Signed: Financial Controller

21 Environmental and social issues

Text references. Chapter 12.

Top tips. Although it may seem difficult to find enough to say about this question, once you remember that environmental reporting impacts significantly upon reputation risk and think about the impact of stakeholder viewpoints, you can score well. One reason for disclosure is that the consequences may be worse if disclosure doesn't happen, as discussed at the start of the answer.

In (a) a good way of thinking through the environmental consequences is to go through the inputs, processes, outputs model and consider the likely environmental consequences at each stage. The social issues discussion is a good illustration of why background reading is useful; you can bring in topics that are currently areas of concern such as low-cost labour.

In (b) the range of business activity covered will depend on what is significant. The discussion about how the business can impact on its suppliers is an important acknowledgement that sometimes these issues cannot be tackled in isolation.

(c) draws a contrast between a compliance approach (hence data is needed to ascertain whether the business has complied) and a competitive approach (where the business is trying to improve and hence setting challenging targets, the board therefore requiring data about whether these targets have been met).

Easy marks. No particularly easy marks in this question.

REPORT

To: The Board
From: Management accountant
Date: 1 October 20X4
Subject: Environmental and social reporting

Problems with disclosure

As the Chief Executive has observed, our Annual Report contains all the disclosures currently required. Any additional disclosure may be to the **benefit of our competitors** and could draw **attention to any perceived weaknesses** in our performance in this sensitive area. Despite such arguments, we cannot ignore the increasing pressure on us to include environmental and social issues within our Annual Report.

Reasons for the inclusion of environmental and social issues in the Annual Report

Competitor disclosure

As the non-executive directors have observed, **many comparable companies** already **do include such issues** in their Annual Report and we may attract adverse publicity if we do not follow this trend.

Attracting investments

There may be **positive benefits** to reporting such issues too. For example, an increasing amount of attention is being devoted to environmental and social issues. **'Green' and 'ethical' fund mangers** have increasing funds available for investment and we may be able to demonstrate that we are suitable for such investment, thereby increasing our share price.

Strategic considerations

Moreover, the Board should be constantly scanning the environment in which the organisation operates, including social and environmental areas, in order to assess the impact of any **changes on the future of the business.**

Government pressure

There have also been recent comments by a government minister that 'if all companies do not make progress', legislation on environmental and social issues will be introduced. If we were to include such issues in our Annual Report we **avoid being forced into providing damaging disclosures required by a more stringent regime.**

(a) **The range of environmental and social issues to cover**

Obtaining copies of annual reports

A first step should be to **view copies of annual reports of companies who positively report** on such issues in order to familiarise ourselves with current best practice, thereby identifying **benchmarks** against which we might be measured. We also need to be aware of current high-profile pressure groups, and a regular review of the press should highlight these 'popular' concerns.

Consumption of raw materials

The greatest focus from an environmental point of view is likely to be on our **consumption of raw materials from tropical areas**. We may wish to consider the concept of **'sustainability'** – are we replanting at a rate equal to or greater than that at which we are harvesting. If so, we are likely to be viewed favourably.

Costs of processing

The **costs of processing** should also be considered, in particular the percentage of **energy** coming from renewable and non-renewable sources and the steps we have taken to increase the efficiency with which we use energy.

Packaging

Packaging is of increasing concern to many consumers. The proportion of both our products and their packaging made from recycled material should be measured, as should the ease with which they can be **recycled after use**.

Social issues

Social issues to cover include minimum rates of pay, the minimum age of child labour, working conditions and living conditions, such as the availability of health care and education. The public's interest in our consumer markets tends to focus on the **discrepancies between 'living standards' in their affluent market compared to those in less developed countries**. In setting standards we need to gather data about these issues in the source countries. Rates of pay expressed in relation to UK earnings may seem derisory but when expressed in relation to the local average they may seem much more acceptable. Using children aged just 14 as part of the labour force may seem less offensive if local schooling is provided up to the age of 12 and the company provides additional education as part of its benefits package.

Nature and extent of reporting

How well our actual performance compares with what we consider to be acceptable standards will determine the nature and extent of any reporting on these issues. If we believe our performance is above average we may well make extensive disclosures in order to gain maximum benefit. The poorer our performance, the less we may choose to disclose. If there are any single issues that, were they disclosed would lead to adverse publicity, we may choose to make no disclosures until these issues are resolved to an acceptable level.

Changing viewpoints

It should be noted, however, that the **popularity** or otherwise of environmental and social issues moves constantly with **changes in public opinion and government policy**. We should endeavor to **anticipate the demands of our stakeholders**, however, rather than appear to be simply reacting to the current 'popular' issues.

(b) **Determining the range of business activity**

Factors to consider

The value chain

A first step could be to **identify the value chain** within the organisation, thereby allowing for all activities (from the sourcing of raw materials through to the selling activity) to be **assessed for their current and future impact on social and environmental issues**. High-risk areas are those that are likely to have a significant impact on profitability if appropriate contingency plans are not in place.

Business partners

We also need to consider **whether to report on the activities of Z plc alone or on those of all of our business partners**, including those from whom we source our raw materials and the sub-contractors we employ during production. It could be argued that we cannot control our sub-contractors, and therefore should not include their activities within our report. For example, it could be deemed unfair if we were held responsible for contractors employing young children without our knowledge.

It is **unlikely that 'we didn't know' would be accepted as a defense were damaging information made public**, however. Once the range of performance benchmarks is established, we should therefore provide it to all of our sub-contractors and advise them that we expect them to conform to such standards. These could be included as a requirement in the **supplier tendering process**.

Impact of stakeholders

Problems are likely to centre on **identifying those issues that will be of concern in the future to stakeholders**. We shall also need to balance the demands of shareholders for maintaining a profitable activity with the concerns of pressure groups over the activity in question.

(c) **Assessing the information requirements at Board level**

Impact of attitude

The **additional information** to be supplied at board level will **depend on the company's ongoing attitude to environmental and social issues**.

Legal compliance

The company may take the view that environmental and social issues are of **no concern**. The company should therefore only be interested in ensur**ing that current legal requirements are met and that the costs of adverse publicity are avoided**. If this is the case, I would recommend that an **individual becomes responsible for monitoring social and environmental developments** and advises the Board if or when the company is required to take additional steps. Disclosure would be kept to a minimum, and would concentrate on practices that are of benefit to the community at large, rather than those that may be of interest to competitors.

Competitive advantage

Given that there is substantial interest amongst consumers and investment fund managers in doing business with companies who are environmentally and socially responsible, we may intend to **report on environmental and social issues as part of our competitive strategy**. The information requirements at board level would then increase significantly. A **study** would need to be conducted into establishing what is considered to be **best practice**. This would identify the **investment requirements of the ethical investment**

funds and the **current thinking on environmental and social issues by the various pressure groups**, such as Amnesty International and Greenpeace.

Impact on reporting

The company should then establish a **formal code of challenging targets** (such as 95% of packaging used should be made from recycled materials) to be achieved on these environmental and social issues and a **report on how these targets are being met should be included as part of the normal internal reporting package**. Areas in which we are particularly successful and which are not commercially damaging (such as a change in product design) could then be included in the Annual Report

Conclusion

I believe that the impact of social and environmental issues will grow in importance and I would be happy to provide any help the Board may require in developing our environmental and social reporting systems.

Signed: Management Accountant

22 Edted

Text references. Chapters 2, 10 and 12

Top tips. It would not be that difficult to set a 25 mark question on corporate citizenship, so you only have time to summarise the main issues in (a). As (a) is only worth 5 marks, this indicates that what is wanted is little more than a definition and a quick summary of the main elements of citizenship. This question is a good illustration of how the question verbs will work in P1. The verbs for (a) (explain and identify) are at a lower level than the verbs for (b) (assess) and (c) discuss.

Good knowledge is required for (b) but the use of assess means that you have to consider how much EMAS will impact upon what Edted does.

The verb discuss in (c) means that you have to consider both sides of the viewpoint. We have done this by saying that there are factors that can influence the ethical positions of staff differently, but then arguing that Edted can use, or have some influence over, these factors. Note the importance of ethical education; (c) can certainly be read as demonstrating how useful ACCA's ethics module will be!

Easy marks. As mentioned above, corporate citizenship is a fairly elastic concept so if your answer was along the lines we discussed, you should have been well-rewarded.

REPORT

To: Directors Edted

From: Consultant

Date: 16 May 20X7

Subject: Corporate citizenship

Introduction

Companies have choices as to how they manage their businesses. These choices can be many and varied but the choices that are made can determine whether or not the company is seen as a good citizen. Many of the world's companies are setting high standards of behaviour in many aspects of business and in a wider social context.

(a) **Corporate citizenship**

Definition

The concept of citizenship **shapes the values** that directors and employees are influenced by when participating in business and engaging with others outside the organisation. The concept of corporate citizenship recognises that there is a connection between the **everyday activities** of companies and the **wellbeing of society** as a whole, including minimising harm and maximising benefit. In recent years companies have adopted a more comprehensive approach to corporate citizenship in general, and this includes social and environmental responsibility.

Stakeholders

Directors now accept that they are not only responsible to the shareholders, the owners of the company, but also to a wider selection of **other stakeholders** which will include employees, customers, business partners, suppliers, the community and government. This however raises various difficult issues, including who **exactly stakeholders are,** what is the **extent of responsibilities** towards each class of stakeholder and how should an organisation **judge between the competing claims** of different stakeholders.

Main elements

It can be argued that corporate citizenship particularly impacts upon the following areas:

- **The basic values, policies and practices of a company** and its business at home and abroad

- The **management of environmental and social issues** within the value chain of business partners

- The **voluntary contributions** made by a company to community development around the world

Extent

Businesses who are seeking to be good corporate citizens must decide the extent to which they will participate in society. Will the main emphasis be on **interaction with employees and local communitie**s, or will the organisation take a wider view of social and political citizenship, seeking to respect and promote the rights of all citizens in the society.

(b) **Significance of EMAS**

Registration under EMAS demonstrates a **commitment to rigorous policies** for controlling the organisation's interaction with the environment. Companies that have adopted the EMAS scheme, particularly in countries where EMAS has not been widely used, are demonstrating the environmental aspects of corporate citizenship very seriously.

Internal procedures

Businesses should base what they do on an **environmental policy statement** that commits to **continuous environmental performance improvement** and goes beyond **compliance with legislation.** When EMAS is introduced, businesses should undertake an on-site environmental review. The management systems that businesses introduce have to be clearly linked to the policy statement and the review results; feedback must impact on policies.

Audit requirements

Feedback will not just come from internal review, but external environmental audits taking place every three years. **Rigorous external verification** is a principal reason why EMAS is regarded as a robust system. The audit does not just **test compliance,** but produces feedback that influences future objectives and targets. The environmental policy and management systems cannot therefore remain static, but must evolve in the light of the feedback from auditors.

Disclosure requirements

Disclosure requirements are the other key elements of EMAS, since the scheme is based on the idea of **rigorous public scrutiny.** Companies need to make detailed disclosure requirements about policy, management systems and performance in areas such as pollution, waste, raw material usage, energy, water and noise. Again external verification is required, **review of environmental statements** by **accredited environmental verifiers.** The disclosure requirements may (are perhaps designed to) make businesses confront tough choices. Will they seek to fulfil targets at the expense of profit maximisation, or will they risk falling short of their environmental targets if it means maintaining profit levels.

ISO 14000

The ISO 14000 group of standards encourages businesses to adopt many of the same elements as the EMAS standards, including an **environmental policy statement**, an **initial environmental review** and an **environmental management system**. However under these standards the system is policed by internal audit making reports to senior management. Disclosure requirements are less rigorous with the central requirement being a statement of compliance with ISO 14001. Critics have claimed that the ISO 14000 standards place excessive emphasis on systems, and do not emphasis sufficiently the need for **better performance.**

(c)   **Basis for finance director's viewpoint**

The finance director's viewpoint is based on the idea that the ethical influences that individual employees have experienced over their lives are all-important, and that Edted cannot overcome these influences. The **level of personal integrity** staff have will have a significant impact, and there may be a number of influences on staff's ethical outlook. However Edted may be able to use some of these influences as a means of encouraging staff to act ethically.

National and cultural beliefs

Nations and cultures vary in the importance they give to different ethical issues, and it is likely that some of these variations will exercise a significant influence on individuals' attitudes. For example national society may place a lot of emphasis on **individual autonomy and fulfilment** rather than the individual striving towards group community goals. The extent to which **money and possessions** are valued in society as opposed to **people and relationships** will also be significant.

The directors may have difficulty overcoming deep-rooted cultural factors, but may be able to promote positive ethical culture by a mission statement, also **setting a good example.** Staff may be more likely to act ethically if their managers are driving good ethical behaviour.

Education

The individuals' education and the **degree to which citizenship** has been emphasised may also have a significant influence. However Edted can of course provide **ethical training** for individuals itself, and make ethical behaviour part of the **appraisal** system.

Cognitive moral development

Using the categories developed by **Kohlberg,** individuals with low moral development are unlikely to be influenced by concepts such as citizenship but by whether they will be **rewarded or punished** for particular actions. At a higher level, individuals' actions will be determined by what is **expected** of them by society so if concepts of citizenship are emphasised by society, individuals will try to be good citizens. At the highest levels, individuals will be making their **own decisions** about whether and how to act as good citizens.

However Edted's board can analyse the level of moral development that individuals have and tailor policies accordingly. **Disciplining staff** who act unethically should work well if staff are perceived to have low (pre-conventional) levels of moral reasoning. **Establishing the right culture,** communicating to staff that 'we don't do that sort of thing round here' should influence staff who see ethics as fitting in with whatever is accepted behaviour where they work. **Education and training** should be geared towards encouraging staff towards a higher level of moral development.

Locus of control

Individuals' **locus of control** may have a significant influence on how active their ethical position is. Individuals with a high internal locus believe that they can have a **significant influence over their own lives.** This could well mean that they are prepared to take more responsibility and hence are more likely to take an active ethical position (a high Kohlberg level) than those who believe that their lives are shaped by accident or circumstances that they can't control.

Edted's managers may have problems overcoming a very **deep rooted locus of control.** However the overall management system may have some influence. If the systems are very bureaucratic, then individual ethical beliefs will be of little consequence, overridden by rules and regulations. If however staff are allowed more autonomy, a system that promotes individual discretion and rewards ethical behaviour could persuade staff that their own actions could make a difference.

Moral imagination

Moral imagination is the **level of awareness** that individuals have about the moral consequences that could arise from their actions. **Education and previous experience** may have a significant influence on moral imagination. Moral imagination is likely to be a significant factor in ethical situations that are not clearcut, where for example individuals have to choose between options that all may have ethical problems.

Again education and training, also ethical guidance and codes that emphasise the need for individuals to consider difficult situations carefully may promote higher awareness.

23 Code of conduct

Text references. Chapter 11.

Top tips. The verb discuss generally means that you should discuss both sides of a case. Although the advantages of establishing an audit committee are numerous, there are one or two disadvantages of which you should be aware.

In (b) you need to consider what level of involvement internal audit ideally should have and what might be the problems limiting that involvement. The other steps are very important features of control systems. You will probably have to discuss them in any question scenario where directors are looking to improve the general control environment.

Easy marks. Hopefully you should have been able to come up with plenty of advantages of establishing an audit committee.

(a)   **Membership of audit committee**

An audit committee normally consists of the independent **non-executive directors** of the company, though there is no reason why other senior personnel should not attend on occasions.

The committee needs to consist of people who are senior enough to appreciate the delicacy of the position of defence companies in both security and political terms and therefore would have foreseen problems such as this.

Advantages of setting up an audit committee

Awareness of executive directors

The existence of an audit committee should make **executive directors** more **aware** of their **responsibilities**.

Contribution of outsiders

The audit committee should normally consist of **non-executive directors**, drawn from outside the company. They can apply their **experience** of other companies in recommending how problems such as failures of communication can be overcome.

Deterrent

The audit committee can act as a **deterrent** to the commission of **illegal acts** by **executive directors**, and may discourage directors from behaving in ways which could be **prejudicial** to **shareholders' interests**.

Liaison with auditors

The audit committee can act as a forum for **liaison** with the **external** and **internal auditors**. The auditors will have an opportunity to express any concerns or problems they might have, such as inability to obtain information or lack of confidence in executive management.

Review of financial information

The audit committee can **review financial documents** such as the year-end accounts or interim statements.

Review of systems

The audit committee can use their collective experience to **review objectively** the **operation** of **internal control and risk management systems** from a perspective outside any operating considerations.

Disadvantages of setting up an audit committee

Lack of transparency

Since the findings of audit committees are rarely made public, it is not always clear **what they do or how effective** they have been in doing it.

Brake on business

The audit committee's approach may prove somewhat **pedestrian**, resolving little of consequence but acting as a **drag** on the drive and entrepreneurial flair of the company's senior executives.

Audit committee assistance

Prevention of problems

Prevention could have been achieved by a **review** of the company's operations, including sales reports and review of authorisation systems to ensure their adequacy.

Detection of problems

Detection could have been achieved by providing a **confidential listening post** for suppliers, customers and members of the public, but most particularly for employees. These roles would be carried out in tandem with the internal audit function.

Investigation of problems

After discovery of this kind of problem the committee has a role as **'independent' investigator**. The resources at the audit committee's disposal will be both internal and external audit. The investigation will try to discover **how** such **sales** came to be **made**, on what was obviously a fairly regular basis, **who knew** about it and whether anyone on the board knew. The committee can also investigate how the **internal control** and **reporting function failed** to alert the board to the problem.

Management of outcome

The audit committee should also be in a position to help the company decide **what to do** about the situation. The sensitive nature of this area means that the company's public image may be badly affected and contracts, particularly with the government, may be threatened. In such a politically sensitive arena, the committee's **expertise** should be **invaluable**.

(b) **Involvement of internal audit**

Monitoring compliance

Whether the internal audit department is directly involved in ensuring compliance with the code depends to a great extent on the department's **terms of reference**. Normally, the central function of internal audit is to test the system of internal control. Ideally, the department should have been involved in **designing** the code and then **monitoring compliance** with the code. This seems unlikely to have happened here.

Reaction to breaches

It is more likely that internal audit will **react** to **reported breaches** of the code, or breaches uncovered by normal internal audit work on the control system. At worst, internal audit may have no reference to the code, although it is possible that the department is involved in occasional studies.

Problems with code

The ideal type of involvement of internal audit may be developed in future, but there are problems, particularly where the code is a very vague 'be good' document. **Internal audit** will need more **specific rules** in the code so that compliance can be judged more objectively.

Evidence seeking

Internal audit may also need to **abandon** the **usual standards** of **documentation** and **proof** as breaches of the code are unlikely to be very public or documented at all. The department is being asked to behave like a private detective, rather than an internal audit department.

Other steps

Given the difficulty of implementing an ethical culture, a good code of conduct and of monitoring the situation, the following should be carried out.

Review and amend the existing code

The code should be amended as necessary to be as **specific and comprehensive** as possible.

Check that the code is disseminated

The code should be **distributed throughout the whole company**, from board level downwards. Board members and staff should acknowledge that they have **received a copy** and that they **agree to adhere to its principles.**

Whistleblowing

The company should **implement** a **confidential reporting system** for staff, using the audit committee, internal audit department and possibly other more informal routes.

Internal processes

The board should **ensure staff** are **trained** in ethical matters and that ethics are included as a component in all managerial decision-making, including budgeting and reporting.

Rewards and deterrents

The board should **introduce** a **formal punishment and reward structure**. Staff should know that they will be punished for ethical breaches, but also that there is a positive reward for being ethical and reporting any breaches of the code.

Board support

The main board and the audit committee must clearly communicate to the rest of the company that the code has the **full authority** of the board and the committee behind it.

24 Drofdarb

Text references. Chapters 3,4 and 11.

Top tips. (a) starts with a straightforward test of knowledge of the ethical principles; however the second half of (a) is more demanding and is a particular concern of the examiner, how an ethical culture is promoted. (b) requires focus on the role of the board in risk management, and an acknowledgement of the limitations of what the board can ensure.

Note in (c) that the independence issues are not clearcut and hence need some discussion. The grounds for making the recommendation are that there are too many potential threats to independence.

Easy marks. You need to learn the fundamental principles if you struggled with the first part of (a) as they really do represent core knowledge. Likewise the four main roles of the non-executive directors has been stressed by the examiner as important knowledge.

Marking scheme

			Marks
(a)	1 mark per principle up to a maximum of 6, plus up to 3 marks for discussion of codes of conduct and visibility		9
(b)	1 mark per point discussed up to a maximum of 4; up to 3 marks for reasons why risks may not be fully eliminated; 1 mark available if mention of links to best practice	max	6
(c)	1 mark per point discussed on role of NED up to a maximum of 4; up to 6 marks for discussions of suitability of NED candidate and conclusion		10
			25

(a) **ACCA's ethical code**

ACCA's ethical code contains the following basic principles.

Integrity

A professional accountant should be **straightforward and honest in performing professional services**. A professional accountant should not be party to the falsification of any record, or knowingly or recklessly supply any information or make a statement that is misleading, false or deceptive in a material particular.

Objectivity

A professional accountant should be **fair** and should **not allow prejudice or bias** or the influence of others to override objectivity.

Professional competence and due care

In agreeing to provide professional services, a professional accountant implies that there is a level of competence necessary to perform those services and that his or her knowledge, skill and experience will be applied with **reasonable care and diligence**. A professional accountant is expected to **present information fully, honestly and professionally,** so that it will be **understood in its context**. She/he also knows, understands and follows **technical standards** and should ensure that all professional services are carried out in accordance with those standards.

Professional behaviour

A professional accountant should behave in a manner consistent with the good reputation of the institute. ACCA requires that its members **refrain from any conduct that might bring discredit** on the institute, especially with regard to their responsibilities towards employers, clients, third parties, other members of the accounting profession, employees and the general public.

Confidentiality

A professional accountant should **respect the confidentiality of information** acquired during the course of performing the professional services and should not use or disclose any such information without proper and specific authority, or unless there is a legal or professional right or duty to disclose.

Action by business

Commitment from business

The use of an ethical code for any business should tie in good behaviour by staff with the overall success of the company. In order for any ethical guide to be successful, **commitment** from senior finance managers is required, along with **visible evidence** that **those** who follow the code **prosper** while those that do not will be **disciplined.**

Need for ethical code

As well as organisational ethical guidance, there probably needs to be an ethical code specifically for the finance staff. Staff need to understand that there is a **clear rationale** for the code. The code should consist of a combination of **specific guidance** and **general expectations** on what constitutes acceptable and unacceptable behaviour. The code must be **freely available** to all staff.

Action by Mr McKenna

Mr McKenna needs to be asked what he has done to ensure this form of control is adopted and maintained within his department, and whether any departures from this code have either occurred or been missed in the last year. His assertions that there is no problem need to be based on more than just perception and supposition; **facts and evidence** need to be collected.

(b) **Risk-based approach**

The UK's Turnbull Report is a good example of best practice. The Turnbull guidance follows a risk-based approach, highlighting the need for organisations to **identify and prioritise risks** and **deploy suitable controls**.

Board review

The Turnbull report suggests that boards should carry out regular and wider-ranging annual reviews of the effectiveness of **risk management and control systems.** The reviews should **cover all material controls** in respect of **financial, operational and compliance risks**. Boards should aim to ensure that **safeguards exist against loss of either assets or information** and that companies **comply with the relevant provisions** of the **Combined Code.**

Audit committee and audit

In addition to an annual review, the Turnbull guidance suggests that there should be an **audit committee** staffed by at least three NEDs with an **internal audit** function made up of employed staff. **Regular review of the systems of internal controls** by **internal audit** and **consultation with external audit** will help the organisation demonstrate that it is managing risks effectively.

Limitations of risk-based approach

The Turnbull guidance acknowledges the need to **manage risks by suitable internal controls.** However, it also acknowledges that there is **no perfect system** and that despite the best efforts of many key stakeholders, **risk** can only be **reduced**, not wholly eliminated. The reasons for this include **poor decisions** being made that result in losses. **Human error** can reduce the effectiveness of internal controls. There may be **deliberate circumvention of controls** by staff intent on fraud, malicious damage or **management override** for reasons of fraud or self – preservation. Controls may only be geared to **normal circumstances** and may not be able to cope with **unforeseeable circumstances.**

At best, a system of internal controls can only give **reasonable, not absolute, assurance** that systems are sufficient. It is up to the Drofdarb board to assess regularly the **uncertainties surrounding their business** to see how likely it is that systems will no longer be sufficient.

(c) **Contribution of NED**

The role of Non-Executive Directors (NED) was addressed by the UK Higgs report. They are an integral but complicated part of running a company because they **should form part of a board of directors** that has **clear responsibilities for running the company.** They also should be **independent**, having an **enquiring mind** and will need to be **well informed** and authoritative; these will enable them to **monitor the activities of executive directors** and the company's systems of risk management and internal control.

Role of NEDs

The Higgs report identifies four roles of NEDs.

(i) They should **aim to participate in setting the strategy** of a company, in particular challenging the proposals of executive directors.

(ii) They should **scrutinise the performance of executive management** in meeting goals and objectives, and monitor the reporting of performance.

(iii) They are responsible for seeing that **risk issues are addressed** within the company, in particular that **financial information** is **accurate** and **financial management** and **systems of control** are **robust.**

(iv) They should be **involved in the people side** of running the company, including their roles on the remuneration and nomination committees. They therefore participate in setting the remuneration of executive directors and the appointment of new directors, also succession planning for senior management over time.

Independence criteria

Cross-directorship

Before Mr McDermott can be considered for the vacant post of NED at Drofdarb, his **independence** needs to be considered. His position as executive director of Sdeel plc calls into question whether he can keep information obtained in the course of his business at both Drofdarb and Sdeel separate and not suffer a **conflict of interest** This is known as **cross directorship**.

Audit partner

His previous position as **audit partner** for Drofdarb shows him to have had a **material business interest** in Drofdarb, although he would not necessarily have had the company's interests in mind, rather those of the shareholders instead. This is less easy to query independence over than cross directorships. The length of time since he has been an audit partner (two years) also means that this is less of an issue.

Family connections

Given that Mr McDermott has **family connections** with the Sdeel and Drofdarb founders, more would need to be known about these connections before his independence could be assessed.

Shareholding

A shareholding in the company is not normally a threat to a non-executive director's independence, as one of his roles is to **represent the interests of other shareholders.**

However a very material shareholding might influence him significantly, particularly if he wants to dispose of it in the near future.

Conclusion

Difficulties in recruitment mean that there are only a limited number of non-executive directors, and sometimes compromises have to be made in order to recruit them. However, because of the **threats to independence**, it is unlikely that Mr McDermott can be entirely independent and as such his appointment as NED is not recommended.

25 Purchasing and entertainment

Text references. Chapters 6, 8 and 11.

Top tips. The key point in (a) was a recognition of the risk of collusion between purchasing staff and suppliers. The answer should have concentrated on controls which minimised this risk, particularly authorisation and monitoring. You needed to draw on your previous auditing studies to help you answer (a).

In part (b), we have looked at the ways in which the code can be seen as acceptable and the ways in which it can be seen as unacceptable and have then suggested ways in which it could be improved.

You may have simply concentrated on the factors within the code that required amendment and have redrafted it, or alternatively you may have defined and justified the code as it stands. Any reasonable approach will be rewarded.

Easy marks. There are plenty of controls that could be suggested in (a).

(a) The following features of the system should help minimise the risk of fraud.

   (i) **Risk assessment**

   Examples of purchase fraud include **rigged tendering**, **goods being supplied** for **private purposes** and **fraudulent transactions** with **connected companies**. In setting up a control system therefore, management should be aware of what kinds of fraud the business may be at risk of experiencing.

   One possible danger is **collusion** between the person authorising purchases and suppliers. Once purchases have been authorised, there may be nothing further that can be done to prevent fraud. The important controls therefore are normally those which are aimed at identifying unusual suppliers or circumstances.

(ii) **Monitoring of suppliers**

The risk of collusion between suppliers and employees can be minimised in a number of ways.

(1) The person using the goods should only be able to choose suppliers from an **approved list**.

(2) The use of new suppliers should be **authorised** by **someone other** than the person using the goods. The person authorising new suppliers should be particularly wary of any of the following:

- Abnormal terms
- Suppliers providing goods which they would not normally supply
- Suppliers which appear small compared with the proposed volume of purchases

(3) In addition these should be **regular monitoring** by management of arrangements with suppliers. Warning signs should be investigated, such as suppliers handled directly by senior staff, or suppliers handled outside the normal control systems.

(iii) **Controls in the payment cycle**

(1) **Segregation of duties**

Segregation of duties can reduce certain risks. **Segregating** the **cheque-signing role** from the **payment authorisation** role can reduce the risk that payments are made out to certain types of bogus supplier, for example those with abbreviated names. Part of the process of reviewing suppliers can be carried out at the payment stage, by checking that **individual** or **total payments** do **not appear excessive**.

(2) **Documentation**

Requirements for **full documentation** should be linked to segregation of duties. Full documentation would include **purchase requisitions**, **purchase orders** and **purchase invoices**. These can help prevent purchases for private use.

Documentation of returns is also important; **credit notes** should always be obtained from suppliers when goods are returned in order to prevent inventory losses through bogus returns.

(iv) **Contract management**

There are a number of different types of contract fraud including fixing the contract tendering process and undue payments in advance. Ways of preventing contract fraud include the following.

(1) An open **competitive tendering** process.

(2) Interim payments being made on **certification** from **independent valuers**.

(3) Any **changes to terms** being **authorised independently** of the person who deals with the contractors on a day to day basis.

(v) **Organisation and staff controls**

(1) **Personnel**

References should be obtained for all new staff, and details retained of previous employers so that possible collusion can be checked.

(2) **Ethics**

A **business code of ethics** can remind staff of what constitutes unreasonable inducements.

(vi) **Internal audit**

Internal audit can play a role in a number of the above checks, particularly the following.

(1) **Detailed checks** of documentation.

(2) **Scrutiny** of suppliers and payments for suspicious circumstances.

(b) As with many codes of conduct adopted in practice, there are both acceptable and unacceptable aspects to the code in question.

Aspects of the code which are acceptable

(i) The organisation has adopted a code of conduct which attempts to **conform** with **customary business practices**. It wishes to behave in a manner consistent with that of others in the market.

(ii) The code appears to imply that employees can take **slight risks** and go beyond behaviour that might be construed as strictly correct in order to secure sales. It would be logical and reasonable to do this in order to gain a sales advantage.

(iii) The conduct of the members of the staff working in the **purchasing function** is **controllable** by the organisation and so the organisation can determine the code of conduct which should apply. The code of conduct covering the **selling operation** has to meet the **expectations** of the **market** and **customers**, however. The organisation has **no control** over its **potential customers**, who can decide whether or not they should accept any gifts, favours or entertainment offered. That part of the code of conduct relating to the purchasing activity is therefore necessarily stricter and more stringent than the part relating to the sales activity.

(iv) Any **gifts**, favours and entertainment **provided** by a **supplier benefits** an **employee** whereas those provided for **customers benefit** the **customer** rather than the employee (unless the entertainment is lavish). There are therefore stricter controls over purchasing staff than sales staff.

Aspects of the code which are unacceptable

(i) The code **fails to provide sufficient guidance**. For example, it does not specify the nature of customary business practices, common courtesies and so on. Employees have no idea about whether they can offer a potential customer a glass of wine, a bottle of wine or a case of wine.

(ii) The code gives **no information** about the **repercussions** for employees for contravening the code. There is therefore no indication of the seriousness with which the organisation views breaches of the code.

(iii) The penultimate sentence about 'favours or entertainment, appropriate in our sales programmes' implies a **double standard** and may encourage sales personnel to adopt a position which could damage the good name of the organisation.

(iv) The unclear nature of the code relating to sales means that, because **behaviour is not actually illegal**, it may be **adopted** because it increases the organisation's short-term profits (despite the fact that it might have longer-term repercussions).

(v) If **performance measures** are based on **short-term profit**, **employees** may feel **pressurised** into adopting unethical or even illegal behaviour.

Suggested amendments to the code of conduct

Given the above comments there are various amendments which could be made to the code of conduct to increase its acceptability.

(i) **Ambiguous terms** should be **clarified**.

(ii) **Penalties** for contravening the code could be **included**.

145

(iii)   It could be drastically **simplified** and the entire section on business courtesies deleted since the information provided in the remaining section provides an adequate and concise code of conduct.

(iv)   The **code relating** to the conduct of employees working in the sales function could be **rewritten** with the intention of making it as **strict** and **clear** as that covering the purchasing function employees (no entertainment, no gifts and so on). There are commercial problems associated with such an approach, however; the market and customers may expect a more liberal attitude.

Such changes would produce an **unambiguous**, **clear** and **concise code of conduct** which will **protect** the **integrity** of the organisation and allow **employees** to be **confident** that their efforts for the organisation will remain within acceptable limits.

26 JH Graphics

Text references. Chapters 1 and 10.

Top tips. (a) is a good example of how ethical theories may be applied to a situation. The difference between being ethical because one should be (normative view) and being ethical because it achieves a financial/strategic end (instrumental view) is very important in this exam. (b) is also a good example of how ethical theory is applied in practice. The key distinction here is between being ethical because of benefit/harm considerations (pre conventional) and being ethical because one should conform with norms (conventional).

Ethical factors are of significance in (c), but you also need to think about strategic issues and reputation risk – very significant in a situation like this. Assess in this context means saying something about the significance of these factors.

To score well in (d) you need to say why the religious group may have a claim. Whatever your personal views, you also should acknowledge that other frameworks may be used to make this decision.

Easy marks. (c) may have been the easiest part of this question as you could generate some ideas from your general business awareness rather than having to concentrate strictly on ethics.

ACCA examiner's answer. The examiner's answer to this question is included at the back of this kit.

Marking scheme

			Marks
(a)	1 point for each relevant point made on normative	4	
	1 point for each relevant point made on instrumental	4	
			8
(b)	1 mark for evidence of understanding the terms	2	
	1 mark for application for each to case	2	
			4
(c)	2 marks for each relevant point made		10
(d)	1 mark for each relevant point made		3
			25

(a) **Jenny's view**

Jenny's view is based on a **normative view of ethics**, that the company should behave in an **ethical way as an end in itself**, and not a means to another end. Hence JH Graphics should not hesitate to adopt the code because it signifies that ethical behaviour is at the core of what it does. Her motivation is **altruistic** rather than **business strategic**.

The moral framework that supports this view is derived from **Kant's** notion of civic duties. Kant argued that these duties are required in maintaining good in society. Amongst these duties is the **moral duty to take account of others' concerns** and opinions; not to do so will result in a failure of social cohesion and everyone being worse off.

Extending the normative view to stakeholder theory, Jenny's view is that JH Graphics should accommodate stakeholder views because of its **moral duties** to its stakeholders, not because accommodating stakeholder concerns will help it achieve its own economic or other concerns.

Alan's view

Alan's view is based on an **instrumental view of ethics**. This sees the company taking ethical positions into account only when they are consistent with the overriding economic objective of **maximising shareholder value**. Hence Alan is concerned with the **strategic implications** of the code (will not adopting it place JH Graphics at a competitive disadvantage) and the **costs of drawing it up and implementing it**.

The instrumental view in relation to stakeholders suggests that shareholder concerns should be accommodated if not doing so threatens its ability to maximise shareholder value. Thus taking account of shareholder opinions is a **means to the end of maximising economic value**, not an end. Thus stakeholders are judged not in terms of whether it is ethically right to respond to their concerns, but how powerful they are in terms of how much influence they can have on JH Graphics achieving its economic objectives.

(b) **Conventional viewpoint**

Kohlberg identified the conventional viewpoint as one of the levels of moral reasoning. Using this perspective, individuals judge ethical decisions in terms of what is **expected of them** in terms of the norms of society or organisation. In this example Jenny would take into account what would be considered **good practice** in the industry; would other companies use similar images even if they did cause offence. She would also consider society's viewpoint as expressed in the law; would the images possibly break laws relating to good taste. Another viewpoint would be whether **members of society other than those belonging to the religious group** would find the image offensive.

Pre-conventional viewpoint

The pre-conventional reasoning viewpoint sees reasoning in terms of the **rewards or punishments** that will result from a particular act. The factors influencing the decision would be whether JH Graphics would suffer a **legal penalty** through its association with the advert, whether it would **lose business** because of the offence taken by potential client or whether (as Alan argues) it would **gain business** through the **free advertising**.

(c) **Variety of factors**

The board will take into account a number of different considerations, some of which are not easily comparable. However one means of aiding the decision would be to consider the various stakeholders affected, and to analyse their viewpoints in terms of **Mendelow's stakeholder influence**, considering their **relative degree of power and influence**.

Relationship with customer

One obvious stakeholder with a strong economic relationship to JH Graphics is the **customer**. The board would need to consider whether business with the customer would be **threatened** if the advertisement was withdrawn and what the consequences would be in terms of **lost sales**. Another viewpoint would be that the customer's interests, that have been secured by paying the advertisement, should take precedence over the religious group's interest, as the religious group has **no economic relationship**. Of course the customer might prefer the advertisement to be withdrawn because it was damaging its interests. JH Graphics would presumably have to comply with the request, although then the issue would be whether there should be an apology.

Negative reputation consequences

The offence caused by the advertisement is an example of a reputation risk materialising, and the board therefore has to assess the consequences in terms of what stakeholders will do. Firstly would a **boycott by members of the religious group be significant**. More widely would actions taken by the **religious group and adverse press coverage** generated lead to other organisations **being unwilling to use JH Graphics** with further lost sales. The board will need to judge the **balance and strength of the coverage**.

Positive reputation consequences

However there may be an **upside to the reputation risk**. JH Graphics may **gain business** as a result of the advertisement with more clients being willing to use the company because it is seen as **forward-looking and daring**. Alan Leroy believes that the advertisement will be good for business. This may be jeopardised if the advert is withdrawn and an apology issued.

Organisational field

The board's decision may be affected by the organisational field of the advertising industry, the common **business environment**, **norms** and **values** within the industry. These appear to work in different directions however in this situation. On the one hand a lot of large companies are emphasising their **ethical commitment**; however there may be pressures within the industry to be **challenging and innovative**.

National culture

The board may also consider the **place of religion in the national culture**, how strongly religious ideas affect people's beliefs and actions.

Strategic considerations

Important strategic considerations include JH Graphics' positioning relative to its competitors. Does it wish to gain a **competitive advantage** through being seen as more ethical, or through being seen as more innovative or perhaps more subversive.

Company objectives

One particularly significant aspect of strategy is whether the objective of **profit maximisation** should be given precedence over everything else or whether JH Graphics exists to fulfil other significant considerations. This could be a very important decision for JH Graphics as there is evidently a dispute between the **purely capitalist, revenue-driven view** of Alan Leroy and the view of Jenny Harris that JH Graphics should express **ethical values through what it does**. The decision may end up having a significant influence on the company's future direction.

(d) **Narrow stakeholders**

The religious group's viewpoint would be that they are **narrow stakeholders**, meaning that JH Graphics' activities seriously affected their own interests. They argue that the content and design undermines their system of beliefs and threatens the promotion of their faith.

How valid this claim is viewed as depends on **how widely corporate accountability** and **stakeholder recognition** are **defined**. Certainly it seems that the advertisement may have affected the religious group's position. However some would claim that the religious group's position is weakened by their not having a **direct economic relationship** with JH Graphics. Another viewpoint is that offence taken by a stakeholder does not imply that JH Graphics has a responsibility towards them.

27 CER

Text references. Chapters 3, 6, 8 and 10.

Top tips. It's likely that P1 exam scenarios will often focus on large international organisations with a diverse range of activities and facing a variety of risks. However, in this particular example, the organisation in question is a charity providing international aid. You shouldn't be surprised about this as questions can be set in a variety of contexts, both profit-making and not-for-profit.

In (a) planning is important to make sure that you do not duplicate any of your answers to risks faced purely at home or away, or both home and away. It's easiest to answer (a) (i) and (ii) together here, evaluating each risk and then recommending how to mitigate it. (a) also illustrates that it's important to think beyond dishonesty/integrity and to consider other risks arising from poor control systems and risks arising from the wider environment. Reputation risk is more significant for a charity than for many limited companies. The professional marks will be awarded for how realistic overall your recommendations are for this charity.

(b) needs you to remember that corporate governance is not mandatory (unless the organisation is a listed company) but it is good practice; poor corporate governance won't help the charity's reputation.

(c) is a good illustration of how the accountant's role in society might be examined. It might be supposed that the auditors of charities have greater responsibilities towards stakeholders than company auditors. The discussion shows why, how they might fulfil their responsibilities and what might be the limitations on their doing so. Professional marks will often be awarded for the quality of your arguments. As the question says discuss, you must put both sides of the case fairly with roughly equal treatment of each side.

In (d) you need to make sure that you identify not only how the bank can be happy that CER will not default on its loan, but that you understand why the bank would be concerned about lending money to CER in the first place. One point that you may have come across in the context of financial management is worth repeating in the context of risk management. If the bank believes that CER is likely to default it should not lend money at all (avoid the risk); this is stronger risk management than obtaining security (reducing the impact if the risk materialises).

Easy marks. The points in (b) are all mainstream corporate governance issues that could apply to charities.

Marking scheme

				Marks
(a)	For each risk		2	
	Method of mitigating risk		1	
	Total per risk		3	
		max	18	
	Professional marks – Judgement on how successfully risks can be mitigated	max	2	
				20
(b)	For each area of corporate governance	max	2	
		max		8
(c)	For each point in favour or against	max	2	
	Max for points		10	
	Professional marks – Balanced discussion with some well-argued points for and against the viewpoint	max	2	
				12
(d)	Introduction to bank risk		2	
	Each factor to limit risk	max	2	
		max		10
				50

ANSWERS

(a) **Risks in home country**

Income (reputation and business risk)

CER depends almost entirely on donations and shop revenues for its income. There is a risk that donors /potential donors will stop giving to the charity because CER **loses credibility in its work** (reputation risk) or because other charities become more attractive (business risk). Giving may also fall if **disposable income decreases** as a result of interest rate rises, for example (economic risk).

CER could attempt to mitigate this risk by **collecting donations via direct debits** or other similar collection options.

Expenditure on board & finance

CER needs to ensure as high a percentage as possible of its income is actually spent on charitable work rather than being **lost in administration and finance operations**. The business risk is that donors will **stop giving to the charity** if too much of their donations seem to be used for administrative and finance functions.

CER could mitigate this risk by **publishing clear information on its expenditure** and showing that board remuneration, for example, is comparable with, or less than similar commercial organisations.

Integrity of volunteers

CER relies heavily on volunteers to both collect income via house-to-house collections and provide staffing for its shops. There is significant operational risk that **income** will be **understated** either because staff are **insufficiently trained and make errors** in collection of income (particularly in shops) or because volunteers are not **completely honest** regarding the amount of income collected.

This risk could be mitigated by **providing basic training on internal controls** expected within shops or ensuring volunteers have **suitable references** from their current or previous employers.

Charity fatigue

There is a general reputation risk that the work of charities is **not seen to be particularly efficient or effective**, decreasing the overall level of income for all charities (eg disaster appeal funds not reaching their intended recipients). Alternatively there may be a feeling that **sufficient money is already being given** to charities, limiting the amount new or existing donors wish to give the CER.

This risk is difficult to mitigate, unless as with income risk above, donors are encouraged to **donate via monthly direct debits** or **standing orders.**

Political risk

About 18% of CER's income is derived from **tax rebates on charitable donations**. This income stream is dependent on the government maintaining this tax benefit.

CER can attempt to mitigate this risk by continuing to **inform the government and the general public** of the amount of good work it is carrying out. If the income stream appears to be threatened, then more detailed information on the good causes that CER cannot assist because of this move could be given.

Integrity of board (business and reputation risk)

The **lack of appropriate corporate governance structures**, and sometimes experience of board members, could limit the apparent ability of CER either to **implement appropriate control systems** or **show its overall integrity** to third parties. Potential donors may be unwilling to donate to CER simply because they are unsure that their donation will be used for appropriate charitable purposes.

This risk could be mitigated by putting into place an appropriate system of corporate governance.

Risks in home country and overseas work

Legislation /political risk

There is a joint risk that legislation in either CER's home country or the country CER is providing assistance to, does **not allow transfer of resources** in the form of money, people or equipment etc. This would effectively curtail CER's operations in the recipient country.

There is very little that CER can do to mitigate this risk, apart from **generate publicity** to show what **good work cannot be done** as a result of the adverse legislation.

Internal control risk

Due to potential inexperience of staff, there is a risk in the home country or abroad that **income is lost** or that **expenditure is incurred** which is **not completely in accordance with CER's aims.** In other words, the **internal control systems** within CER are not sufficiently robust to identify loss of income or inappropriate expenditure.

This risk can be mitigated by **improving the control systems.** As with any other change, the **cost of the improvement** must be **weighed against the perceived benefit.**

Expenditure on supplies

Care is needed, both at home and overseas, that **purchases are obtained** for an **appropriate price.** There is the risk that suppliers could take advantage of CER's lack of controls to charge too high a price (although of course some suppliers may decrease prices to assist the charitable work of CER).

This risk can be mitigated by **comparing prices charged by suppliers** on a regular basis.

Trustworthiness of volunteers

In many situations CER uses volunteers to organise distribution of aid, whether this is in the form of money or goods. There is a risk, both in the home country and overseas, that the **aid does not reach the intended donors** because it is taken by volunteers or used for other purposes. The extent of the risk depends mainly on the ethics and level of corruption within the individual jurisdiction.

Again, it is difficult to mitigate this risk, unless CER decides to send aid only to countries with apparently low levels of corruption.

Risks in overseas work

Sufficient resources (demand > supply);

It may be difficult for CER to actually determine **what aid is necessary** in individual recipient countries. Other charities may also be providing aid, duplicating supply, or actual demand may be unclear because there is **not the expertise** to measure it correctly. There is therefore a risk that CER either sends aid to countries that do not require it or does not send aid to countries actually needing it.

The risk can only be mitigated by trained CER staff **assessing the situation** 'on the ground' in the individual country.

War (political risk)

There is a risk that distribution of aid is **disrupted by war** in the overseas country (the likelihood of war in this respect in CER's home country being deemed to be low). This provides the risk that aid will not be sent or provided to the expected donees but either lost, impounded or at worst taken by warring factions for their own use.

The risk can only be mitigated by CER **ceasing aid as soon as war is considered possible** or declared.

Cultural issues (local pride vs. need)

There is some cultural risk that aid will not be accepted due to the **pride of the intended recipients.**

There is little that CER can do to mitigate this risk, except attend to provide assistance where it is deemed to be necessary. Another possibility would be to **channel aid through independent organisations** such as the Disasters Emergency Committee in the hope that it will be received from them.

(b)   **Corporate governance**

Corporate governance is not mandatory for the CER charity but could be seen as **best practice** (especially to help in the loan applications).

Examples of good corporate governance that could be used within CER include:

Separate chairman and chief executive officer

This will help to enhance the overall control systems within the charity (no one person having too much power on the board) as well as placing one individual specifically in charge of ensuring that the **objectives of the charity** are **being met.**

Appointment of one or more non-executive directors

This will provide an **independent check** on the working of the board of directors. Again, control systems will be enhanced as the non-executive directors will be checking that the **objectives** of the **charity** are **being met.**

Properly briefed board

Board information at present appears to be **sketchy and incomplete.** Provision of enhanced reporting systems (eg level of donations reported within a few days of the month end) will help the board decide how much money can be used for charitable donations, rather than leaving this to 'guesswork' as is the current case.

Good internal controls for sound decision-making and accountability

Enhancing the control systems where possible will **improve the image** of CER, and provide additional re-assurance to donors that their money is being used for charitable purposes.

Provision of an internal audit function

Many large charities (eg Oxfam) have internal audit departments. Simply having the department will **improve the application of overall controls** as staff and volunteers realise that some basic checking of operations is being carried out.

Relations with stakeholders

Stakeholders for CER include not just the donors, but suppliers, recipients of aid and volunteers, employees working for CER. CER can at least start to **provide more information to these stakeholders** on its operations, and may eventually have some form of stakeholder committee to oversee CER and suggest new areas of activity.

(c)   **Arguments in favour of wider auditor involvement**

Responsibility to society

The basic argument in favour of greater auditor involvement is founded on the stakeholder view of companies and other organisations. The view is that society **allows organisations to carry out activities** and that in return organisations must consider all whom its activities affect, all its stakeholders. The audit should act as a check on whether organisations are doing this.

Position of charities

The stakeholder argument is evidently stronger for charities than it would be for limited companies who are obliged to consider the wishes of shareholders to maximise their income. Charities are constituted by their **trust deeds to fulfil certain purposes. Donor stakeholders** have contributed money on the basis that the charity will fulfil these purposes; the charity is obliged by its trust deed to consider whether the interests of recipient stakeholders have been met. There is also the wider argument that money not spent for 'proper purposes' is being diverted from other, worthier, causes.

Judgements

In response to the criticism that auditors **lack the ability** to make judgements about the use of money, the counter-criticism can be made that an audit is about making judgements. Above all a key part of the auditors' role is to judge whether accounts are fair; accounts that do not present a full view of charities' activities, highlighting contentious areas, cannot be considered to be fair.

Available audit techniques

A further argument is that auditors are perfectly able to carry out audits other those relating to the financial information in the accounts. In particular well-developed methodologies exist for considering the **value for money** of an organisation's activities.

Arguments against wider auditor involvement

Accountability

One argument against a wider audit role is the issue of **accountability**. Auditors are in the first place accountable to the **members** or **trustees** to whom their report is addressed. Any wider responsibility is defined by government or the regulatory bodies that prescribe the framework within which auditors report. The idea that auditors have a wider responsibility to society beyond governments or regulatory bodies that represent society begs the question what exactly is society.

Work auditors already do

The expressed opinion ignores the fact that auditors are required by auditing standards in most jurisdictions to consider **breaches of laws and regulations** that may impact upon the financial statements. Breach of its trust deed by a charity using money for improper purposes may ultimately threaten the charitable status of that charity and therefore its existence; thus auditors have to be alert for any such breaches and be aware of what forms these could take. In addition auditors may have specific responsibilities to report to charity regulatory bodies if charities use monies for improper purposes.

Evidence problems

It may be difficult for auditors to **obtain very strong evidence** about how charities' income is being spent. The auditors may have to **rely on reports** from the charity's operatives. Seeing for themselves how the charity's money is being spent may be impractical on anything other than a very limited basis because of the area over which the charity's activities are dispersed. The costs of visiting these activities, and hence the audit fees, may be considered higher than is desirable for the charity to bear, unless the view is taken that auditors should carry out charity audits for free or for limited fees as part of their 'wider duty to society.'

Political opinions

Finally the criticisms that money is not being spent effectively and is going to the wrong people may well be impossible to judge against the charity constitution or any objective standards. They may instead reflect the **political opinions** of those who make the judgements, and auditors are not employed to validate political opinions.

(d) **Risk avoidance – Intercontinental bank**

Problem of inflows

The main issue for the bank lending money to the CER charity is the **lack of definite cash inflows** to guarantee funds for repayment of the loan and accumulated interest. In many situations it is unusual for charities to ask for significant loans (Oxfam for example has no loans at all) although the need to diversify to protect income streams is valid from CER's point-of-view. The bank will want to **limit its risk exposure**, that is ensure that any loan to CER **fits the bank's risk profile** and is **not excessive** for the risk category of charities/non-commercial organisations.

Ultimately if the bank does not feel sufficiently sure that the money will be repaid, it should not make the loan.

Risk reduction

Assuming the bank feels that the **risk of non-repayment** is at an **acceptably low level**, it can gain assurance that it will receive money by the following methods.

Security for loan

The obvious form of **security for the loan** is a charge on the properties to be purchased by CER. Furthermore, if property prices are rising then this security will serve to both repay capital and accumulated interest should CER default on the loans.

Cash flow forecast-shops

CER should be able to obtain details of previous cash flows from the shops and from this extrapolate expected future income. The results of similar shops could be looked at in an attempt to confirm the accuracy of the forecasts. Overheads may well be less (use of some volunteer staff to clear tables etc) meaning that net cash inflows will be higher than other commercial coffee shops. This information will help the bank **check CER's ability to repay interest.**

Cash flows – further considerations

 The actual income generated from the coffee shops may well be dependent on their location. **Further analysis** is required to show where the coffee shops are, and how shopping trends in those areas will change in the future to confirm the accuracy of the cash flows. For example, a shop located in a "high street" which is being challenged by a new indoor shopping centre may expect to lose income whereas a shop in the new development would be expected to gain income.

Business plan for CER, charity shops and coffee shops

 Presenting a business plan showing expected income for CER and the coffee shops will help to provide some confidence on the **level of support from CER's other trading activities** (it is unlikely that donations would be available to repay loans for commercial ventures – donors normally expect their money to be used for charitable causes).

Separate limited company

Finally, the bank could encourage CER to establish the coffee shops as a **separate limited company** (possibly limited by guarantee). Establishing a separate company would ensure, for example, that **board members with commercial experience** were appointed and that **appropriate internal control systems** were established. This would provide the bank with confidence that the investments were being managed wisely, rather than have a 'charity' run the coffee shops with the implication, rightly or wrongly, that control systems would be weaker.

28 VCF

Text references. Chapters 1, 3, 4, 5 and 10.

Top tips. In (a) it is difficult to get away from the fact that the company is overwhelmingly dependent on Viktor but you have to try to make maximum use of the information in the scenario. The question is quite a test of your ability to assess a number of different types of control.

In (b) remember that this report is addressed to the board, in particular of course Viktor. Therefore you need to explain your recommendations in terms that make it likely that the board will accept them. However the company is listed, and therefore needs to introduce more formal systems and not be so dominated by a single individual. There are some fairly obvious indications of poor corporate governance. The risk part can (as often) be tackled by following through the main aspects of the risk management cycle. The controls discussion links into (a).

The professional marks would be available for putting your report in the right format and the persuasiveness of your answer.

(c) covers comprehensively the main concepts underpinning corporate governance that the syllabus emphasises. As you'd get two (possibly three) marks for discussing each concept you wouldn't have needed to have discussed all of them to obtain full marks. A quick definition of each is helpful; however to get full marks you need to relate the concept to the scenario and demonstrate why applying the concept in practice would be beneficial for VCF. Given that the answer argues that VCF should be applying the concepts because doing so fulfils its own (economic) interests, it's clear that an instrumental viewpoint is being taken.

Easy marks. Identifying the controls in (a) should hopefully have been straightforward but remember you also have to evaluate them, which is more challenging.

(a)   **Introduction**

The main features of the controls are much dependence on one person, and limitations in management accounting and human resource systems.

Dependence on Viktor

The main control and also the main weakness of the system is its **dependence** on **Viktor's knowledge and experience**. The biggest danger the company faces is that something happens to Viktor, perhaps as a result of the personal risks he takes, and the other directors and the company are left to cope without him.

Role of board

The board appears to play little if any role in **actively supervising** the company's activities. Viktor's reports appear to be unquestioned, and the rest of the board appears to have little involvement in decision-taking.

Sensitivity analysis

The **analysis undertaken** by Viktor to **manage cash flow** does **not appear to be linked** in with any **budget** and **management accounts** being produced. In addition VCF seems very dependent on this **analysis** being **reasonable**, particularly as costs are tight.

Pricing

The pricing system seems based on **customers' willingness to accept high prices**. If there is a risk of economic recession, customers may not be prepared to pay these prices and VCF will be forced to adopt **more sophisticated pricing methods**.

Balanced scorecard

Viktor is making some attempt to use a balanced scorecard to assess performance. A model scorecard focuses on four perspectives:

(i)   **Customer satisfaction** is being addressed, but it is difficult to see how it is being measured

(ii) **Internal processes**; as suppliers are responsible for delivery of outsource service, VCF's processes are concerned with **how relations with suppliers are managed**. This issue does not appear to be considered very much, and may leave VCF vulnerable to problems with suppliers

(iii) **Innovation and learning**; VCF invests heavily in research and development but how the performance of research and development is assessed is unclear, apart from the vague measure of **maintaining technological leadership**

(iv) **Financial**. Financial measures are a **major element** in **performance assessment**, but the weakness is that shareholders and the stock market may be more concerned with profit measures than Viktor is

Assessment of managers

Manager assessment appears to depend on Viktor's personal involvement; there seems to be no formal system of **appraising managers**. This is more of a problem as the achievement of **many of the responsibilities of management** cannot be measured in monetary terms; other than **Viktor's knowledge of competitors**, it is difficult to see how standards of **after-sales service** and **customer satisfaction** are being measured. In addition **cost control** does not appear to be a major element in the assessment of managers' performance.

Human resources

Identifying and dismissing staff who are 'not committed to the company's objectives' may be problematic unless carried out **formally**, and could result in **unfair dismissal claims** and **dissatisfaction** amongst staff who remain. VCF appears to rely on the assumption that staff will be happy as they are being paid well, which may not be correct.

Research and development controls

The fact that **research and development** is **not linked** into any product but is expensed suggests the link with specific product development lacks clarity and the benefits of R&D activity are uncertain. Some uncertainties are inevitable given the nature of the industry; however there seems to be risks that **activity is wasted** on projects that provide **no benefits**, that projects **fail to deliver the planned benefits** and **costs** are not adequately controlled.

Patent protection

The main control is the institution of legal proceedings but this may be a more effective control for limiting losses than **avoiding the risks of competitors** using VCF's technology in the first place. There do not appear to be any restrictions placed on **staff moving to competitors** and taking knowledge with them that competitors can use; the chances of this happening may be enhanced by Viktor's dismissal of unhappy staff.

(b)   **Report**

To: Board, VCF
From: Consultant
Date: 1 August 20X5
Subject: Improvements in governance, risk management and internal controls

Introduction

This report offers recommendations for a number of ways in which systems can be improved, to enhance the efficiency of operations, manage risks more effectively and fulfil investor and stock market operations.

(i) **Corporate governance**

VCF fails to fulfil several aspects of **corporate governance best practice**. These should not just be seen as box-ticking requirements, but as contributing to the **well-running** of the company and its appeal to shareholders. The failure to follow requirements may mean that VCF is seen as riskier than it need be, and hence less appealing to investors, resulting in a lower share price.

Board

The board does not appear to be meeting often enough to be exercising effective supervision over the company. The governance reports recommend that in order to operate well, the board should **meet regularly (more than once a quarter)** and that the board's constitution should specify that certain major business decisions such as significant investments must be formally taken by the whole board.

Lack of division of responsibilities

Currently the board's operation is completely dependent on Viktor, and serious problems may occur if he is unable to **fulfil his responsibilities**. Viktor acting as **chairman and chief executive** does not fulfil the requirements that there is a clear division of responsibilities at the head of the company, with different directors acting as chairman and chief executive.

Non-executive directors

Although two out of four directors are non-executives, the connections both have with the company means that they cannot be classified as independent. Governance guidelines state that a majority of non-executive directors should be **independent**, and be able to contribute an **objective view** of the company.

In addition there is no indication that either of the non-executive directors has significant **financial expertise**; at least one non-executive director ought to have an accounting qualification to be able to analyse the accounting information with appropriate knowledge.

Committees

VCF does not operate the committee structure recommended by corporate governance guidance:

(1) A **nomination committee**, made up of **non-executive directors** whose role is to oversee the process for board appointments. The committee needs to consider carefully the best structure of the board including the balance between executives and non-executives, the range of skills possessed by the board, the need for continuity and the appropriate size of the board.

(2) An **audit committee** made up of independent non-executive directors. This committee would be responsible for certain control tasks including reviewing financial information and VCF's system of risk management, and liasing with, and reviewing, the work of external audit.

(3) A **remuneration committee**, again consisting of independent non-executive directors. Though salaries paid to directors could well be justified, the increased transparency that use of a remuneration committee can mean should deflect possible shareholder criticism of high salary levels.

Views of shareholders

There appear to be no mechanisms for **seeking the views of shareholders**, and damaging conflict may arise if shareholders are particularly concerned with short-term profitability.

(ii) **Risk management strategy**

Overall VCF does not appear to have a clear risk management framework. Identifying risks is one of the many responsibilities of Viktor, but risk identification and mitigation will be enhanced if VCF formalises its risk management procedures.

Risk appetite

It seems that the directors are prepared to tolerate a high level of risk being taken, but **do not appear to have a clear idea** of whether the **returns** the company is achieving justify the level of risks being taken. In addition the board does not appear to have considered whether the **benefits** of countering certain risks outweigh the costs – are the costs and resources required to pursue legal action for infringement of patents worth the benefits?

Risk identification

A key aspect of risk identification is **Viktor's analysis** of likely threats to cash flow. As this is so important, this analysis ought to be checked by someone else who reviews the figures, and considers the reasonableness of the assumptions made and whether there are any other possible scenarios that have not been analysed.

Risk acceptance

The **decisions** made on whether to accept exchange risk have been determined by historical balancing out of gains and losses, whereas VCF should also be considering the **likely future movements of exchange rates**.

Effectiveness of risk reduction methods

Outsourcing and personal contact may **not be very effective methods** for addressing some of the main risks the company faces. Even if Viktor has good contacts with customers and competitors, these will not do much to mitigate major economic risks. In addition competitors are themselves likely to have very stringent methods for **protecting their own technology** and it may be difficult for VCF to stay ahead if competitors develop market-winning technology.

Failure to reduce certain risks

In addition VCF does not appear to have mitigated the impact of certain risks. Although the company has tight cash flow quite often, there does not appear to be any identified source of **contingency funds**. There also appear to be **no contingency arrangements** if supplier problems arise.

(iii) **Internal controls**

Overall the control system needs to **depend less** on **Viktor's involvement** and have more formal procedures in place.

Role of board

Expanded board membership should enable the whole board to exercise more effective supervision over the company. This includes carrying out a formal process of **risk identification**, and **monitoring and considering** the **effectiveness** of **internal control**, including a formal annual review of internal control.

Internal audit

A small internal audit department could be established. Not only would it fulfil the requirements of corporate governance guidelines, but it could be used to review the **value for money** of a number of aspects of operations, including supplier procurement, marketing and research and development, thus potentially saving the business considerable costs.

Accounting system controls

Comparisons need to be made of actual costs with **budgeted costs** and **variances investigated.** A more formal **system of responsibility accounting** needs to be introduced with costs allocated to cost centres and ultimately to individuals for control purposes.

Scorecard

The system Viktor uses needs to be modified with more consideration being given to supplier performance and cost measures.

Area managers

The **responsibilities** of area managers need to be **clarified**; there appears to be confusion resulting in the managers being bypassed. The system for **appraising managers** needs to be formalised, and the scope of assessment widened, covering control over costs as well as the aspects currently appraised.

Staff controls

All staff ought also to be **formally appraised** and feedback obtained to ascertain whether staff are happy, since departure of dissatisfied staff to competitors may jeopardise VCF's **competitive position**. VCF should ensure that staff contracts are drafted as tightly as possible as regards use elsewhere of knowledge of VCF's operations, and **joining competitors**, although local employment law may limit how effective these restrictions can be.

Summary

Overall the company would benefit from more **formalised governance procedures**, a wider base of **directors** and developments in **accounting**, **human resources** and particularly **risk management** systems.

(c) **Corporate governance ethical concepts**

Fairness

Fairness means taking into account the interests of all stakeholders that have a legitimate interest in VCF. The board certainly considers the interests of **shareholders** (the emphasis on cash flow) and **customers** (the emphasis on customer satisfaction). However whether all interests of employees are taken into account is less clear; Viktor appears to assume that all staff are interested in is high salaries, when they may also be interested in developing their own careers and contributing to decision-making in a way that is not allowed for by Viktor's personal rule. Perhaps staff potential exists that is not being fully realised.

Accountability

The board does not appear to recognise the significance of **accountability to shareholders,** nor that accountability extends beyond making high profits. Now that VCF is listed, and given that Viktor does not own a majority of shares, other significant shareholders who are discontented could combine and raise their concerns at general meetings or even seek changes on the board in attempt to limit Viktor's power. They might do so because they are **unhappy** about the **risk-return** relationship that is available from investing in VCF. Although sales may appear to be doing well, cash flows are tight, and the company's future success is dependent upon the outcome of uncertain research and development.

Transparency

Shareholders should be **reassured** if VCF fulfils another key concept, that of transparency. This not only means fulfilling all the requirements of law and accounting standards in relation to the content of annual accounts, but **maintaining a regular dialogue with shareholders and perhaps voluntarily reporting** on certain activities. Transparency may be limited to some degree by the need to maintain commercial confidentiality about research and development to keep the information from competitors. However the board may be able to give more details about their risk management processes and their long-term strategy; if shareholders are reassured that VCF has a **clear vision**, they may believe that the risks linked with strategy will be managed successfully.

Independence

The lack of independent non-executive directors means a lack of scrutiny not only of what the board is doing (which shareholders may be concerned about) but also the company's **risk and business analysis processes**. A non-executive director with experience of markets outside the Pacific home country may be able to contribute to suggesting improvements in the way VCF does business in those markets. An **IT specialist** may be able to monitor the activities of the research and development department in a way that current board members cannot because of their lack of expertise.

Responsibility

Responsibility means being able to correct and hold managers to account for poor management. This appears to be happening at **lower levels of VCF's management structure** but does not appear to be happening at board level; there is no method of assessing whether the board is running as **efficiently and effectively** as it could be. In the absence of independent non-executive directors, possibly the board could ask the non-executive director with consultancy experience to assess the way the board is currently working, comparing this with other ways of running the board, and **appraise the performance** of each of the other directors.

Judgement

Judgement means the board making decisions that **enhance the prosperity of the organisation.** Ultimately it depends on the experience and sense of the directors; however the governance reports also stress the importance of the board having **formal decision-making processes** that VCF does not appear to have. Instead board meetings seem to be for reporting progress rather than taking decisions. Formal processes may act as a necessary brake on Viktor, given his **high risk appetite**.

Probity and integrity

Probity and integrity are linked concepts; probity means **honesty**, integrity means **straightforward dealing and completeness.** Obviously in relationships with customers, this means not promising what VCF is unable to deliver, but this does not seem to be a significant issue as VCF is able to charge high prices because of the good service it provides. There is no suggestion that Viktor is **dishonest in his dealings** with managers and staff; however the fact that he frequently bypasses managers suggests that they may find it difficult to trust him. This may result in the managers feeling **demotivated** and also uncertain about what they can do because they may be overridden by Viktor.

Reputation

VCF's reputation will depend on the factors described above. The directors' concern for VCF's reputation will therefore be demonstrated by the extent to which they fulfil the principles and requirements of other corporate governance codes. Given that VCF is traded now on the stock exchange, a **reputation for poor corporate governance** may have an adverse impact on its share price.

Ethical viewpoint

Instrumental viewpoint

The ethical viewpoint that regards good corporate governance as an mechanism for helping to ensure high profits is the **instrumental viewpoint.** This reflects the view that Viktor holds that organisations exist to fulfil **mainly economic responsibilities** towards shareholders plus the **legal responsibilities** that it needs to fulfil in order to continue trading. Thus the business does not have its own moral viewpoint; it adopts ethical attitudes towards corporate governance because not to do so would upset its stakeholders. Thus the instrumental viewpoint requires an assessment of the power and interest of stakeholders, and identification of the stakeholders that it cannot afford to provoke.

Normative viewpoint

The instrumental viewpoint can be contrasted with another key ethical viewpoint, the **normative viewpoint.** This sees ethical behaviour as reflected for example in good corporate governance as an end in itself and not the **means to the end** of making more money. Failing to take an ethical position leads ultimately to the breakdown of the cohesion that society requires to operate effectively.

29 Ronald Co

Text references. Chapters 2,5,6,11.

Top tips. The categories of risk described in Chapter 6 of the text are a good way of organising the threats that Ronald faces in (a). The 2 marks are available for the higher level skill of making reasoned assessment, based on financial impact, of the consequences for Ronald.

(b) is a good test of your knowledge of the main points of Sarbanes-Oxley, but you would not pass this question part without discussing how well Ronald complies. Note that application by Ronald is not simple yes or no; even where Ronald does comply, the answer discusses any doubts and qualifications eg yes there is an audit committee but it's not doing a very good job.

The professional marks in (c) are awarded for the skill of being able to come up with reasonable solutions to the ethical problems that are in accordance with ethical guidance. The ethical threats will have been covered in your previous studies; in this exam you are less likely to be told which threats are relevant and the solutions may not be clearcut.

(d) does not represent an invitation to write all you know about what audit committees do without making any mention of Ronald. Your answer should be based on the information you're given in the scenario, and you should discuss what the audit committee should be doing in the context of what you're told. Don't forget that the audit committee's liaison with internal **and** external audit, also its acting as a contact point for whistleblowing staff, are very important parts of its role.

Easy marks. There are plenty of clues to help you identify the risks in (a), but as explained in Top tips, you need to assess their impact as well.

(a)   **Risks**

Finance risk/ going concern risk

This is potentially the most serious risk facing Ronald, that the company will not be able to operate as a going concern. Specific going concern indicators include:

- **Competitors** who are not exposed to the same manufacturing and exchange rate risks as producing is carried out after the transport of cloth rather than before
- **Falling sales**
- **Increasing borrowings**
- **Cash management** issues

Ronald is likely to require a detailed **profit and cash flow forecast** in an attempt to clarify the company's going concern status.

Currency risk

Currency risk occurs when companies trade with customers or suppliers in other jurisdictions. The risk relates to exchange rate movements that **affect the value of debts or payments to overseas companies.** Ronald is exposed in both areas as the company both imports finished goods and then exports those goods to other countries.

It appears that Ronald has been affected by **increasing customer balances** with exchange rates moving in the customers' favour. This decreases the amount of home currency that Ronald can expect from a given debt. Ronald has also been affected by **increases in import prices** that it cannot easily pass on to its customers. Competitors are partially protected from this increase by manufacturing clothes in their home jurisdiction.

Interest rate risk

This risk relates to changes in interest rates, particularly where a company has borrowed money. The risk is **interest rates will increase**, adversely affecting repayments (unless the terms of the loan are for a fixed rate of interest). Ronald is exposed to interest rate risk on the new borrowings taken out if the interest rate increases.

Credit risk

This is the risk that customers **fail to meet their obligations to pay invoices on time**. The new cash management system appears to have been overstating collections from customers, so collections are not as good as expected. Lack of cash collections affects Ronald in three ways:

- **Cash receipts fall**, meaning that less cash is available to pay company expenses

- Delays in payments mean that **adverse exchange rate movements** decrease the amount of home currency obtained

- There may be an **increased incidence of bad debts**, further decreasing cash collections

Liquidity risk

This is the risk that a company **cannot pay its debts as they fall due** to a mismatch between inflows and outflows. The increase in short term loans being taken out by Ronald implies the company is having difficulty meeting its debts. The fact that short term borrowings have had to be secured on long term assets would tend to confirm this view.

Financial risk

Financial risk in this area normally relates to the need to **restate financial information due to errors or irregularities in accounting systems**. In the case of Ronald there appear to be some irregularities as the auditors are considering a qualification in their audit report. The irregularities appear to affect cash, receivables and possibly payables figures with the qualification indicating that this weakness is **material**.

(b) **Impact of Sarbanes-Oxley**

The Sarbanes-Oxley Act affects the Ronald Company due to its parent company being **located in the USA**. The Act applies to all companies listed on a USA stock exchange, as well subsidiaries of those companies, no matter where in the world those subsidiaries are located.

Off-balance sheet financing

Sarbanes-Oxley requires **appropriate disclosure** of all transactions affecting a company. Those transactions cannot be kept off-balance sheet in an attempt to make the company's financial statements look better. The provision was introduced due to the extensive off-balance sheet financing in Enron, effectively hiding many of the debts of the company.

In Ronald the **non-provision of financial support** by Ronald's parent company and the subsequent obtaining of the bank loan does not appear to be in breach of the Act. A parent company can choose not to provide financial support to a subsidiary. As long as the debt from that subsidiary is **properly consolidated** in the parent company accounts (and there is no indication that Ronald has decided not to do this) then the loan and disclosure are legal.

Auditors providing other services

Auditors are **not allowed to provide other services** to an audit client (except for a few exceptions such as provision of taxation services). The provision of other services is disallowed to **avoid conflicts of interest**; auditors will be tempted not to qualify financial statements in case that qualification loses not only the audit but the lucrative other services also provided.

Ronald's auditors have provided other services in the form of **specifying and implementing the cash management system**. This provision of Sarbanes-Oxley has therefore not been met.

Audit committee

Ronald **has an audit committee**. This is a requirement of the Sarbanes-Oxley Act so in this sense Ronald complies with the Act.

However, it is unclear whether this committee is **working effectively**. All non-audit work undertaken by auditors should be **authorised by the committee**. Furthermore, the provision of services in terms of setting up or recommending controls from the company's auditors is specifically banned under the Act. The audit committee should have **identified this breach** and informed the board.

Removal of auditors

The action of the board to **consider removing the auditors from office** is not correct. Under the Act, the external auditors are appointed by the audit committee, and so it is that committee that should remove the auditors. At the least, the issue of **audit independence and problems with audit/other services** should be discussed with the audit committee prior to the directors taking any stance on this issue.

Corporate responsibility

The **chief executive officer and chief finance officer should certify the appropriateness of the financial statements** and that those financial statements **fairly present the operations and financial condition** of the issuer. If the company has to prepare a restatement of accounts due to material non-compliance with standards, the chief finance officer and chief executive officer should **forfeit their bonuses**.

It is not clear how bad the internal control weakness is in Ronald. However, there is a **risk of restatement** so the CEO and CFO should be more interested in ensuring that the **financial statements** are **correct**, not ensuring that the financial statements are not qualified. At the extreme, the reports provided by the CEO and CFO will have to **state the control weaknesses**. However, if those weaknesses are resolved and any necessary adjustments made to the financial statements, then a qualification can be avoided.

Internal control reporting

Annual reports, as well as interim reports where necessary, should contain internal control reports that **state the responsibility of management for establishing and maintaining an adequate internal control structure and procedures for financial reporting**. The directors of Ronald have attempted to meet this responsibility by establishing the control systems and in particular the system to track cash balances.

Unfortunately, the system is defective, and the directors should have recognised the risk of using external auditors for this work. The directors need to ensure that the **weakness is remedied** (as noted above) and **file the necessary forms** with the SEC now in respect of that weakness.

(c)　**Audit firm ethics**

Qualification of audit report

The directors of Ronald Co have threatened to remove the audit firm if the audit report is qualified. This is an **intimidation threat** against ARC & Co as the client is attempting to force their auditors to **take action against their professional standards**. However, the situation is complicated by the **self-interest threat** (ARC & Co presumably do not wish to lose audit income) and the **self-review threat** identified below. The directors appear to be arguing that the qualification would not have occurred had ARC & Co implemented an appropriate cash monitoring system.

It is difficult to determine the outcome to this matter as it rests on the directors' opinion compared to the auditors. The directors may assert that the system was flawed, and the auditors may assert that the controls were used incorrectly. Whatever the outcome, the auditors should **follow professional ethical guidance and qualify the audit report**. However, as noted below, this action may be irrelevant given the self-review threat.

Systems changes

ARC & Co designed a new control system to manage cash in Ronald Co. This is a **self-review threat** because ARC & Co is now reviewing controls that it designed. In other words ARC & Co is **not providing an independent view** of the control system and may even choose to hide any weaknesses it finds because of the negative impact on ARC. The implementation of the control system was also in contravention of the Sarbanes Oxley Act.

In this situation ARC & Co would be **advised to resign as auditors**; their position is compromised and this action is actually recommended under Sarbanes-Oxley. An **independent firm of auditors** must take over the audit. It is unfortunate that the audit carried out by ARC is nearly complete, as a lot of audit work may have to be duplicated. Further negotiation may be required with Ronald Co to determine who will pay for this work.

Staff entertaining

An audit senior at ARC & Co has been entertaining a senior member of the accounts department at Ronald. While the board maintains that the senior was attempting to **elicit information on control weaknesses**, the issue for the audit firm is one of a **familiarity threat**. The audit senior may be tempted **not to apply professional scepticism** because of the close association with the member of the accounts department.

In this situation, ARC & Co would be advised to **replace the audit senior** and have any **work of that staff member reviewed** to check its integrity. The allegation of **attempting to obtain inside information** should be discussed with the senior. If this was the case then **disciplinary action** should be **considered**, also reporting to the appropriate authorities. Depending on the information obtained from the senior, the audit partner must **discuss the matter with the directors** to rebuild confidence in the audit firm.

Shares

As well as the issue above, the audit senior also holds 5% of the share capital of Ronald's parent, although this was not initially disclosed to the partner in ARC & Co when the audit started. This is a **self-interest threat** because the senior will have a conflict between ensuring that the shares in Ronald's parent increase in value while at the same time attempting to ensure that accounts show a true and fair view. If the profit in Ronald's parent group accounts is overstated (as it may be regarding the bad debt reserve) then the senior is less likely to report this due to the adverse impact on the value of the shares held.

In this situation, the senior must be **removed from the audit**. For subsequent years, work on Ronald Co would only be allowed if the shares had been sold. ARC & Co may require the shares to be sold anyway as many audit firms do not allow staff to hold shares in any audit client.

(d) **Purpose of audit committee**

The main purpose of an internal audit committee is, according to commentary on the Sarbanes Oxley Act, to **provide 'moral compass'** for a company. In other words the committee will provide **an independent view** on many of the activities of the board and the company as a whole.

Areas of work

These include **reviewing financial statements and systems to ensure their accuracy and compliance with any Sarbanes-Oxley disclosure requirements**. As we have mentioned, liaison with the external auditors is important, including appointing the auditors and discussing the contents of any communications between the company and the auditor (eg audit report and management letters). The audit committee should also **review internal audit** to ensure their work is carried out efficiently and effectively and **review the internal control systems** to ensure they are working correct and comply with statutory obligations

Regarding the problems outlined in Ronald, the audit committee should have been able to prevent some of them, and may be able to advise now on others.

Non audit services

The changes to the control system should have been **authorised by the audit committee**. Hopefully, the work would have been identified as not being allowed under Sarbanes-Oxley and would therefore have been **undertaken by a different professional firm**.

The committee may help now by **ordering an independent review** of the cash management system to determine whether the directors were correct in their assertion that the control system was flawed.

Audit removal

The directors have threatened to remove the auditors. As noted in part (b) the **audit committee should be involved in this decision** as they, in theory, appointed ARC & Co.

Internal control reporting

The committee have **responsibility for checking the financial statements** and other Sarbanes-Oxley reports, including details of control weaknesses. If weaknesses have occurred, then these must be reported.

The committee can assist by ensuring that the **relevant disclosures are made** in a **timely manner** rather than have the parties simply disputing who is responsible.

Whistle-blowing

The committee has the **responsibility to hear representations** from employees concerning potential inaccuracies in the accounting systems, control weaknesses etc. This fact should be publicised within Ronald.

In this situation, the junior clerk should be **advised to talk to the chair of the audit committee in confidence** to explain the concerns about the cash management system. The chair can then decide what, if any, action needs to be taken on the information provided. The concerns of the clerk regarding the directors manipulating the financial statements may or may not have been justified. However, the audit committee provides the appropriate independent view on the matter to ensure that the concerns are addressed.

Mock exams

ACCA Professional Level

Paper P1

Professional Accountant

Mock Examination 1

Question Paper	
Time allowed	
Reading and Planning Writing	**15 minutes** **3 hours**
This paper is divided into two sections Section A This ONE question is compulsory and must be attempted Section B TWO questions only to be attempted	
During reading and planning time only the question paper may be annotated	

DO NOT OPEN THIS PAPER UNTIL YOU ARE READY TO START UNDER EXAMINATION CONDITIONS

Section A – This question is compulsory and must be attempted

Question 1

SeaShells is a small company operating from an island near continental Europe. SeaShells is a private company with 25 shareholders; its shares are not traded on any stock exchange. However, the board is constituted in accordance with good corporate governance practice with an appropriate balance of executive and non-executive directors. There are also remuneration and audit committees.

The main business of SeaShells is packaging of fresh seafood (fish, oysters, crab etc.) and selling these to supermarkets and other retailers. The company employs 150 people, mainly in the packing departments. Packing is labour intensive due to the need to clear and prepare fish etc. by hand prior to packing. Supplies of seafood are obtained from the island's fishing fleet, whose only significant customer is SeaShells. Given that there are only 9,000 living on the island, this makes SeaShells one of the island's major employers. There is some concern that SeaShells' increased demand for seafood is causing over-exploitation of some fish species, and that the population of these fish may "crash" or decrease dramatically in the near future.

In the last few weeks, the directors of SeaShells have decided to transfer almost all of the packaging of seafood to another country. The seafood will be moved by refrigerated ships to this other country, packaged by workers there and then moved back by ship to SeaShells for resale as before. The rationale behind this move is that labour costs are only 1/10th of the costs on the island. Even taking into account transportation costs, this move will halve the packaging costs of SeaShells. As a result of the move, the workforce will decrease to 35 people. The decision has resulted in significant adverse publicity for SeaShells on the island, although the reaction from customers has been positive as the company can offer reduced prices on many products.

The directors of SeaShells believe that the decision to transfer the packaging of seafood is correct because, as the CEO explained, the decision is "best for the company, best for the shareholders and best for the directors". The comment concerning directors can be justified in terms of directors' remuneration – 75% of the total remuneration package of the directors is based on performance related pay, the main element of this being the net profit of SeaShells. The remaining 25% of remuneration relates to salary and is based on a 3 year contract with SeaShells. Other (non-salary) remuneration includes company contributions to a pension scheme and a share option scheme, with options being exercisable in 5 years based on the share price 1 year ago.

Required

(a) Explain Mendelow's theory of stakeholder power. Identify the stakeholders involved in the decision to transfer packaging of seafood to another country, and discuss the response of each group to this decision.

(14 marks)

(b) Using Gray, Owens and Adams' viewpoints on social responsibility as a framework for your answer, evaluate the decision to transfer packaging seafood to another country. **(14 marks)**

(c) Prepare a memo for the board that explains the concept of ''sustainability'', and evaluates the extent to which SeaShells' activities can be considered sustainable and discusses methods of reporting that can be used by SeaShells to explain the environmental impact of its activities.

(14 marks)
(including 2 professional marks)

(d) Discuss corporate governance best practice in terms of directors' remuneration and assess the extent to which remuneration in SeaShells meets these requirements, making any recommendations you consider appropriate. **(8 marks)**
(including 2 professional marks)

(Total = 50 marks)

Section B – TWO questions ONLY to be attempted

Question 2

HiT is an information technology company set up in the Dotcom boom in the late 1990s. Unlike many other companies, it did not expand too quickly at first as the proprietors were cautious and hence did not seek external funding other than venture capital. As a result the company has been well-placed to pick up business that has become available in the IT sector and has done well since the millennium.

The directors have now decided on a policy of expansion both internally and by acquisition. They appreciate that they will need more external funding, and believe the company will soon be in a healthy enough position for them to seek a stock market listing. They understand that this will mean that the company's corporate governance structures need to become more formal. Previously the board has just consisted of the original shareholders plus a representative from the venture capitalists. The directors appreciate that if the company is listed, they will need to recruit some non-executive directors to the board, but are unclear about their role and why most of them need to be independent.

Required

Prepare a memorandum to the board of HiT:

(a) Explaining the position, qualities and role of non-executive directors in the corporate governance of a listed company. **(7 marks)**

(b) Defining the distinction between independent and non-independent non-executive directors. **(3 marks)**

(c) Discussing the main areas for a potential conflict of interest between the external shareholders of a company and its directors, and how non-executive directors can help deal with this problem. **(11 marks)**

(d) Discussing the objections to paying non-executive directors in shares or share options. **(4 marks)**

(Total = 25 marks)

Question 3

HOOD sells a wide range of coats, anoraks, waterproof trousers and similar outdoor clothing from its 56 stores located in one country. The company is profitable, although the gross profit in some stores has declined recently for no apparent reason.

Each store uses EPOS to maintain control of inventory and provides the facility to use EFTPOS for payments. However, about 55% of all transactions are still made by cash. Details of sales made and inventory below re-order levels are transferred to head office on a daily basis where management reports are also prepared.

Inventory is ordered centrally from Head Office, details of requirements being obtained from the daily management information provided by each store. Orders are sent to suppliers in the post, inventory arriving at each store approximately 10 days after the re-order level is reached.

Recent newspaper reports indicate one of the chemicals used to waterproof garments releases toxic fumes after prolonged exposure to sunlight. The board of HOOD are investigating the claim, but are currently treating it with some degree of scepticism. The product range has generally sold well, although there has been little innovation in terms of garment design in the last 4 years.

Required

(a)   Identify the different risks facing the HOOD Company, placing the risks into suitable categories.

(10 marks)

(b)   Evaluate the potential effect of each risk on the company and recommend how the impact of that risk can be minimised.   **(15 marks)**

(Total = 25 marks)

Question 4

LMN is a charity that provides low-cost housing for people on low incomes. The government has privatised much of the home building, maintenance and management in this sector. The sector is heavily regulated and receives some government money but there are significant funds borrowed from banks to invest in new housing developments, on the security of future rent receipts. Government agencies subsidise much of the rental cost for low-income residents.

The board and senior management have identified the major risks to LMN as: having insufficient housing stock of a suitable type to meet the needs of local people on low incomes; making poor property investment decisions; having dissatisfied tenants due to inadequate property maintenance; failing to comply with the requirements of the regulator; having a poor credit rating with lenders; poor cost control; incurring bad debts for rental; and having vacant properties that are not earning income. LMN has produced a risk register as part of its risk management process. For each of more than 200 individual risks, the risk register identifies a description of the risk and the (high, medium or low) likelihood of the risk eventuating and the (high, medium or low) consequences for the organisation if the risk does eventuate.

The management of LMN is carried out by professionally qualified housing executives with wide experience in property development, housing management and maintenance, and financial management. The board of LMN is composed of volunteers with wide experience and an interest in social welfare. The board is representative of the community, tenants and the local authority, any of whom may be shareholders (shareholdings are nominal and the company pays no dividends). The local authority has overall responsibility for housing and social welfare in the area. The audit committee of the board of LMN, which has responsibility for risk management as well as internal control, wants to move towards a system of internal controls that are more closely related to risks identified in the risk register.

Required

For an organisation like LMN:

(a)   Analyse the purposes and justify the importance of risk management and explain its relationship with the internal control system.   **(9 marks)**

(b)   Evaluate the importance of a management review of controls for the audit committee.   **(5 marks)**

(c)   Explain the principles of good corporate governance as they apply to the board's role:

   (i)   in conducting a review of internal controls; and
   (ii)   reporting on compliance.   **(11 marks)**

Illustrate your answer with examples from the scenario.

(Total = 25 marks)

Answers

DO NOT TURN THIS PAGE UNTIL YOU HAVE
COMPLETED THE MOCK EXAM

A plan of attack

We know you've been told to do it at least 100 times and we know if we asked you you'd know that you should do it. So why don't you do it in an exam? 'Do what in an exam?' you're probably thinking. Well, let's tell you for the 101st time. **Take a good look through the paper before diving in to answer questions.**

First things first

What you must do in the first five minutes of reading time in your exam is **look through the paper** in detail, working out **which questions to do** and the **order** in which to attempt them. So turn back to the paper and let's sort out a plan of attack.

We then recommend you spend the remaining time analysing the requirements of **Question 1** and highlighting the key issues in the question. The extra time spent on **Question 1** will be helpful, whenever you intend to do the question, If you decide to do it first, you will be well into the question when the writing time starts. If you intend to do it second or third, probably because you find it daunting, the question will look easier when you come back to it, because your initial analysis should generate further points whilst you're tackling the other questions.

The next step

You're probably either thinking that you don't know where to begin or that you could have a very decent go at all the questions.

Option 1 (if you don't know where to begin)

If you are a bit **worried** about the paper, remember you'll need to do the compulsory question anyway so it's best to get it over and done with.

- You can score well on part (a) of **Question 1** if you use the information in the scenario – there is plenty of information about the stakeholders. There's also enough detail about remuneration to jog your memory in part (d) about corporate governance remuneration requirements.

- If you have think you have some knowledge of non-executive directors, **Question 2** could be a good choice. However a couple of the parts bring in wider practical and ethical issues so it's not just a straightforward test of knowledge.

- Although the scenario in **Question 3** may appear quite short, there is in fact lots of information about potential risks. If you think widely and make realistic suggestions in (b) that clearly link into your answer in (a), you can score well on this question.

- There's a number of fairly basic points you make in part (a) of **Question 4,** and you can get significant credit in (c) for setting out your knowledge of the corporate governance guidelines. Think when you're planning how you can bring the scenario information in.

What you mustn't forget is that you have to answer **Question 1** and then two questions from Section B.

Option 2 (if you're thinking 'I can do all of these')

It never pays to be over confident but if you're not quaking in your shoes about the exam then **turn straight to the compulsory question** in Section A. You've got to do it so you might as well get it over and done with.

* Make sure you make the most of the information you're supplied with in parts (a) and (d) of **Question 1**; a general answer won't score well. You may well have very good knowledge of the issues covered in parts (b) and (c) but allocate your time carefully; it's important not only to avoid running over time for each question part, but also to ensure you cover a sufficient breadth of points within the time allowed.

Once you've done the compulsory questions choose two of the questions in Section B.

* Although **Question 2** may look straightforward, parts (c) and (d) require a bit more thought about wider governance issues, so be careful if you choose this question.

* Careful reading of the question and planning is the key to success in **Question 3**. Make sure you identify all the risks hinted at for part (a) and provide realistic suggestions for managing those specific risks in part (b).

* If you've got good knowledge of the corporate governance requirements relating to control reviews, you can score well in **Question 4**. Part (a) is about the fundamentals of risk management, so knowledge of these basics will help you as well. However make sure that you include references to relevant scenario information.

No matter how many times we remind you...

Always, always **allocate your time** according to the marks for the question in total and for the parts of the questions. And always, always **follow the requirements exactly**.

You've got free time at the end of the exam.....?

If you have allocated your time properly then you **shouldn't have time on your hands** at the end of the exam. If you find yourself with five or ten minutes spare, however, go back to **any parts of questions that you didn't finish** because you ran out of time.

Forget about it!

And don't worry if you found the paper difficult. More than likely other students would too. If this was the real thing you would need to forget the exam the minute you leave the exam hall and **think about the next one**. Or, if it's the last one, **celebrate**!

Question 1

Text references. Chapters 3, 10 and 12.

Top tips. It's a good idea to draw the matrix in (a) as a starter. The way to approach planning the rest of (a) to list all the major stakeholders (and the question makes it clear that the 'usual' stakeholders are all important) and then decide where they fit on the matrix.

If you struggled with (b), go and learn these viewpoints! The examiner has stressed their importance and may well set similar question parts in the exam. Note that the scenario will have to give you issues that would interest all seven viewpoints. The key questions to ask when considering things from each viewpoint are:

- Do the company's activities have a significant impact?
- Do the impacts they have matter?
- Why do they matter?
- What can the company do to reduce or eliminate the impacts, or provide compensation?

There are various hints to help you answer on sustainability in (c). The issue about unnecessary use of transport is topical, and it's certainly worth keeping an eye on continuing sustainability debates. This question part should represent the maximum amount of detail you need to bring in about sustainability reporting. The main thing to remember is the basics of each framework; what numbers are involved and the narrative element. If you can remember the basics, you should be able to come up with enough examples of the detail in the reports.

(d) is quite a good question part on remuneration as some of the issues involved aren't clearcut. It's good for example for remuneration to link with performance, but not so good for it to depend largely on short-term financial performance. Asking yourself what the potential problems are and then the key question – why? should enable you to generate sufficient depth of discussion. What you must avoid are simple this is acceptable or unacceptable statements without explanation.

Easy marks. Depends on how well you know the social responsibility material in Chapter 12. There's enough information on remuneration in (d) to give you a number of points to discuss.

Marking scheme

			Marks
(a)	Up to 3 marks for explanation of Mendelow's matrix	3	
	Up to 2 marks for each stakeholder identified and discussed	12	
	max		14
(b)	Up to 2 marks for each Gray, Owen and Adams position discussed		14
(c)	Up to 2 marks for definition of sustainability	2	
	Up to 5 marks for evaluation of whether company's position is sustainable	5	
	Up to 7 marks for discussion of methods of reporting – to achieve high marks detail must be given of a number of different methods	7	
	Up to 2 professional marks for the form of the answer (memo in which content is laid out in an orderly and informative manner)	2	
	max		14
(d)	Up to 3 marks for each relevant point. To achieve 3 marks points must include application to company and recommendations		
	2 professional marks for reasonableness of recommendations		
	max		8
			50

(a) **Mendelow's matrix**

Mendelow classifies stakeholders on a matrix (shown below). The matrix is used to identify the type of relationship the organisation should seek with its stakeholders, and how it should view their concerns. The two axis show:

- The **level of interest** the stakeholder has in the company
- The **amount of power** that stakeholder has to influence the decisions of the company

Using these two axes, stakeholders can be divided into four groups as follows:

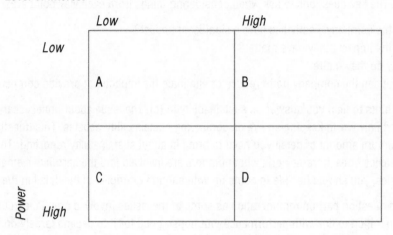

Section A

Stakeholders in this section have a **low level of interest** in the company and have **minimal power** to influence the decisions of the company.

Government

For SeaShells, Section A stakeholders may include the **government** of the island. As long as SeaShells pays the correct amount of taxes, the government may not be able to interfere with the company.

Section B

Stakeholders in this section have a **high level of interest** in the company, but have **minimal power** to actually influence its activities. This group will normally attempt to influence the company by lobbying groups that have high levels of power.

For SeaShells, stakeholders in this category include the following.

The local community

SeaShells is a major employer on the island. This means the community has an interest in the company **maintaining that level of employment**. It is unlikely therefore that the community will agree with the decision to decrease the number of jobs at SeaShells. However, apart from applying pressure in terms of adverse publicity, the community cannot actually stop SeaShells taking this action.

Suppliers

SeaShells purchases from the fishing fleet on the island. As SeaShells appears to be the **only major customer** of the fleet, then the fleet has little power to affect SeaShells. While in theory the fleet could refuse to sell to SeaShells, the lack of an alternative buyer decreases the effectiveness of this option.

Employees

This group is obviously **interested in the success of the company** as they receive a salary from SeaShells. However, the only method of influencing SeaShells is by **withdrawal of labour**; this is ineffective given that transferring the packing to a different country has this effect anyway for Seashells. The only other option for influencing the company appears to be generating bad publicity, as for the local community above.

Section C

Stakeholders in this section have a **low level of interest** in the company, although they have the **ability to exercise power** over the company if they choose to do so. The group will have to be kept satisfied to ensure that their power is not used.

Shareholders

In SeaShells, this group is likely to include the shareholders. As long as the **return on investment** from SeaShells is **acceptable**, and the directors are running the company effectively, then the shareholders will be happy. Certainly the decision to decrease input costs will be acceptable if this also means increased profits and dividends. Given that knowledge of cost savings is now available, it can be argued that the directors must take this option, or else the shareholders may become dissatisfied and attempt to remove the directors.

Section D

Stakeholders in this section have a high level of interest in the company and also a high level of power. These stakeholders are therefore able to influence the company. For SeaShells, this group will include customers and directors.

Customers

Customers have high power because they can presumably **obtain supplies of seafood from other companies**. SeaShells must therefore keep this group satisfied or lose important sources of income. The decision to decrease packaging costs will be supported by customers as SeaShells' prices will also fall.

Directors

Directors can influence SeaShells because they **make decisions regarding the running of the company**. In this sense, moving packaging to a different country is in the interests of Seashells, as it provides the company with additional competitive advantage in terms of price and therefore helps ensure its survival.

(b) **Viewpoints of social responsibility**

Gray, Owen and Adams in their book *Accounting and accountability* identify seven viewpoints of social responsibility. These viewpoints can be applied to many situations, including the actions of companies, as explained below.

Pristine capitalists

Pristine capitalists support the idea that in a liberal economic democracy, the **private property system** is the best system. This means that companies **exist to make profits and seek economic efficiency**. Businesses therefore have **no moral responsibilities** beyond their obligations to shareholders and creditors.

In terms of moving packaging to another country simply on the basis of cost, then SeaShells has acted in terms of this belief; the obligation to maximise shareholder profit has been met and the social issues of making people redundant and the adverse effect on the island community are irrelevant.

Expedients

Expedients believe in a modified liberal economic democracy, noting that economic systems do generate some excesses. This means that businesses have to **accept some, albeit limited, social legislation** and moral requirements, particularly if this is in the businesses' best interests.

Seashells is potentially caught between two countries here. On the one hand in its home country Seashells does not appear to be acting morally because the loss of jobs will adversely affect employment and the island's overall economy. However, in the country to which the packaging is being moved, more jobs will be created, potentially in areas of lower employment. In these terms Seashells is acting morally.

Proponents of the social contract

Proponents of the social contract believe in a **contract between society and organisations**. Both parties must therefore **interact to their joint benefit**.

Seashells is continuing to provide employment in terms of purchasing fish etc from the fishing fleet – and the island is providing support services to Seashells (some employment, land etc.). Seashells has possibly breached the contract by removing some employment from the island; some adverse impact in terms of bad publicity is therefore expected.

Social ecologists

Social ecologists note that **economic processes** that **result in resource exhaustion, waste and pollution must be modified**. In other words, the transfer of seafood to another country for packaging only to be returned to SeaShells for distribution is not environmentally friendly. To be responsible in this area Seashells should continue to package the seafood at its current location.

Socialists

Socialists see two classes in society – **capitalists owning businesses exploiting workers**. Within this framework, equality is difficult to achieve. In Seashells, shareholders and directors appear to be capitalists because they stand to "win" from the packaging decision. However, the workers on the island stand to "lose" in that their employment is terminated (although other workers will gain in the overseas country).

Radical feminists

Radical feminists see a trade off between **masculine qualities such as aggression and conflict** and **feminine values of cooperation and reflection**. Moving the packaging work to another country does appear to create conflict. However, whether the feminine view of cooperation is better is unclear – even if say only half the packaging function was moved, there would still be conflict on the island. Similarly, not moving the packaging function could create resentment in the other country as Seashells is not taking advantage of their cost advantage in terms of labour wages.

Deep ecologists

Deep ecologists believe that human beings have **no greater rights to resources or life than other species**. At the extreme therefore the entire business of SeaShells cannot be justified, especially where fish populations are threatened. Similarly, the economic decision to move packaging cannot be justified in environmental terms. The viewpoint that businesses cannot be trusted to maintain something as important as the environment is therefore correct.

(c)

To:	Board
From:	Accountant
Date:	23 May 20X7
Subject:	Sustainability and environmental reporting

Sustainability involves developing strategies so that the company only **uses resources at a rate** that **allows them to be replenished**. This means that those resources will continue to be available into the foreseeable future. Similarly, emissions of waste are confined to levels that do not exceed the capacity of the environment to absorb them.

In other words, sustainability has been defined as ensuring that development meets the needs of the present without compromising the ability of the future to meet its own needs. **Sustainable development is development that meets the needs of the present without compromising the ability of future generations to meet their own needs**.

In terms of the activities of SeaShells, they could be termed to be not sustainable on two counts.

Demand on fish stocks

In terms of capitalism, the fishing fleet will continue to try to meet this demand and SeaShells will continue to sell seafood as both parties are making a profit from these activities. However, the warning that some **fish stocks may crash** indicates that fishing and the economic activity of SeaShells as a company are not sustainable. How activities can be amended to be sustainable is unclear, unless there is some way to limit demand for fish or limit the amount of fish actually used by SeaShells.

The transport of seafoods for packaging in another country

The use of fuel simply to take seafood to a different location and back again to be packaged does **not appear to be justifiable economically**, and is not sustainable given that oil is a limited resource.

Disclosures

The extent to which SeaShells may actually want to disclose the environmental impact of its activities is unclear; in other words **entirely voluntary disclosure is unlikely**, particularly in view of the lack of sustainability referred to above. Methods of reporting the environmental impact of SeaShell's activities include the following.

Financial accounts

The basic financial accounts of SeaShells will disclose **the financial impact of its activities**, although these will only show the direct costs in terms of fuel used to transport fish for packaging etc. As many environmental costs are intangible e.g. pollution or potential over-fishing, these will not be included in the financial accounts, making this method of reporting incomplete.

Full cost accounting

This is a system that allows current accounting to include all **potential/actual costs and benefits** including environmental and possibly social externalities. The aim is to arrive at a 'full cost' of the activities of an organisation.

While the idea is good, it is not necessarily clear what the 'full cost' of an organisation's activities are. Full cost accounting suggests various 'tiers' of costs from the tangible through to the intangible. Using this system SeaShells would disclose

- **Actual costs** incurred (transport, wages etc.)

- **Hidden costs** of maintaining environmental monitoring systems

- **Liability costs**, such as fines for any environmental damage

- **Intangible costs**, including loss of customer goodwill (possible given the packaging policy) and reputation risk (again this risk will be there with the packaging policy). However, it is unclear how these costs will be 'measured'.

- **Environmentally focused costs** – that is cost of ensuring the company's activities have a zero environmental impact. The transport of seafood for packaging is likely to be environmentally negative; there is then the query of how these costs are 'offset' – should SeaShells plant trees to offset CO_2 emissions?

The emphasis on costs and the difficulty of estimating some of those costs again implies that this method of disclosure may not be effective.

CSR / GRI

An alternative to financial reporting is to provide information in a separate, predominantly narrative, report. The Corporate and Social Responsibility (CSR) report in the UK or the recommendations of the Global Reporting Initiative (GRI) are examples of this type of report. The GRI has a vision that reporting on economic, environmental and social importance should become as routine and comparable as financial reporting. The emphasis is therefore on **voluntary disclosure**, but based **on some ethical standards**. The additional information is expected perhaps by society, and therefore companies should provide it.

SeaShells appears to be under some pressure at present, although this is more in terms of economic pressure on jobs than on environmental reporting. Either additional legislation or social pressure appears to be required to ensure that additional environmental reporting is provided.

(d) **Remuneration**

The overriding requirement is that **adequate remuneration** has to be paid to directors in order to attract individuals of sufficient calibre. Remuneration packages should be structured to ensure that individuals are **motivated to achieve performance levels that are in the company and shareholders' best interests** as well as their own personal interests.

Within SeaShells it is difficult to determine whether total **remuneration is sufficient** to meet this objective. However, the fact that there does not appear to be any problems recruiting directors indicates that remuneration is sufficient, or may even be excessive.

Setting remuneration

Directors' remuneration should be set by a **remuneration committee**, which SeaShells has. The reason for this is to ensure that there is **no bias in setting remuneration levels**. The only concern with SeaShells is that the scenario just states there is a remuneration committee – not that this is correctly appointed with non-executive directors. Some element of bias may remain.

Performance related remuneration

Corporate governance guidelines indicate that a **significant proportion of the rewards** should be focused on **measurable performance**, which SeaShells does. What is meant by a significant amount is not always stated but 50% is a reasonable figure. A 75% amount may again be considered as excessive.

The other element of guidance regarding the performance element of remuneration is that this should be **balanced and not relate to the short term only**, as short term performance can be manipulated. The current focus simply on net profit is therefore inappropriate.

Share options

Share options give directors the right to **purchase shares at a specified exercise price over a specified time period in the future**. If the price of the shares rises so that it exceeds the exercise price by the time the options can be exercised, the directors will be able to purchase shares at lower than their market value. This provides a good incentive to the directors to increase share prices.

However, corporate governance regulations normally suggest a **three year maximum term** for share options. The five year term in SeaShells may be unrealistic as the **term is too far in the future** to motivate the directors now. Decreasing the term for future option grants should be considered.

Service contract

Length of service contracts can be a particular problem. If service contracts are too long, and then have to be terminated prematurely, directors may receive **excessive payments for breach of contract**. Most corporate governance guidance therefore suggests a 12 month term.

The **current length of service contracts** in SeaShells of three years therefore appears to be **excessive**. Although there is no indication that directors are looking for compensation for loss of office, decreasing the term to one year would be advisable.

Question 2

Text references. Chapter 3.

Top tips. Whilst ACCA has stated that it's most important that you're aware of the general principles of corporate governance without getting too involved in the details of individual reports, it is fine to quote **selectively** from them as we have done. The length of each part of your answer should roughly reflect the marks available.

Note how the system of committee (audit, remuneration, nomination) is designed to counter key threats to independence. The most basic control though is recruiting sufficient independent non-executive directors, so look out for threats to non-executive independence if you are given scenarios about the corporate governance situation in a particular organisation.

Easy marks. All parts require some thought: even in (a) you could obtain a few marks through quoting the corporate governance reports, but would need to go beyond these for higher marks.

Marking scheme

			Marks
(a)	Position of NEDs	3	
	Qualities of NEDs	3	
	Role of NEDs	3	
	max		7
(b)	Up to 3 marks for relevant discussion, answer should stress lack of connection		3
(c)	Up to 2 marks for each relevant point. To obtain high marks answer must contain discussion of problems and solutions that alleviate problems identified		
	max		11
(d)	Problems with shares	2	
	Problems with share options	2	
			4
			25

To: Directors of HiT
From: Consultant
Date: 3 February 20X4
Subject: Non-executive directors (NEDs)

(a) Position of NEDs

The board of directors of a listed company has the purpose of leading and controlling the company. The board will normally be made up of **executive directors** who work full time for the company and have specific roles, such as finance director or sales director. The board should also consist of **some NEDs** who will be part-time and have no specific operational role in the company.

The board should include a **balance of executive and NEDs** (and in particular independent NEDs) such that no individual or small group of individuals can dominate the board's decision taking. Some corporate governance guidelines suggest that at least half the board should be NEDs.

Qualities of NEDs

NEDs should be **independent in judgement** (even if they are not independent according to governance guidance) and have **enquiring minds**. They need to be **well-informed** about the **company and the external environment** in which it operates, with a strong command of issues relevant to the business.

Role of NEDs

The main roles of NEDs are **to develop strategy** and **monitor performance**.

(i) **Development of strategy**

In terms of their strategic role they are working with the executive directors in order to **determine the future** of the company.

(ii) **Monitoring**

The monitoring role of NEDs takes on many forms. In general terms they are there to **challenge the decisions** of executive directors where they do not agree and to highlight any bad practice or poor performance.

NEDs should also **satisfy themselves** on the **integrity of financial information** and that **financial controls and systems of risk management** are robust and defensible. They therefore need to ensure that **sufficient, accurate, clear and timely information** is **provided** sufficiently in advance of meetings to enable thorough consideration of the issues facing the board.

(b) **Non-independent NEDs**

A NED is not independent if he or she is on the board **representing** the **interests** of a **major shareholder**, because the views given by the director will be made in the interests of that shareholder. Similarly, it is debatable whether a director is independent when he or she has a **close relationship** with the company or any other executive director. For example, a former chief executive of a company might be given a non-executive role after retirement. He would not be independent.

Independent NEDs

In contrast, an independent NED is a person who has no connection with the company other than as a non-executive director, and who should be able to give an **independent opinion** on the affairs of the company, without influence from any other director or any shareholder.

(c) **Conflicts of interest**

A potential conflict of interest occurs when the executive directors or senior management of a company might be inclined to take decisions that would not be in the **interests** of the **company's shareholders**. Although there are several areas where a conflict of interest could arise, the major problem areas are those of remuneration of the directors and senior managers, financial reporting, and nominations of new board members.

Remuneration

If executive directors are allowed to decide their own remuneration, they could be inclined to pay themselves as much as possible, without having to hold themselves to account or to justify their high pay. Where incentive schemes are in place, there is a risk that incentive schemes devised by the executive directors for themselves will be linked to **achieving performance targets** that are not necessarily in the shareholders' interests. For example, rewarding directors with a bonus for achieving profit growth is of no value to shareholders if the result is **higher business risk** and a **lower share price**.

Remuneration committee

Corporate governance in many countries, such as the UK's Combined Code, calls for a remuneration committee of the board to be established to decide on **directors' pay**, including **incentive schemes**, and for

BPP
LEARNING MEDIA

this committee to comprise at least three, or in the case of smaller companies two, members, who should all be **independent non-executive directors**.

The remuneration committee should have **delegated responsibility** for **setting remuneration** for all **executive directors** and the chairman, including pension rights and any compensation payments. The committee should also recommend and monitor the **level and structure** of **remuneration** for **senior management**. The NEDs should, in principle, be able to devise fair remuneration packages that include an incentive element, in which the performance targets bring the objectives of the executive directors more into line with those of the shareholders.

Financial reporting

A second potential area for conflict of interest is financial reporting. The executive directors might be tempted to '**window dress**' the results of the company, in order to **present the financial results** in a way that reflects better on themselves and their achievements.

Audit committee

There should be an **audit committee** of the board, consisting of non-executive directors, whose task should be to consider issues relating to financial reporting and financial control systems. This committee **should be responsible for maintaining regular liaison** with the external auditors. The Combined Code says that the audit committee should **comprise at least three**, or in the case of smaller companies two, members, who should all be **independent NEDs**. The board should satisfy itself that at least one member of the audit committee has recent and relevant financial experience.

Nominations to board

A third potential area for conflict is **nominations of new board members**. A powerful chairman or chief executive could be tempted to appoint their supporters or 'yes men' to the board, and so strengthen their position on the board. The Combined Code recommends that there should be a nominations committee of the board, manned by NEDs.

Other areas

Other areas of potential conflict of interest can be identified, such as **succession planning**, and the board's decisions on **making acquisitions** or in preparing defences against a takeover bid. In each of these areas, NEDs should be able to provide a counter-balance to the self-interested views of executive directors.

(d) **Share payments**

In many companies, NEDs receive a fixed cash payment for their services, without any incentives. However, some companies pay their NEDs in shares.

They would argue that the more equity the NEDs hold, the more likely they will be to look at issues from the point of view of the shareholders. There is a risk that a NED holding shares could become more concerned with **short-term movements** in the share price and the opportunity of making a **short-term profit from selling their shares**. However, a suitable precaution against this could be to obtain the agreement of a NED **not to sell his or her shares** until after leaving the board.

Share options

The argument that NEDs should be rewarded with share options is more contentious, but it has been widely practised in the UK and is even more common in the US. The argument against rewarding NEDs with share options is that this form of remuneration could align the interests of the NEDs more closely with the executive directors, who also hold share options. NEDs should give independent advice, and it can be argued that it is therefore not appropriate to incentivise them in the same way as the executives.

The Combined Code points out that holding of share options could be relevant to the determination of a non-executive director's independence. It states that remuneration for non-executive directors **should not include share options**. If, exceptionally, options are granted, **shareholder approval** should be **sought in advance** and any shares acquired by exercise of the options should be held until at least one year after the non-executive director leaves the board.

Question 3

Text references. Chapter 5, 6 and 8.

Top tips. The framework used in (a) is a good way of identifying the most important risks. Other frameworks may be used, although it will be important to ensure that the risks identified are clearly related to the situation outlined in the scenario.

For (b) if you are faced with a question of the format:

Part (a) Identify risks

Part (b) Discuss effects of identified risks and what the organisation can do to mitigate them, ensure your answer plan shows consistency in format. Your answer to (b) needs to be a mirror image of your answer to (a).

Don't worry also if you haven't thought of, or had time to discuss, all the possible risks we have. Remember a score of 15 out of 25 is a comfortable pass.

Easy marks. Evidence suggests most students find it easier to identify risks than to come up with ways of reducing and controlling them. However to improve your chances of passing, you must be able to come up with realistic ways of tackling risks at some stage in your answer.

Marking scheme

		Marks
(a)	Up to 2 marks for each distinct risk identified.	10
(b)	Up to 3 marks for discussion of effect and reduction of each risk identified. To gain three marks, both effect and reduction should be discussed. Risks discussed should be those described in (a).	15
		25

Answer plans

(a)

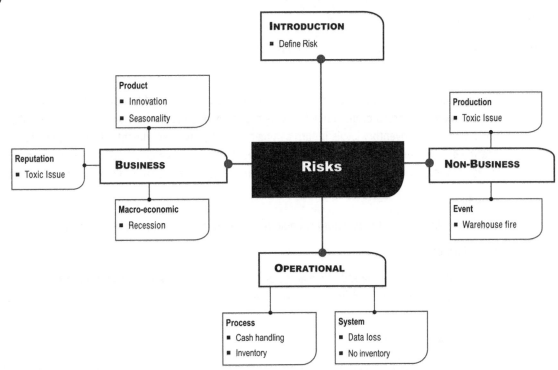

(b)

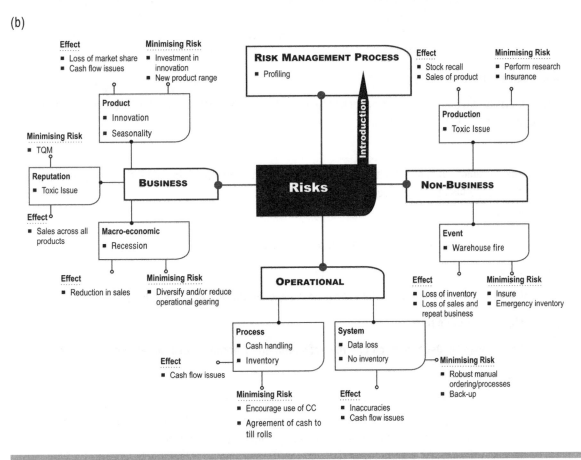

Risk can defined as the possibility that events or results will turn out differently from is expected.

(a)   The risks facing the HOOD Company are outlined below.

Operational risks

These are risks relating to the business's day-to-day operations.

(i)   **Accounting irregularities**

The unexplained fall in gross profit in some stores may be indicative of **fraud** or **other accounting irregularities**. Low gross profit in itself may be caused by **incorrect inventory values** or loss of **sale income**. Incorrect inventory levels in turn can be caused by **incorrect inventory counting** or **actual stealing of inventory** by employees. Similarly, **loss of sales income** could result from **accounting errors** or employees **fraudulently removing cash** from the business rather than recording it as a sale.

(ii)   **Systems**

Technical risks relate to the **technology** being **used by the company** to run its business.

(1)   **Backup**

Transferring data to head office at the end of each day will be **inadequate for backup purposes**. Failure of computer systems during the day will still result in loss of that day's **transaction data**.

(2)   **Delays in ordering**

Although inventory information is collected using the EPOS system, **re-ordering of inventory takes** a **significant amount of time**. Transferring data to head office for central purchasing may result in some discounts on purchase. However, the average 10 days before inventory is received at the store could result in **the company running out of inventory**.

Non-business risks

These are risks that arise for reasons beyond the normal operations of the company or the business environment within which it operates.

(i)   **Production**

The possibility of sunlight making some of HOOD Company's products potentially dangerous may give rise to **loss of sales** also inventory recall.

(ii)   **Event**

HOOD may be vulnerable to losses in a warehouse fire.

Business risks

External risks relate to the **business**; they are essentially **uncontrollable** by the company.

(i)   **Macro-economic risk**

The company is **dependent on one market sector** and **vulnerable to competition** in that sector.

(ii)   **Product demand**

The most important social change is probably a **change in fashion**. HOOD has not changed its product designs for 4 years indicating some lack of investment in this area. Given that fashions tend to change more frequently than every four years, HOOD may experience falling sales as customers seek new designs for their outdoor clothing. HOOD may also be vulnerable to **seasonal** variations in demand.

(iii)   **Corporate reputation**

Risks in this category relate to the overall **perception of HOOD in the marketplace** as a supplier of (hopefully) good quality clothing. However, this reputation could be damaged by **problems with the manufacturing process** and a consequent high level of returns.

(b)   **Profiling**

By identifying and profiling the effects of the risks, HOOD can assess what the consequences might be, and hence what steps (if any) are desirable to mitigate or avoid the consequences.

The potential effects of the risks on HOOD and methods of overcoming those risks are explained below.

Operational risks

(i)   **Accounting irregularities**

The potential effect on HOOD is **loss of income** either from inventory not being available for sale or cash not being recorded. The overall amount is unlikely to be significant as employees would be concerned about being caught stealing.

The risk can be minimised by introducing additional controls including the necessity of producing a **receipt for each sale** and the **agreement of cash received** to the **till roll** by the shop manager. Loss of inventory may be identified by more frequent checks in the stores or closed-circuit television.

(ii)   **Systems**

(1)   **Backup**

The potential effect on HOOD is relatively minor; **details of one shop's sales** could be lost for part of one day. However, the cash from sales would still be available, limiting the actual loss.

Additional procedures could be implemented to **back up transactions** as **they occur**, using online links to head office. The **relative cost of providing these links** compared to the likelihood of error occurring will help HOOD decide whether to implement this solution.

(2)   **Delays in inventory ordering**

The potential effect on HOOD is **immediate loss of sales** as customers cannot purchase the garments that they require. In the longer term, if running out of inventory becomes more frequent, **customers may not visit** the store because they believe inventory will not be available.

The risk can be minimised by letting the stores **order goods directly** from the manufacturing, using an extension of the EPOS system. Costs incurred relate to the provision of Internet access for the shops and possible increase in cost of goods supplied. However, this may be acceptable compared to overall loss of reputation.

Non-business risks

(i)   **Production**

The effect on HOOD is the possibility of having to **reimburse customers** and the loss of income from the product until the problems are resolved.

The risk can be minimised by HOOD taking the claim seriously and **investigating its validity**, rather than ignoring it. For the future, **guarantees** should be obtained from suppliers to confirm that products are safe and **insurance** taken out against possible claims from customers for damage or distress.

(ii) **Event**

The main effects of a warehouse fire will be a **loss of inventory and** the incurring of costs to replace it. There will also be a **loss of sales** as the inventory is not there to fulfil customer demand, and perhaps also a loss of subsequent sales as customers continue to shop elsewhere,

Potential losses of sales could be avoided by **holding contingency inventory** elsewhere, and losses from the fire could be reduced by **insurance.**

External risks

(i) **Macro-economic risk**

The potential effect on HOOD largely depends on HOOD's **ability to provide an appropriate selection of clothes**. It is unlikely that demand for coats etc. will fall to zero, so some sales will be expected. However, an increase in competition may result in **falling sales,** and without some diversification, this will automatically affect the overall sales of HOOD.

HOOD can minimise the risk in two ways: by **diversifying into other areas**. Given that the company sells outdoor clothes, then commencing sales of other outdoor goods such as camping equipment may be one way of diversifying risk. It can also look to resume **operational gearing**, fixed cost as a proportion of turnover.

(ii) **Product demand**

Again the **risk of loss of demand and business to competitors** may undermine HOOD's ability to continue in business.

This risk can be minimised by having a **broad strategy** to **maintain** and **develop** the **brand** of HOOD. Not updating the product range would appear to be a mistake in this context as the brand may be devalued as products may not meet changing tastes of customers. The board must therefore allocate appropriate investment funds to updating the products and **introduce new products** to maintain the company's image.

(iii) **Corporate reputation**

As well as **immediate losses of contribution from products** that have been returned, HOOD faces the consequence of loss of future sales from customers who believe their products no longer offer quality. Other clothing retailers have found this to be very serious; a **reputation for quality**, once lost, undoubtedly **cannot easily be regained**. The potential effect of a drop in overall corporate reputation will be falling sales for HOOD, resulting eventually in a **going concern problem**.

HOOD can guard against this loss of reputation by **enhanced quality control procedures**, and introducing processes such as **total quality management**.

Question 4

Marking scheme

			Marks
(a)	Up to 3 marks for analysis of purposes of risk management	3	
	Up to 3 marks for justification of importance of risk management	3	
	Up to 3 marks for explanation of interaction of risk management and internal control system	3	
			9
(b)	Up to 3 marks for need for, and significance of, management review	3	
	Up to 2 marks for other sources of assurance	2	
			5
(c)	Up to 8 marks for explanation of different elements of review. To obtain high marks, answer must include details of regular and annual review and relate to information in the scenario	8	
	Up to 4 marks for explanation of different disclosures. To obtain high marks, answer must include statement of board's responsibilities, what has been done to manage risk and that board has reviewed risk management	4	
	max		11
			25

(a) **Purposes of risk management**

Alignment of risk appetite and strategy

LMN's board should consider what risks it is prepared to **tolerate** in the light of the organisation's strategy. Risk management comprises the systems and processes for dealing with the risks that the board is prepared to tolerate in order for LMN to fulfil its **strategic objectives**.

Develop a consistent framework for dealing with risk

A coherent risk management framework can help LMN compare risks with **obvious financial consequences** (poor cost control, loss of income due to bad debts) with risks whose financial consequences are less obvious (dissatisfied tenants). It also should provide guidelines that can be applied by staff operating across all areas of LMN's activities.

Develop risk response strategies

The risk management process should **identify and evaluate risks** (for example by the high-medium-low method described) and therefore provide the information necessary for management to decide what the best **response to risk** should be – bearing, reduction, elimination or transfer.

Importance of risk management

Improve financial position

The risk management framework can provide a means of judging the costs of **treating the risks** measured against the **benefits**. It can also help LMN's directors judge whether to take advantage of opportunities, for example property investment.

Minimize surprises and losses

By identifying risks in the **risk register**, the risk management process should reduce the occurrence of unexpected shocks. For example identifying property maintenance as a risk issue should encourage a programme of regular maintenance designed to deal with the risks associated with the types and ages of property.

Maintain reputation

As LMN is a charity, its reputation as a good corporate citizen is very important. Risk management should help it avoid risks to its reputation such as **poor treatment of tenants** or failing to comply with **regulatory requirements**.

Risk management and the internal control system

Internal control is action taken by management to achieve organisational objectives and goals. Internal control thus is bound up with the organisation's strategies, and is therefore also bound up with risk management that is dependent upon the organisation's strategies. Internal control is made up of two elements:

(i)   The **control environment**, the framework within which controls operate and within which attitudes towards risk are an important elements. **Communication** between directors and employees is a key element of the control environment.

(ii)   **Internal controls**, which should be operated when their **benefits outweigh costs**; controls focused on dealing with the most significant risks will have obvious benefits. Because risks as here affect different areas of activity, controls of different types will be required; financial controls, although significant, will not be enough.

Given the risks LMN faces, key controls will include **debtor management**, **maintenance inspections and logs**, **financial appraisal of new investments** and **tenant satisfaction questionnaires**, as well as **accounting**, **compliance** and **cost limitation** controls.

(b)   **Audit committee's role in internal control**

Under corporate governance guidelines audit committees are responsible for creating a **climate of discipline and control.** To do this, they have to obtain assurance that internal control is working **effectively** and providing an **adequate response** to the **risks** faced.

Importance of management review

The management review provides the audit committee with evidence of whether the **control systems** appear to be effectively managing the most significant risks. It also gives the audit committee an indication of the **scope and quality** of management's monitoring of risk and internal control; does the report appear to be an

adequate review given the risks faced. The review should provide **feedback** that the audit committee should confirm has led to improvements in the control systems.

Other sources of evidence

However management's review of internal control is only one source of evidence that the audit committee should use to gain assurance. The committee should also receive reports from **staff** undertaking important and high-risk activities such as property investment. They should also receive reports from **control functions** such as human resources or internal audit (if any). Feedback from external sources such as **external audit** or **regulatory visits** will also provide information.

(c) (i) **Review of internal controls**

The UK's Turnbull committee emphasises the importance of a regular review and an annual review of internal control as part of an organisation's strategy for **minimizing risk, ensuring adherence to strategic objectives, fulfilling responsibilities to stakeholders** and **establishing accountability at its senior levels.**

Regular review

Regular review is an essential part of the strategy for minimizing risks. The audit committee is likely to have responsibility for this review, and as best practice recommends at least **three audit committee meetings a year**; this is thus how often the review should take place. Its findings should be communicated to the board.

The review should cover the following areas:

(1) Whether LMN is **identifying** and **evaluating** all key risks, financial and non-financial. This is a very significant task given the variety of risks faced, and also the need to devote limited resources to the most important risks.

(2) Whether **responses and management** of risks are **appropriate**; for example what level of risks should LMN bear without taking any steps (just low likelihood, small consequences risks or any others).

(3) The **effectiveness of internal controls** in countering the risks. The board should consider how much controls could be expected to **reduce the incidence** of risks, any evidence that controls have **not been operating effectively** and how **weaknesses are being resolved**. The board would consider evidence such as incidence of bad debts, records of property occupation and complaints from tenants.

Annual review

The annual review of internal control should be more wide-ranging than the regular review, taking into account the **strategic objectives of the charity** and undertaken by the **whole board** rather than just the audit committee. It should examine controls and risk management systems in all major areas, covering in particular:

(1) The **changes** since the last assessment **in risks faced**, and the charity's ability to **respond to changes in its environment**. For example the board would consider any changes in the charity's credit ratings, also longer-term trends such as changes in the incidence of low income earners.

(2) The **scope and quality of management's monitoring of risk and control**, also whether internal audit is required. In particular the review should consider whether the **scope and frequency of the regular review** should be increased.

(3) The **extent and frequency of reports** to the board; should reports on high incidence, high likelihood risks be made more regularly.

(4) **Significant controls, failings and weaknesses** that may materially impact on the financial statements, for example problems over its property portfolio management.

(5) Communication to stakeholders of **risk objectives, targets** and **measures** taken to counter risks.

(ii) **Disclosures in the annual report**

The report on compliance is a key part of the annual report by which LMN demonstrates its **compliance with regulations** and how it has **fulfilled the differing requirements of its stakeholders**.

Responsibility

The board should also **acknowledge its accountability** for LMN's system of control and **reviewing its effectiveness**.

Risk management

The Turnbull report recommends that as a minimum the board should disclose what has been done to **manage risk** and how the board has **reviewed the effectiveness of the risk management process**. The board should explain the limits of the process (it aims at risk management rather than risk elimination) and disclose any **material problems** or **weaknesses** that have been found.

ACCA Professional Level

Paper P1

Professional Accountant

Mock Examination 2

Question Paper	
Time allowed	
Reading and Planning Writing	**15 minutes** **3 hours**
This paper is divided into two sections	
Section 1 This ONE question is compulsory and must be attempted	
Section 2 TWO questions only to be attempted	
During reading and planning time only the question paper may be annotated	

DO NOT OPEN THIS PAPER UNTIL YOU ARE READY TO START UNDER EXAMINATION CONDITIONS

Section A – This question is compulsory and must be attempted

Question 1

Pacific Goods is a large retail company, selling a wide range of goods from small household items such as cleaning materials to garden tools and a limited range of gifts and chocolates. The company was founded in the 1800's and now trades in 23 countries with more than 250 stores. The company's image is one of being 'cheap and cheerful' – that is staff are always happy to assist customers, although the goods themselves are moderately priced.

Over the past three years, Mr Carson (the CEO) has attempted to take Pacific Goods more 'up-market'. Ranges of cheap goods were discontinued and more expensive items placed on sale. A new company logo and corporate slogan were implemented in an attempt to re-brand the company. The board of Pacific Goods provided Mr Carson with unanimous support, effectively ignoring warnings from some store managers concerning the demographic profile of their customers and how the move would adversely affect that profile.

The risk committee was also concerned that this decision was not fully evaluated. However, the committee was not provided with the time or information to make an effective evaluation. The committee comprises one non-executive director and three store managers. In terms of corporate governance, Pacific Goods also maintains an appointment committee and an audit committee. Each committee comprises two executive directors and one non-executive director. Mr Beckett, the Chairman of Pacific Goods and a major shareholder, has always maintained that it is important to follow the principles of corporate governance rather than follow rigorous regulations. The fact that Pacific Goods is not a quoted company confirms his belief that it is the 'spirit' of corporate governance only that needs to be followed.

To compliment the new image, Mr Carson required store managers to provide detailed reports on achievement of profit and insisted on downsizing the number of shop staff to achieve an enhanced level of profit. Remaining staff were also required to work longer hours with only minimal pay increases on an annual basis. Store managers were also to refer a range of decisions (although the exact list was never published) to the newly appointed human resources director, the son of Mr Carson. Mr Carson jnr has just graduated from business school and was seen by the board as having all the necessary skills to assist store managers in their difficult task of managing budgets and people. The appointment of Mr Carson jnr was made without the involvement of the appointments committee.

Unfortunately, the store managers (rather than the board's optimism) were proved correct and the move upmarket was disastrous. Sales at Pacific Goods have fallen by around 25% in the last two years. Mr Carson (snr and jnr) resigned their positions and the remaining board members are attempting to 'rescue' the company. Mr Beckett collapsed from a heart attack at about the same time and is now convalescing; he does not expect to work for at least six months.

In response to the problems facing the company, the appointment committee has taken the unusual step of appointing Mr Staite to be the company's chairman and CEO. Mr Staite has had significant previous experience in re-focusing corporate strategy; it is the appointment committee's belief that this is the most effective way of ensuring Pacific Goods survives as a going concern over the next few years.

Required

(a) Prepare a memorandum for the board explaining what is meant by the term 'control environment' and evaluating the control environment within Pacific Goods.

(14 marks)
(including 2 professional marks)

(b) Explain the principles-based approach to corporate governance, describing the advantages of this approach. Discuss whether the approach is appropriate for Pacific Goods.

(14 marks)

(c)   Define strategic and operational risk. Identify and describe the strategic and operational risks facing Pacific Goods. **(14 marks)**

(d)   Discuss the ethical and corporate governance issues resulting from Mr. Staite's position on the board of Pacific Goods plc, recommending how the issues can be resolved. **(8 marks)**

(including 3 professional marks)

(Total = 50 marks)

Section B – TWO questions ONLY to be attempted

Question 2

Hammond Brothers, a road haulage company, is likely to be seeking a stock exchange listing in a few years' time. In preparation for this, the directors are seeking to understand certain key recommendations of the international corporate governance codes, since they realise that they will have to strengthen their corporate governance arrangements. In particular the directors require information about what the governance reports have achieved in:

- (i)   Defining the role of non-executive directors
- (ii)   Improving disclosure in financial accounts
- (iii)   Strengthening the role of the auditor
- (iv)   Protecting shareholder interests

Previously also the directors have received the majority of their income from the company in the form of salary and have decided salary levels amongst themselves. They realise that they will have to establish a remuneration committee but are unsure of its role and what it will need to function effectively.

The directors are also considering whether it will be worthwhile to employ a consultant to advise on how the company should be controlled, focusing on the controls with which the board will be most involved.

Required

(a)   Briefly evaluate what the main corporate governance reports have achieved in the areas (i) – (iv) listed above.

(9 marks)

(b)   Explain the purpose and role of the remuneration committee, and analyse the information requirements the committee will have in order to be able to function effectively.   **(9 marks)**

(c)   Explain what are meant by organisation and management controls and recommend the main organisation and management controls that the company should operate.   **(7 marks)**

(Total = 25 marks)

Question 3

You are a manager in the internal audit department of TB1, a large listed company employing 7,000 staff in your country including an internal audit department of 30. During the course of the audit of the computer-based financial control systems, you have discovered that €1.1 billion of revenue expenditure has been treated as capital spending. You have reported this finding to the head of internal audit and then to the chief accountant, but as far as you are aware, no action has been taken by the company. The external audit is due to commence in 7 days, and you have been instructed by the head of internal audit not to disclose this information to the external auditors.

Required

(a)   Explain the composition and the role of the audit committee in a listed company.   **(8 marks)**

(b)   Discuss reasons why whistleblowing has become more important in recent years.   **(6 marks)**

(c)   Evaluate the alternative actions available to you now, and how these may conflict with ACCA ethical guidance.   **(11 marks)**

(Total = 25 marks)

Question 4

LP manufactures and supplies a wide range of different clothing to retail customers from 150 stores located in three different countries. The company has made a small net profit for the last three years. Clothes are made in three different countries, one in Europe, one in South America and the last in the Far East. Sales are made via cash, major credit cards and increasingly through the company's own credit card. Additional capital expenditure is planned in the next financial year to update some old production machinery.

In order to increase sales, a new Internet site is being developed which will sell LP's entire range of clothes using 3D revolving dummies to display the clothes on screen. The site will use some new compression software to download the large media files to purchasers' PCs so that the clothes can be viewed. This move is partly in response to environmental scanning which indicated a new competitor, PVO, will be opening an unknown number of stores in the next six months.

As a cost cutting move, the directors are considering delaying LP's new range of clothes by one year. Sales are currently in excess of expectations and the directors are unwilling to move away from potentially profitable lines.

Required

(a)   Describe a process for managing risk that could apply to any company of a similar size to LP.   **(10 marks)**

(b)   Evaluate the business risks affecting LP and describe how these risks can be managed.   **(15 marks)**

(Total = 25 marks)

Answers

DO NOT TURN THIS PAGE UNTIL YOU HAVE
COMPLETED THE MOCK EXAM

A plan of attack

We've already established that you've been told to do it 101 times, so it is of course superfluous to tell you for the 102nd time to **Take a good look at the paper before diving in to answer questions.**

First things first

Remember that the best way to use the 15 minutes reading time in your exam is firstly to **look through the paper** in detail, working out **which questions to do** and the **order** in which to attempt them. Then spend the remaining time analysing the requirements of **Question 1** and highlighting the key issues in the question.

The next step

You may be thinking that this paper is a lot more straightforward than the first mock exam; however, having sailed through the first mock, you may think this paper is actually rather difficult.

Option 1 (Don't like this paper)

If you are challenged by this paper, it is still best to **do the compulsory question first.** You will feel better once you've got it out the way. Honest.

- There are a lot of application marks in **Question 1** and some fairly distinct question parts. Having read the requirements carefully, mark against each paragraph the part of the question to which it relates. Use this as the basis of your plan as hopefully the material in the scenario will jog your memory about the corporate governance theory that you need to discuss.

- The scenario in **Question 2** gives you the framework you need for your answer to part (a); you just need to flesh it out with some ideas. In (b) there's quite a lot you could say about the role of the remuneration committee. Whether you choose this question may depend on whether you think you can attempt part (c); if you are struggling to define these controls or think of relevant examples, you may choose to avoid this question.

- Part (a) of **Question 3** may appear to be one of the easiest sections of the paper. However you will also need to think about wider issues in (b) when discussing whistleblowing and make practical recommendations in (c). Remember in (c) that you have to discuss a number of possible solutions and will get two to three marks for each.

- Part (a) of **Question 4** is fairly general, but you do have to bear the company's details in mind. Although the scenario is quite short, there are lots of ideas in it that you can use to generate points for (b).

Option 2 (This paper's alright)

Are you **sure** it is? If you are then that's encouraging. You'll feel even happier when you've got the compulsory question out the way, so why not **do Question 1 first**.

- Although **Question 1** appears to require some fairly basic knowledge, you won't get all that many marks for it. Make sure therefore by marking the question that you identify the relevant issues in the scenario for each part of the question and that you maximise your score by including them within your answer.

- Yes, there is potentially lots to write for **Question 2.** However read the question and scenario carefully to make sure that you realise all the elements that your answer has to contain. Check when you've completed your plan that your answer is complete. Also make sure when answering part (c) that the examples of controls that you suggest are relevant.

- You may think you know enough about audit committees to tackle a 25 mark question on the subject. However part (a) of **Question 3** is only worth 8 marks so take care! You have to discuss wider issues in (b) when considering whistleblowing, and discuss a number of alternatives in (c), coming up with some practical arguments.

- Remember to bear in mind the circumstances of the company when answering part (a) of **Question 4**, although your answer can be fairly general. Analyse the scenario carefully in part (b) to ensure you've identified all relevant risks.

Once more

You must must must **allocate your time** according to the marks for the question in total, and for the parts of the questions. And you must must must also **follow the requirements exactly.**

Finished with fifteen minutes to spare?

Looks like you slipped up on the time allocation. However if you have, make sure you don't waste the last few minutes; go back to **any parts of questions that you didn't finish** because you ran out of time.

Forget about it!

Forget about what? Excellent, you already have.

Question 1

Text references. Chapters 2,3,4,6 and 11 all contain relevant material.

Top tips. (a) illustrates how the control environment ranges widely over committee and reporting structure, and overall culture. Note that the problems arise as a consequence of specific poor decisions, through failures in the environment and through existing mechanisms not functioning effectively. Culture requires careful consideration, since the examiner has stressed its importance.

In (b) ease of application is the main reason why a principles-based approach is preferred, and this has a number of aspects that the answer discusses. However with Pacific Goods ease has meant easy to ignore, because the principles-based approach has been effectively seen as a soft option.

Note how (c) draws out certain risks such as liquidity and legal risks which may not be obvious from the scenario. In questions of this sort, you need to consider a variety of risks, but ensure that your answer includes enough explanation about what they are and their consequences. When planning you need to assess which are the most significant risks and spend most time discussing them – but don't spend too long on any individual risk.

Note in (d) the ethical implications of this classic corporate governance problem. The answer is based on the simple model of identifying the issues, considering alternative solutions, and making reasoned recommendations.

Easy marks. There are a few easy marks for definitions, and hopefully in (b) the advantages of a principles-based approach should have provided easy marks as well; make sure you learn these if it didn't.

Marking scheme

			Marks
(a)	Up to 3 marks for definition of control environment	3	
	Up to 2 marks for each issue evaluated in company's control environment	12	
	Up to 2 professional marks for the form of the answer (memo in which content is laid out in an orderly and informative manner)	2	
	max		14
(b)	Up to 3 marks for explanation of principles-based approach	3	
	Up to 2 marks for each advantage identified	8	
	Up to 2 marks for each point about application of approach to company	6	
	max		14
(c)	Up to 3 marks for definitions of strategic and operational risk	3	
	Up to 2 marks for each risk described	12	
	max		14
(d)	Up to 3 marks for identification of issues	3	
	Up to 4 marks for alternative solutions suggested	4	
	Up to 3 professional marks for reasoned recommendations	3	
	max		8
			50

(a)

Memo

To: Board
From: Consultant
Date: 5 May 20X8
Subject: Control environment in Pacific Goods

Control environment

The **control environment** is the **overall attitude**, **awareness and actions** of directors and management regarding internal controls and their importance in the entity. The control environment encompasses the **management style**, **corporate culture and values** shared by all employees. It provides the **background** against which the various other controls are operated.

Control environment Pacific Goods - overview

The control environment within Pacific Goods appears to be weak. While there appear to be the **correct structures** in place to **identify and implement control systems** in terms of the risk committee, the committee does not appear to be effective. Specific matters that need to be addressed are noted below.

Risk identification

The risk committee appears to be ineffective because it **lacks clear strategies** for either identifying or dealing with those risks that have been identified. For example, the strategy of attempting to move Pacific Goods 'upmarket' was not fully considered, and the **possibility of failure** was **not considered** by the board.

Company culture

Pacific Goods' standard of customer service has been good. The fact that staff were prepared to assist customers provided a **good company reputation** and **repeat business**. However, the new emphasis on **profitability and cutting of expenses** (including the number of staff in each store) will have **adversely affected the company's image** and **contributed to falling sales**. Similarly, basing store manager performance entirely on **profit** rather than a range of indicators has meant a cultural emphasis on profit, again decreasing the good customer service ethic.

Reporting requirements

The **requirement to send monthly reports on profitability** with detailed comments on variances further implies a change in the company's culture. The detailed review implies a **lack of trust in the store managers**, which will also **decrease the motivation** of those managers. Staff **motivation will also have fallen** as they see an **increased focus on selling** rather than customer service, to say nothing of **redundancies** further decreasing motivation.

Consequences of poor appointment

The appointment of Mr Carson jnr may have been a mistake. While business school will provide some skills, the director **lacked the real world experience and therefore credibility** within the role. It was unlikely that store managers would trust Mr Carson jnr with the effect that they may not have deferred decisions to him and neglected to implement his advice.

Authority levels

The **lack of clear explanation of what decisions** would be made by Mr Carson jnr was also not helpful. Store managers would have been in the situation of being **accountable for their budgets**, but **not having the authority** to make the decisions they need to manage those budgets effectively. Not only will this have further decreased their motivation, but also it will have **decreased the store manager's credibility** with shop staff as the managers would have been seen to lack the authority to run the store.

Appointment committee

There are two specific weaknesses within the control environment at Pacific Goods in relation to corporate governance. Firstly, the appointment committee can be **over-ridden by the board of directors**. The appointment of Mr Carson jnr clearly shows this. There is the risk that inappropriate staff/directors will be appointed into the company, increasing the risk that their duties will not be carried out appropriately.

Risk committee

Secondly, the **risk committee appears to be ineffective** regarding the identification or evaluation of risks. This is due partly to lack of information provision, but also to lack of sufficient senior staff on the committee. Even if a full evaluation of the change in company image had taken place, it is unlikely that one non-executive director could sufficiently influence the rest of the board.

(b)   **Principles-based approach to corporate governance**

The principles based approach focuses on **objectives of corporate governance** rather than **enforcing the mechanisms** by which those objectives should be achieved. The idea is that principles are easier to integrate into strategic planning systems than detailed rules and regulations.

Advantages of principles-based approaches

Difficulty of applying rules

The principles-based approach is particularly useful where **rules cannot easily be applied**. For example, it is relatively straightforward to define rules for internal control systems, but not for areas such as organisational culture or maintaining relationships with stakeholders. Similarly, principles can be **applied across different legal jurisdictions** rather than being based on the legal regulations of one country.

Comply or explain basis

Principles-based approaches are also normally in force in corporate governance terms **on a comply or explain basis**. The extent to which a principle has or has not been applied can therefore be clearly explained, rather than simply stating that a rule has not been followed.

Ease of implementation

The approach is also **easier and cheaper to implement**. Being able to state principles removes the need for detailed or complicated legislation to attempt to cover every possible eventuality and is therefore cheaper from the legislative point-of-view. The law making body of each jurisdiction does not have to spend large amounts of time (and money) producing detailed legislation. From the point of view of companies, the benefit is less 'red-tape' or form filling.

Flexibility for companies

Using principles allows **each entity to decide how to implement those principles**, without having to follow detailed rules or guidelines that may simply not be applicable to that entity.

Investors' decision-making

The principles-based approach means that **emphasis is placed on investors** to decide what a company is doing, rather than the company providing lots of data about rules being followed, but no overall impression of the success or otherwise of the company.

Appropriateness for Pacific Goods

It is unclear whether the principles-based approach is applicable for Pacific Goods. Clearly, the benefits of the approach should apply to the company in terms of being able to **implement procedures appropriate** for the company, particularly in softer areas such as stakeholder communication and employee management.

Lack of commitment

However, the risk of this approach, as identified in Pacific Goods, is that the company may either choose **which principles to apply** from the longer list, or apply those principles in de-minimis form rather than being serious about corporate governance. For example, Pacific Goods does have an appointment committee and risk committee, but the members of those committees **do not have sufficient power to carry out their duties** correctly. Having only one non-executive director on each committee for example means a 'uphill' battle in persuading the board into a course of action and leaves the executives with the easy option of vetoing any suggestions.

Use of rules-based approach

Taking the alternative, a rules-based approach may be more appropriate for Pacific Goods as **compliance** with a set of rules would have to be stated. In other words, the extent of compliance would not be left up to the company; the **extent** would be **inherent within the rules or regulations**. Taking this approach would mean, for example, that the appointment committee had the 'correct' numbers of non-executive directors. Obviously areas such as internal controls would still be difficult but at least 'lip-service' could not be paid.

Conclusion

Overall, a principles-based approach would be appropriate if the directors **actually followed the appropriate corporate governance guidelines**. Without that compliance, a rules based approach may be preferred, at least in the short term.

(c) **Strategic risks**

Strategic risks are risks that relate to the **fundamental and key decisions** that the directors take about the future of the organisation.

Company strategy

The main strategic risk relates to the **change in company strategy** at Pacific Goods. The directors have in effect risked the entire business in the attempt to move the company 'upmarket'. A strategy change in this way is notoriously difficult (for example even after the attempt to move 'upmarket' Skoda cars are still considered cheap and unreliable even though the company has won reliability awards). As the scenario appears to indicate, it has not worked.

Company culture

There has also been a significant change in company culture. There have been two key changes in this area; firstly the additional requirements placed on store managers and secondly the overall philosophy of customer service being reversed. The new emphasis on profit may succeed although there has been **considerable damage to morale** with respect to redundancies and treatment of store managers.

Liquidity risk

There is some liquidity risk relating to the falling sales, although **no financial information** is **available** to identify any effect on cash flow. However, a fall in volume may indicate that overheads **take a higher proportion of expenses**. In the longer term, Pacific Goods may have **cash flow problems** as falling inflows are insufficient to pay for fixed cash outflows.

Legal risk

There is the possibly of **legal risk** in relation to pay and working hours of staff. Most jurisdictions have **legislation on minimum wage and maximum working hours** and Pacific Goods may be in breach of these. There is specific concern regarding extension of working hours with minimal pay increase as the hourly rate payable is likely to fall, and this fall could be below the minimum wage. Breach of legislation would result in adverse publicity for Pacific Goods.

Operational risks

Operational risks relate to matters that can go wrong on a **day-to-day basis** while the organisation is carrying out its business.

For Pacific Goods, operational risks focus mainly on the business of ensuring that the correct goods are available for sale in its shops at the correct time. Given the focus on profit and downsizing, specific risks in the supply chain include:

- Late or **inappropriate orders to re-stock products** (mistakes made in reading inventory levels)

- **Inappropriate orders being placed** (store managers not being aware of the product ranges that could appeal to slightly more upmarket customers)

- **Products not being placed** on shelves quickly enough (insufficient staff for restocking)

In other words, overworked staff may cause an increased number of manual errors.

(d) **Issues arising**

Mr Staite is currently the **chairman and CEO of Pacific Goods plc**. Codes of corporate governance indicate that the roles of chairman and CEO should be taken by different people to avoid excessive power being vested in one individual.

In Pacific Goods plc, there is a risk that Mr Staite could **abuse his power** on the board, either to further his own interests in Pacific Goods, or to adversely affect the strategy of Pacific Goods without proper discussion at board level. Mr Staite will effectively dominate the board meeting.

Alternative options

There are two options available to Mr Staite.

Firstly, he can **resign from being either the chairman or the CEO** as soon as the appointment committee can identify and appoint a suitable replacement.

Secondly, he can **continue to be chairman and CEO** to see out the crisis at Pacific Goods. This course of action is allowed by codes of corporate governance in the short term only and has been used occasionally. For example, in the early 2000's, Marks & Spencer appointed a chairman/CEO in an attempt to revive the company (an action which appeared to succeed).

Recommendations

Given Pacific Goods' current problems and Mr Staite's experience in alleviating similar problems in other companies, then it appears reasonable that he can **continue as chairman / CEO at least in the short term**. However, the appointment committee should be seeking suitable candidates to be CEO within a timescale of say 18 months from now.

This action allows Mr Staite to **attempt to see Pacific Goods through the current crisis**, while at the same time identifying the corporate governance requirement of keeping the roles separate wherever possible.

Question 2

Text references. Chapters 1, 3 and 4.

Top tips. As well as illustrating the key features of governance codes, (a) illustrates some of their limitations, the lack of detailed practical guidance and the realities of board power.

(b) is a good summary of the guidance on remuneration committees. The requirement relating to information is effectively asking what the remuneration committee should consider when setting levels of remuneration.

(c) deals with the SPAMSOAP controls that are of most relevance for this paper, the organisation and management controls.

Easy marks. The role of the remuneration committee should have provided easy marks in (b) even if the information requirements proved more difficult, so make sure you revise this area if you struggled.

Marking scheme

				Marks
(a)	Up to 3 marks for each issue discussed. 3 marks only awarded if limitations of each measure discussed			9
(b)	Up to 2 marks for each relevant point made about role and functioning of remuneration committee	7		
	Up to 4 marks for information requirements	4		
			max	9
(c)	1 mark for definition of organisation controls, 1 mark for definition of management controls			
	1 mark for each reasonable example given of an organisation or management control			7
				25

(a)   **Main concerns**

Most of the corporate governance reports have addressed concerns about the system of **financial reporting** and the **safeguards** provided by **auditors**. This is because of a number of reports have followed corporate scandals where the accounts of companies involved were shown to have misled investors. Other concerns that governance guidance has addressed have included **unexpected failures of major companies** and **lack of accountability of directors** towards shareholders and other stakeholders.

Features of governance reports

(i)   **Role of non-executive directors**

Governance reports have stressed the **role of independent non-executive directors**, particularly in regimes which do not have two-tier boards with a supervisory board. Independent non-executive directors should constitute **a strong presence on a board** (a third or more in numbers, depending on the governance regimes). They should be prepared to challenge the views of executive directors, and also staff the key **board committees** that monitor executive directors (the audit, remuneration, nomination and risk management committees).

However there are a number of examples of companies failing with a **significant non-executive presence** on board. The impact of the governance codes may thus be limited, for the following principal reasons.

Limited nature of role

The role of non-executive directors is essentially a **part-time**, **limited** involvement.

Position on board

Whilst the report recommends that certain tasks should fall specifically within the remit of non-executive directors (membership of the audit and remuneration committees) their impact on the main board depends on the **constitution** of the board and the **division of power** amongst executive directors

(ii) **Improvement of disclosure in financial accounts**

Certain recommendations in the area of financial reporting have been further developed by local statute and by financial reporting standards. Listed companies in some regimes are required to produce an **operating and financial review**; most regimes require the board to comment on the operation of internal controls and the entity's future as a **going concern**. There should be **improved disclosure** of **directors' remuneration**.

Undoubtedly there is more information but its added value remains uncertain. In particular some of the guidance on internal controls does not lay down the form of report, and does **not require** directors to make any statement on **effectiveness**. In addition there is **little guidance** on **design** and **implementation** of controls; industry-specific guidance may be helpful in this area.

(iii) **Strengthening the role of the auditor**

Undoubtedly the codes have demonstrated how **auditor concerns can be raised** with **independent directors**, and have demonstrated the importance of links between the external and internal auditors and the audit committee.

However whether the reforms have increased the value of audits to shareholders is doubtful for the following reasons.

Strength of board position

The audit committee's ability to express concerns will depend on its **members' position and influence** on the **main board**.

Increase in scope of audit

The codes lay stress on the role of the audit committee in selecting and if necessary recommending **changes** in **auditor appointments**. However it is doubtful whether in most instances changing the auditor will mean the scope of the audit will increase significantly. 'Big Four' spokesmen have indicated that their fears about increased exposure to liability mean that they are unwilling to take on extra reporting responsibilities.

(iv) **Protection of shareholders**

The above measures are designed to increase shareholder protection by increased control and availability of extra information. The codes have also stressed that **shareholders** can take advantage of their rights to **speak** at Annual General Meetings. They have also acknowledged the influence of **institutional shareholders**, stressing how institutional shareholders could be a force for good within companies.

However many codes have **not addressed** the question of whether the **interests** of different types of shareholders, would **differ**, and, if so, how each type could be protected.

(b)   **Purpose and role of remuneration committee**

The purpose of the remuneration committee is to provide a **mechanism** for **determining** the **remuneration packages** of executive directors. The scope of the review should include not only salaries and bonuses, but also share options, pension rights and compensation for loss of office.

The committee's remit may also include issues such as **director appointments** and succession planning, as these are connected with remuneration levels.

Constitution of remuneration committee

Most codes recommend that the remuneration committee should consist entirely of **non-executive directors** with no personal financial interest other than as shareholders in the matters to be decided. In addition there should be **no conflict of interests** arising from remuneration committee members and executive directors holding directorships in common in other companies.

Functioning of remuneration committee

Corporate governance such as the Combined Code states that remuneration should be set having regard to market forces, and the packages required to **'attract, motivate and retain'** the **desired calibre** of **director**. The committee should pay particular attention to the setting of performance-related elements of remuneration.

Reporting of remuneration committee

In addition a **report** from the committee should form part of the annual accounts. The report should set out **company policy** on remuneration and give details of the **packages** for **individual directors**. The **chairman** of the committee should be **available to answer questions** at the annual general meeting, and the committee should consider whether **shareholder approval** is required of the company's remuneration policy.

Information requirements

In order to assess executive directors' pay on a reasonable basis, the following information will be required.

(i)   **Remuneration packages given by similar organisations**

The problem with using this data is that it may **lead to upward pressure on remuneration**, as the remuneration committee may feel forced to pay what is paid elsewhere to avoid losing directors to competitors.

(ii)   **Market levels of remuneration**

This will particularly apply for **certain industries**, and **certain knowledge and skills**. More generally the committee will need an awareness of what is considered a minimum competitive salary.

(iii)   **Individual performance**

The committee's **knowledge and experience of the company**, will be useful here.

(iv)   **Organisation performance**

This may include **information about the performance of the operations** which the director controls, or more **general company performance information** such as earnings per share or share price.

(c)   **Main concerns of board**

The board's principal concern is with controls that can be classified as organisation or management.

Organisation controls

Organisation controls are designed to ensure **everyone** is **aware** of their **responsibilities**, and **provide** a **framework** within which lower level controls can operate. Key organisation controls include the following.

(i) **Structure**

The board should establish an **appropriate structure** for the organisation and **delegate** appropriate levels of authority to different grades.

(ii) **Internal accounting system**

The board should ensure that the system is providing **accurate and relevant information** on a regular basis. Good quality information will enable the board to assess whether targets are being met or losses are possible.

(iii) **Communication**

Communication of organisation **policies** and values through manuals and other guidance to staff is essential.

Management controls

Management controls are designed to **ensure** that the **business** can be **effectively monitored**. Key management controls include the following.

(i) **Monitoring of business risks on a regular basis**

This should include **assessment of the potential financial impact** of contingencies.

(ii) **Monitoring of financial information**

Management should also be alert for **significant variations in results** between branches or divisions or significant changes in results.

(iii) **Use of audit committee**

The committee should actively **liase** with the external and internal auditors, and **report** on any **weaknesses** discovered. The committee should also regularly **review** the **overall structure** of internal control, and investigate any serious weaknesses found.

(iv) **Use of internal audit**

Internal audit should be used as an independent check on the **operation** of **detailed controls** in the operating departments. Internal audit's work can be biased as appropriate towards areas of the business where there is a risk of significant loss should controls fail.

Question 3

Text references. Chapter 3 covers corporate governance, Chapter 11 ethical codes.

Top tips. In (a) the role and composition of an audit committee are matters of fact. It is important to recognise the role of NEDs and the internal reporting function of internal audit as the latter ties in with section (c) of the question.

In (b) whistleblowing can be addressed as risks to the company, or as in this situation, why it is currently important. Knowledge of issues such as Enron and the note in the small scenario about computerised accounts provides links to points that can be made in the answer.

In (c) you need to show that some form of disclosure should be made while maintaining the ethical guidance of the Institute. An alternative approach to the answer would be to discuss the different disclosure options and then show how these affected integrity and confidentiality. However, explaining the ethical issues first does allow these to be applied to the reporting alternatives, reducing the amount of potential repetition in the answer.

Easy marks. If you have a reasonable knowledge of corporate governance, you should score high marks on (a).

Marking scheme

			Marks
(a)	Up to 3 marks for membership of audit committee, focusing on independence and financial knowledge	3	
	1 mark for each of the major tasks carried out by the audit committee	5	
			8
(b)	Up to 2 marks per point discussed		6
(c)	Up to 3 marks for identification of problem	3	
	Up to 6 marks for discussion of possible solutions	6	
	Up to 2 marks for recommendation which should be relevant and related to previous discussion	2	
			11
			25

(a)   **Membership of audit committee**

According to the Combined Code, the **audit committee should have at least three members**, all Non Executive Directors. At least one member should have **relevant financial knowledge**; generally this would mean holding an accountancy or similar qualification. A majority of the membership should be **independent NEDs**. The head of the internal audit department and the external auditor may also form part of the committee, especially where internal and external audit reports are being discussed.

Role of audit committee

Review of financial statements and systems

The committee should review both the **quarterly/interim** (if published) and **annual accounts**. This should involve assessment of the judgements made about the overall **appearance and presentation of the accounts**, **key accounting policies** and **major areas of judgement**. The committee should also review the financial reporting and budgetary systems.

Liaison with external auditors

The audit committee's tasks here will include being responsible for the **appointment or removal of the external auditors** as well as fixing their remuneration. The committee should consider whether there are **any threats to external auditor independence,** particularly **non-audit services.** The committee should **discuss the scope of the external audit** prior to the start of the audit and act as a **forum for liaison** between the external auditors, the internal auditors and the finance director.

Review of internal audit

The review should cover **standards** including objectivity, technical knowledge and professional standards, the **work plan** and **scope**. The review should also cover adequacy of **resources, reporting and results** and **liaison** with external auditors. The head of internal audit should have **direct access** to the audit committee.

Review of internal control

Committee members can use their own experience to **monitor the adequacy of internal control systems,** focusing particularly on the control environment, management's attitude towards controls and overall management controls. The committee should also **consider the recommendations of the auditors** in the management letter and executive management's response.

Review of risk management

The audit committee should check whether there is a **formal policy in place for risk management** and that the policy is **backed and regularly monitored** by the board. The committee should also review the arrangements, including training, for ensuring that **managers and staff** are **aware of their responsibilities**. Committee members should use their own knowledge of the business to confirm that risk management is updated to reflect the current business environment and strategy.

(b) Whistleblowing has become more important in recent years for three main reasons:

(i) **Accessibility of information**

Firstly, an increasing amount of information is held on **computer files** that are in turn **accessible to many employees**. Certainly in the use of internal audit techniques where many transactions can be analysed by computer audit programs, the discovery of unusual or potentially incorrect transactions is more likely. Outside of the internal audit department, employees may encounter information inadvertently, simply because it is easily accessible. Whistleblowers are therefore more likely to find potentially unlawful or fraudulent transactions.

(ii) **Loyalty**

There is a **strong culture of loyalty** within many companies so that employees blowing the whistle may be seen as **traitors**. Although many countries have enacted laws to protect whistleblowers, they may still face retaliatory action by the company up to and including dismissal for making potentially false or malicious allegations.

(iii) **Whistleblowers**

Whistleblowers play an important role in uncovering mismanagement. Some recent financial scandals including Enron (2001) and WorldCom (2002) were bought into the public domain partly as a result of the actions of whistleblowers.

(c) **Importance of ethical code**

Actions that the audit manager can take must be **weighed against the ACCA ethical code**. While disclosing information about financial irregularities to a third party may appear to be attractive, the manager must bear in mind the overall ethical principles of integrity and confidentiality.

(i) **Integrity**

The principle of **integrity** implies that the manager will act honestly and that any action can be trusted. Any disclosure must therefore be made in good faith and not for financial gain and without malicious intent.

(ii) **Confidentiality**

The concept of **confidentiality** implies that information obtained during the course of employment in a company will be kept confidential, unless there is an appropriate reason to disclose this information. 'Normal reasons' will include client authorisation, breach of specific laws such as money laundering, and due process of law in a court.

The manager must therefore consider whether any disclose will be believed and whether breach of duty of confidentiality is appropriate in this situation.

Possible actions

Assuming that disclosure is thought appropriate, then the manager can consider the following reporting options:

(i)   The **board of directors or the chairman**

        However, these people may be **swayed by the opinion of the chief accountant** and may not wish disclosure due to the adverse impact on TB1.

(ii)   The **external auditors**

        Disclosure to a third party would appear to **go against the explicit instructions** of the head of internal audit. There is also no guarantee that the external auditors will be able to obtain appropriate audit evidence due to limited audit procedures or alteration of evidence prior to their visit.

(iii)   The **audit committee**

        Given that TB1 is a listed company, then the principles of good corporate governance should be followed. Specifically, there should be procedures within the company to **allow employees with genuine concerns** about the operations of the company to make a confidential approach to the audit committee. As the committee is comprised of non-executive directors, then they should be able to take appropriate investigative action without conflict of interest regarding their stewardship of the running of the company.

Recommendation

It is **therefore recommended** that the **manager makes disclosure** to the **audit committee**. This action will **not breach confidentiality** against the company as **no external disclosure** has been made, and given that disclosure is made in good faith, then it will also **maintain the manager's integrity**.

Question 4

> **Text references**. Chapters 6 and 8.
>
> **Top tips.** In (a) the answer follows a standard method for effective risk management. While the question requirement leaves open the possibility of using other processes, the idea of identifying the risks, assessing the likelihood of occurrence, limiting the risk and control and review should be identifiable in the answer. In (b), the scenario provides some useful hooks on which to base the main points in the answer. However, the list of risks could be applied to many other different companies. Identification and explanation of the risk and coming up with reasonable risk management suggestions is an important skill.
>
> **Easy marks**. (a) is a fairly straightforward discussion and you should score most of the marks you need to pass this question on it.

Marking scheme

			Marks
(a)	Up to 4 marks for description of risk identification procedures	4	
	Up to 4 marks for description of risk evaluation procedures	4	
	Up to 5 marks for description of risk management procedures	5	
	Up to 3 marks for description of risk control and review procedures	3	
	Give credit in all stages for relevant procedures		
	max		10
(b)	Up to 3 marks for each risk. Only award 3 marks if assessment of risk's		
	significance has been made and means of managing the risk have been identified		15
			25

(a)   There are four main principles for effective risk management in a business context.

Risk identification

Any organisation needs a procedure for **reviewing** the **risks** it faces and **to identify what those specific risks are**. The board of the company also needs to be aware that those risks will change over time, so it must be on the lookout for new risks. This is particularly true with more widespread terrorist activities (eg the 11th September attacks in the USA) and changes in the nature of global competition (eg outsourcing of call centres from Europe to the Middle and Far East).

Risks may also **vary depending on the country** in which the company operates. For example it may be difficult to establish a new brand in a new country, or there may be different employment, environmental or other legislation that must be followed.

The use of **internal audit** and **environmental audit programmes** will help to **identify different risks** enabling the company to keep up-to-date on the different risks facing it.

Risk evaluation

Risk evaluation involves the **use** of **various procedures to try and identify the size of the risk**. For a downside risk, the extent of any loss depends on:

(i)   The **probability of the outcome of the loss making event**, and

(ii)   The **size of the loss in the event that the risk crystallises** – that is occurs

Where the probability of the outcome is remote and the actual loss small, then no action may be taken regarding that risk. However, a high probability of the event and potentially large losses will mean that some risk management measures are required.

Risk management measures

Risk management measures are the **responsibility of managers and the board in an organisation**. The actual measure taken vary depending on the risk:

(i)   **Transfer of risk** by **Insurance** may be available so that a third party pays should the event occur, eg loss of company assets.

(ii)   **Avoidance** by removing that risk from the company. For example, a company may avoid the possibility of losses in a subsidiary by selling that subsidiary.

(iii) **Acceptance** of the risk as a feature of business. Some risks such as acts of terrorism may not even be insurable.

(iv)   **Reduction** of the risk. Many financial risks can be minimised, by hedging or use of forward contracts. Other risks such as over-reliance on a single product may be minimised by expanding the product range or purchasing competitors to diversify.

Risk control and review

Control systems should be established to monitor risks and to identify situations where actions are required to minimise new risks or existing risks that are becoming more significant. The Turnbull report indicates that a good system of internal control should be established to monitor risks, but that risk reviews should also be carried out on a regular basis to ensure that the control system is operating correctly.

(b)   **Business risks**

These are risks that a **company's performance could be better or worse than expected**.

(i)   **The new business venture to sell clothes on the Internet using 3D models to display the clothes**.

There is the risk that demand will be far short of that anticipated or that costs of developing the Internet site will significantly exceed budget. Previous experience in this area is not positive, with the dot.com company Boo.com collapsing after only a few weeks trading due to lack of ability of servers to cope with demand.

LP should have assessed the 3D project for feasibility. Budgets should have been established and **actual expenditure** regularly **compared with budgets**. If actual expenditure is unavoidably significantly in excess of budget, the board should consider whether the **project should continue**. Thorough **testing procedures** should have been built into the plan, and these should ensure that the site is capable of coping with anticipated demand. Once the site is operational, LP should monitor the level of sales generated by obtaining customer feedback through the site, and comparing sales generated with the costs of keeping the site updated.

(ii) **Product obsolescence**

The decision to lengthen the time of sale for each product may appear to decrease development costs. However, the board of LP must also take into account **demand** for the goods. The fashion industry tends to issue new clothes and designs every few months, and certainly in temperate climates, fashions will change according to the season. There is a risk that not amending the style of products sold will **reduce sales** far in **excess of the reduction in expenditure**. The overall going concern of the company may also be adversely affected if customers perceive the clothes to be 'out of date' and change to other suppliers.

LP should **monitor the performance of products** in detail, and look for evidence of falling sales and other evidence that its products are viewed as old-fashioned, for example adverse customer or press comment. The board should also consider whether work on developing new products should continue to some extent, so that new lines can be launched quickly if demand falls.

(iii) **New competition**

The new company PVO appears to be aggressively attacking LP's market place. While the overall effect of the new competitor is difficult to determine, having a new range of clothes available is likely to attract customers with little if any brand loyalty to LP.

LP should make sure that **competitor activity** is **carefully monitored** and responses are made to known or predicted competitor activity, for an example an advertising campaign to counter new products being launched by the competitor. LP's board should also **review very regularly the performance of products** which are most vulnerable to competitor activity and decide whether to invest more in these or concentrate on other less vulnerable products.

The overall going concern of the company may again be affected.

Financial risks

Financial risks arise from the **possibility that the financial situation of the company will be different from what was expected**. Financial risks will include:

(i) **Credit risks**

These arise from the use of the **company's store card**. If there is an economic depression then there may be an increased risk of card holders defaulting on their payments.

LP should carry out **credit checks** before consumers are allowed a credit card. The **initial credit limits** should be **set low**, and increased over time if the customer's level of business and repayment record warrant it. The company's systems should **reject payments** that take customers in excess of their credit limits. LP should insist on a **minimum amount** being repayable on the card each month. There should be **specified procedures** for pursuing overdue debts.

(ii) **Foreign exchange risks**

These occur because LP purchases raw materials and some finished products from **overseas**. Depending on how these purchases are financed, there will be a risk of **exchange rate losses** if the main currency LP uses moves adversely compared to the supplying country's currency.

LP's board should consider changing purchasing arrangements, so that more purchases are made in countries where LP has significant sales, thus reducing exchange risks by **matching**. However this should be weighed against the possibility that purchase prices may increase from using different sources. Payments on large purchases not made immediately could be covered by **forward contracts**.

(iii) **Interest rate risk**

This results from an **increase in bank base rates**. An increase in rates may affect LP adversely, especially where there are significant **loans or overdrafts** where the interest rate follows the base rate.

LP's board should review the company's pattern of lending. Ideally if interest rates are expected to rise, it should look to replace **overdraft and floating rate finance** with **fixed rate loans**. LP may also hedge borrowing that will be required in some months' time by means of **interest rate futures and options**.

ACCA Professional Level
Paper P1
Professional Accountant

Mock Examination 3
Pilot Paper

Question Paper	
Time allowed	
Reading and Planning Writing	**15 minutes** **3 hours**
This paper is divided into two sections	
Section A This ONE question is compulsory and must be attempted	
Section B TWO questions only to be attempted	
During reading and planning time only the question paper may be annotated	

**DO NOT OPEN THIS PAPER UNTIL YOU ARE READY TO START UNDER
EXAMINATION CONDITIONS**

Section A – This question is compulsory and must be attempted

Question 1

Chemco is a well-established listed European chemical company involved in research into, and the production of, a range of chemicals used in industries such as agrochemicals, oil and gas, paint, plastics and building materials. A strategic priority recognised by the Chemco board some time ago was to increase its international presence as a means of gaining international market share and servicing its increasingly geographically dispersed customer base. The Chemco board, which operated as a unitary structure, identified JPX as a possible acquisition target because of its good product 'fit' with Chemco and the fact that its geographical coverage would significantly strengthen Chemco's internationalisation strategy. Based outside Europe in a region of growth in the chemical industry, JPX was seen by analysts as a good opportunity for Chemco, especially as JPX's recent flotation had provided potential access to a controlling shareholding through the regional stock market where JPX operated.

When the board of Chemco met to discuss the proposed acquisition of JPX, a number of issues were tabled for discussion. Bill White, Chemco's chief executive, had overseen the research process that had identified JPX as a potential acquisition target. He was driving the process and wanted the Chemco board of directors to approve the next move, which was to begin the valuation process with a view to making an offer to JPX's shareholders. Bill said that the strategic benefits of this acquisition was in increasing overseas market share and gaining economies of scale.

While Chemco was a public company, JPX had been family owned and operated for most of its thirty-five year history. Seventy-five percent of the share capital was floated on its own country's stock exchange two years ago, but Leena Sharif, Chemco's company secretary, suggested that the corporate governance requirements in JPX's country were not as rigorous as in many parts of the world. She also suggested that the family business culture was still present in JPX and pointed out that it operated a two-tier board with members of the family on the upper tier. At the last annual general meeting, observers noticed that the JPX board, mainly consisting of family members, had 'dominated discussions' and had discouraged the expression of views from the company's external shareholders. JPX had no non-executive directors and none of the board committee structure that many listed companies like Chemco had in place. Bill reported that although JPX's department heads were all directors, they were not invited to attend board meetings when strategy and management monitoring issues were being discussed. They were, he said, treated more like middle management by the upper tier of the JPX board and that important views may not be being heard when devising strategy. Leena suggested that these features made the JPX board's upper tier less externally accountable and less likely to take advice when making decisions. She said that board accountability was fundamental to public trust and that JPX's board might do well to recognise this, especially if the acquisition were to go ahead.

Chemco's finance director, Susan Brown, advised caution over the whole acquisition proposal. She saw the proposal as being very risky. In addition to the uncertainties over exposure to foreign markets, she believed that Chemco would also have difficulties with integrating JPX into the Chemco culture and structure. While Chemco was fully compliant with corporate governance best practice, the country in which JPX was based had few corporate governance requirements. Manprit Randhawa, Chemco's operations director, asked Bill if he knew anything about JPX's risk exposure. Manprit suggested that the acquisition of JPX might expose Chemco to a number of risks that could not only affect the success of the proposed acquisition but also, potentially, Chemco itself. Bill replied that he would look at the risks in more detail if the Chemco board agreed to take the proposal forward to its next stage.

Finance director Susan Brown had obtained the most recent annual report for JPX and highlighted what she considered to be an interesting, but unexplained, comment about 'negative local environmental impact' in its accounts. She asked chief executive Bill White if he could find out what the comment meant and whether JPX had any plans to make provision for any environmental impact. Bill White was able to report, based on his previous dealings with JPX, that it did not produce any voluntary environmental reporting. The Chemco board broadly supported the idea of environmental reporting although company secretary Leena Sharif recently told Bill White that she was unaware of the meaning of the terms 'environmental footprint' and 'environmental reporting' and so couldn't say whether she was supportive or not. It was agreed, however, that relevant information on JPX's environmental performance and risk would be necessary if the acquisition went ahead.

Required

(a) Evaluate JPX's current corporate governance arrangements and explain why they are likely to be considered inadequate by the Chemco board. **(10 marks)**

(b) Manprit suggested that the acquisition of JPX might expose Chemco to a number of risks. Illustrating from the case as required, identify the risks that Chemco might incur in acquiring JPX and explain how risk can be assessed. **(15 marks)**

(c) Construct the case for JPX adopting a unitary board structure after the proposed acquisition. Your answer should include an explanation of the advantages of unitary boards and a convincing case FOR the JPX board changing to a unitary structure. **(10 marks)**
(including 2 professional marks)

(d) Explain FOUR roles of non-executive directors (NEDs) and assess the specific contributions that NEDs could make to improve the governance of the JPX board. **(7 marks)**

(e) Write a memo to Leena Sharif defining 'environmental footprint' and briefly explaining the importance of environmental reporting for JPX. **(8 marks)**
(including 2 professional marks)

(Total = 50 marks)

Section B – TWO questions ONLY to be attempted

Question 2

In a recent case, it emerged that Frank Finn, a sales director at ABC Co, had been awarded a substantial over-inflation annual basic pay award with no apparent link to performance. When a major institutional shareholder, Swanland Investments, looked into the issue, it emerged that Mr Finn had a cross directorship with Joe Ng, an executive director of DEF Co. Mr Ng was a non-executive director of ABC and chairman of its remuneration committee. Swanland Investments argued at the annual general meeting that there was 'a problem with the independence' of Mr Ng and further, that Mr Finn's remuneration package as a sales director was considered to be poorly aligned to Swanland's interests because it was too much weighted by basic pay and contained inadequate levels of incentive.

Swanland Investments proposed that the composition of Mr Finn's remuneration package be reconsidered by the remuneration committee and that Mr Ng should not be present during the discussion. Another of the larger institutional shareholders, Hanoi House, objected to this, proposing instead that Mr Ng and Mr Finn both resign from their respective non-executive directorships as there was 'clear evidence of malpractice'. Swanland considered this too radical a step, as Mr Ng's input was, in its opinion, valuable on ABC's board.

Required

(a) Explain FOUR roles of a remuneration committee and how the cross directorship undermines these roles at ABC Co. **(12 marks)**

(b) Swanland Investments believed Mr Finn's remuneration package to be 'poorly aligned' to its interests. With reference to the different components of a director's remuneration package, explain how Mr Finn's remuneration might be more aligned to shareholders' interests at ABC Co.

(8 marks)

(c) Evaluate the proposal from Hanoi House that both Mr Ng and Mr Finn be required to resign from their respective non-executive positions. **(5 marks)**

(Total = 25 marks)

Question 3

At a recent conference on corporate social responsibility, one speaker (Professor Cheung) argued that professional codes of ethics for accountants were not as useful as some have claimed because:

"they assume professional accountants to be rules-driven, when in fact most professionals are more driven by principles that guide and underpin all aspects of professional behaviour, including professional ethics."

When quizzed from the audience about his views on the usefulness of professional codes of ethics, Professor Cheung suggested that the costs of writing, implementing, disseminating and monitoring ethical codes outweighed their usefulness. He said that as long as professional accountants personally observe the highest values of probity and integrity then there is no need for detailed codes of ethics.

Required

(a) Critically evaluate Professor Cheung's views on codes of professional ethics. Use examples of ethical codes, where appropriate, to illustrate your answer. **(12 marks)**

(b) With reference to Professor Cheung's comments, explain what is meant by 'integrity' and assess its importance as an underlying principle in corporate governance. **(7 marks)**

(c) Explain and contrast a deontological with a consequentialist based approach to business ethics.

(6 marks)

(Total = 25 marks)

Question 4

As part of a review of its internal control systems, the board of FF Co, a large textiles company, has sought your advice as a senior accountant in the company.

FF's stated objective has always been to adopt the highest standards of internal control because it believes that by doing so it will not only provide shareholders with confidence in its governance but also enhance its overall reputation with all stakeholders. In recent years, however, FF's reputation for internal control has been damaged somewhat by a qualified audit statement last year (over issues of compliance with financial standards) and an unfortunate internal incident the year prior to that. This incident concerned an employee, Miss Osula, expressing concern about the compliance of one of the company's products with an international standard on fire safety. She raised the issue with her immediate manager but he said, according to Miss Osula, that it wasn't his job to report her concerns to senior management. When she failed to obtain a response herself from senior management, she decided to report the lack of compliance to the press. This significantly embarrassed the company and led to a substantial deterioration in FF's reputation.

The specifics of the above case concerned a fabric produced by FF Co, which, in order to comply with an international fire safety standard, was required to resist fire for ten minutes when in contact with a direct flame. According to Miss Osula, who was a member of the quality control staff, FF was allowing material rated at only five minutes fire resistance to be sold labelled as ten minute rated. In her statement to the press, Miss Osula said that there was a culture of carelessness in FF and that this was only one example of the way the company approached issues such as international fire safety standards.

Required

(a)   Describe how the internal control systems at FF Co differ from a 'sound' system of internal control, such as that set out in the Turnbull guidance, for example.

(10 marks)

(b)   Define 'reputation risk' and evaluate the potential effects of FF's poor reputation on its financial situation.

(8 marks)

(c)   Explain, with reference to FF as appropriate, the ethical responsibilities of a professional accountant both as an employee and as a professional.

(7 marks)

(Total = 25 marks)

Answers

**DO NOT TURN THIS PAGE UNTIL YOU HAVE
COMPLETED THE MOCK EXAM**

A plan of attack

Yes we know you've heard it 102 times but, just in case for the 103rd time **Take a good look at the paper before diving in to answer questions**.

First things first

Again remember that the best way to use the 15 minutes reading time in your exam is firstly to **choose questions to do** and decide the **order** in which to attempt them. Then get stuck into analysing the requirements of **Question 1** and identifying the key issues in the scenario.

The next step

You may be thinking that this paper is OK compared with the previous two mocks; alternatively you may like this paper a lot less than the other two.

Option 1 (Don't like it)

If you are challenged by this paper, it is still best to **do the compulsory question first.** You will feel better once you've got it out of the way. Honest.

- When tackling **Question 1**, read the requirements carefully first, and think about what they mean and what information you are likely to use in each part. Then read the scenario, noting against each paragraph to which question part(s) it appears to relate. There are some marks available for general discussion or explanation (advantages of unitary boards in part (c), explanation of roles of non-executive directors in part (d)); however your answer to part (a) and the first section of part (b) in particular should be structured round what you are told in the scenario.

- **Question 2** offers a number of marks just for knowledge of directors' remuneration and the work of the remuneration committee, before you even bring in the scenario. There are plenty of marks in (a) for the description of the roles of the remuneration committee. In part (c) the scenario sets out the ethical choices you need to discuss; if you consider them, and make a sensible reasoned recommendation, you can easily score close to 5 marks.

- If you don't feel comfortable discussing ethical concepts, you probably won't choose **Question 3** as parts (b) and (c) are worth half the marks. Note that the question verbs require you to show higher level skills, so description and explanation won't get you all the marks you need. In (a) also you will need a few points both for and against the views expressed.

- Given that the scenario in **Question 4** isn't that long, there's actually plenty of material that you can use in your answer. The hints the scenario gives are not very subtle either. If you revised the Turnbull guidance thoroughly, there are a number of marks available in part (a) just for knowledge of that.

Option 2 (It's a pleasant surprise)

Are you **sure** it is? If you are then that's encouraging. You'll feel even happier when you've got the compulsory question out the way, so why not **do Question 1 first**.

- You won't score well in **Question 1** unless you adopt a systematic approach. Therefore analyse the requirements carefully, seeing which require general knowledge and which require application to the scenario and think about what information you're likely to need. Then go through the scenario, determining and marking which information relates to which question parts. Where you do need to apply your knowledge, make sure you clearly link your answer into what you've been told.

- There are lots of marks available for general knowledge in parts (a) and (b) of **Question 2** so make sure you get them. To get the marks related to the scenario, make sure you pick up all relevant details, including Mr Finn's role (and how therefore he may be remunerated).

- Be careful with **Question 3** as the requirement verbs have been chosen deliberately. (a) requires you to consider how strong Professor Cheung's views are, and (c) wants you to clearly show the differences between the two approaches.

- Although there are quite a few marks available in **Question 4** for general knowledge, don't just treat the question as a knowledge dump. There's a lot of material in the scenario that you can bring into your answers for (a) and (b), so make sure you make the most of it

Once, once more

You must **allocate your time** according to the marks for the question in total, and for the parts of the questions. And you must also **follow the requirements exactly.**

All finished and quarter of an hour to go?

Your time allocation must have been faulty. However make the most of the 15 minutes; go back to **any parts of questions that you didn't finish** because you ran out of time.

Forget about it!

Just wipe it from your mind.

Question 1

Text references. Chapters 3, 6, 7 and 12.

Top tips. (a) may well be an example of the sort of governance question that will occur frequently on this paper. The answer combines some obvious points (lack of non-executive directors) with some less obvious points (the family-dominated structure, the oblique reporting). The best way to approach (a) would have been to go through the scenario carefully during the reading time, noting each point that is relevant to corporate governance, and comparing the details you're given with corporate governance best practice.

(b) covers a combination of risks; the extra risks that JPX will bring to Chemco (the environmental risk and the exchange risk), the risks of the acquisition itself (the market risk of the stock) and the risks arising from the processes of change that will be implemented once the merger takes place. Remember when trying to identify risks in the scenario that often a lot of risks will relate to what's about to change; the results of the change and the processes required for change to occur will all have risks attached.

You may see slightly different versions of the risk assessment process described in the second part of (b), but you would get full marks if you described a logical process that was similar to what's described in the answer.

The key advantages in (c) are equal legal responsibility and larger boards meaning that more viewpoints are represented and that the board is less likely to be dominated by a single director or group of directors. In relation to JPX, consistency is also an issue, but you need to show why it's important; the answer contains a good explanation. The answer also stresses the importance of culture change, an aspect of the control environment that the examiner has highlighted as very important.

(d) represents a summary of the role of non-executive directors, usefully grouped under four key headers. In the second part of (d) you need to discuss elements of what does and doesn't make a good board; that the interests of external shareholders should be represented, that all relevant viewpoints should be included and the board shouldn't be dominated by a small group. These points certainly link in with the discussion in (c).

(e) represents the ethical element that the examiner has promised will be part of all compulsory questions. It emphasises the key elements of interaction with the environment. Note that the second part of (e) includes discussion of general corporate governance principles of openness and sufficient explanation; the answer also brings out how reporting can bring home to the company its environmental impact.

Easy marks. There are various general sections that don't need to be related to JPX or Chemco such as the risk assessment process or the role of non-executive directors. These represent core knowledge and should therefore be easy marks.

ACCA examiner's answers. The examiner's answers to all the questions in Mock exam 3 are included at the back of this kit.

Marking scheme

			Marks
(a)	Up to 2 marks per valid point made on the inadequancy of JPX's governance		10
(b)	1 mark for identifying and describing each risk to Chemco in the JPX acquisition	6	
	Up to 1 mark per relevant point on assessing each risk and a further 1 mark for development of relevant points	10	
	max		15
(c)	Award 1 mark for each relevant point made		
	(i) Up to 4 marks for an explanation of the advantages of a unitary boards	4	
	(ii) Up to 5 marks for the case concerning the advantages of a unitary board at JPX	5	
	(iii) Up to 2 professional marks for the clarity and persuasiveness of the argument for change in the JPX board	2	
	max		10
(d)	Award 1 mark for each explanation of the four roles of non-executive directors	4	
	Award 1 mark for each specific benefit of NRDs to JPX up to a maximum of four marks	4	
	max		7
(e)	Memo to Lenna Sharif		
	Explaining environment footprint – 1 mark for each relevant point made	3	
	Explaining importance of environmental reporting – 1 mark for each relevant point made	5	
	Up to 2 professional marks for the form of the answer (memo in which content is laid out in an orderly and informative manner)	2	
	max		8
			50

(a) **Reasons for inadequacies**

The shortcomings in JPX's corporate governance arrangements can be seen as largely due to its **development from being a family-run company**. As JPX has increased in size, its corporate governance arrangements do not seem to have developed.

Non-executive directors

There are no non-executive directors on the boards of JPX. Corporate governance reports recommend that there should be a strong presence of non-executive directors on the board (at least a **third of members is recommended** in many jurisdictions). The result of having no non-executive directors is that JPX's upper board is too **inward-looking** and may well **lack balance in terms of skills**. It is also very difficult to say that JPX's board is **objective**, and this undermines its role as a monitor of JPX's activities.

Chem-Co is also likely to be concerned that there are **no non-executive directors** to **counter the influence of the dominant family clique.**

Board committees

The lack of board committees may indicate that JPX is **paying insufficient attention** to some aspects of corporate governance.

(i)   The **lack of an audit committee** would be against the law in America, and may mean that **insufficient attention** is being paid to **reviewing financial statements, risk management and internal control**. It also means that internal and external audit are **unable to report to independent directors.**

(ii)   The **lack of a nomination committee** may be a factor in the lack of balance of the boards. A nomination committee should address issues such as **director recruitment** and an **enhanced role for department heads.**

(iii)   The lack of a remuneration committee may mean that **inadequate scrutiny** has been made of **directors' remuneration**, and directors may be receiving remuneration packages that shareholders consider unwarranted ChemCo's worries about the level of risk exposure it faces indicates that it will be particularly concerned about the **lack of an audit committee**. Also if it becomes JPX's dominant shareholder, it will wish to ensure that **directors' remuneration** is in line with what it deems to be desirable.

Organisational structure and communication

Corporate governance is also about encouraging a proper control environment. This includes an **appropriate and effective organisational structure.** Although there is a structure in place, the **lack of involvement of department heads in strategic decision-making** indicates **shortcomings in communication** and organisational practice differing from organisational structure – as directors, department heads should be involved in decision-making.

Annual general meeting

Under corporate governance codes, the annual general meeting should be the principal forum for **communication** between the **board and shareholders.** However at JPX's annual general meeting discussion has been stifled.

As controlling shareholder, ChemCo would expect to communicate through other channels as well as the annual general meeting, but may be concerned with the AGM as a **means of communication** if other shareholders still hold shares after the takeover.

Reporting

The limited evidence available of JPX's accounts, the unclear comment about environmental impact, may indicate a **lack of transparency** and **insufficient disclosure** for the purposes of shareholder decision-making. Given that ChemCo is uncertain about the **risks inherent in the investment**, risk disclosures in JPX's accounts may also be inadequate.

(b)   **Risks**

Market risks

Whenever ChemCo invests in JPX, there is a risk that it will be paying a **higher value** for JPX's shares than they are intrinsically worth. This risk could be quite high, because JPX has only recently been floated, and its shares may not **yet have found their equilibrium price;** also ChemCo's **lack of experience** in dealing with the region where JPX is located may mean that it is more likely to make a mistake in deciding an acceptable price to pay.

Exchange risks

As JPX is operating in a different part of the world to ChemCo, the value of ChemCo's investment in JPX may fall. The **present value of future cash flows** from the **investment in JPX** may be reduced by adverse exchange rate movements.

Integration risks

There appear to be a number of risks that may arise from **integrating JPX into the ChemCo group.** These include ChemCo **management time being taken up** dealing with resistance from JPX, that **diseconomies of scale arise** due to the larger group being less easy to control and that **JPX's culture** does not change in the ways that ChemCo's board desires. The results of these risks may result in the investment **yielding lower returns** than were expected when it was made.

Environmental risks

The comment about negative local environmental impact indicates the existence of environmental risk, the risk that the environment will suffer **adverse consequences** through JPX's activities and also that JPX will suffer adverse financial consequences. These may include **legal costs and fines, also clean-up costs**.

Reputation risks

The poor corporate governance arrangements and the potential threat to the environment may also mean that JPX acquires a **reputation** as a company to avoid. This could have various financial consequences. Shareholders, frustrated by the lack of communication, could sell their shares, **forcing the price of shares down. JPX** could be subject to a **consumer boycott** because of its adverse environmental impacts, leading to **falling revenues and profits.**

Risk assessment

There are various frameworks for assessing risks, but most follow similar stages with maybe slightly different terminology

Risk identification

Companies need an awareness of **familiar risks,** also to look out for unfamiliar risks. This implies knowledge of **what conditions** create risk and what **events** can impact upon **implementation of strategy** or **achievement of objectives.** Methods of doing this include inspections, enquiries, brainstorming, also monitoring conditions that could lead to events occurring and trends. With JPX, it is likely to mean consulting with directors, senior managers and other stakeholders.

Risk analysis

Risk analysis means determining what the **consequences and effects** will be of a risk materialising. This includes not just financial losses, but opportunity costs, loss of time.

Risk profiling

This involves making an assessment of the **likelihood** (low or high) of the risk materialising and the **consequences** (low or high) of the risk materialising. This will help the organisation to decide whether the risk is acceptable in accordance with its **appetite** for taking risks. If it isn't acceptable, profiling will help the organisation decide what it should do about the risk (take risk reduction measures, transfer the risk by means of insurance.) Again consultation with managers and stakeholders should help determine the best strategies.

Risk quantification

For more significant risks, this stage involves trying to calculate the **level of risks** and **consequences**. Organisations may wish to **quantify** the **expected results**, the **chances of losses** and the **largest expected losses.**

Risk consolidation

Risk consolidation means aggregating at the corporate level risks that have been **identified or quantified at the subsidiary or divisional level.** This stage may involve further analysis such as **sorting risk into categories.** The consolidation process will support board decisions on what constitute appropriate control systems to counter risks and **cost-benefit analysis of controls.**

(c) **Advantages of a unitary board**

Equal responsibility

A unitary board structure implies that all directors having **equal legal responsibility** for **management and strategic performance**. All directors can be held **accountable** for board decisions. This avoids the potential problem of confusion over responsibilities if more than one board is responsible for performance.

Equal role in decision-making

If all directors attend the same meetings, it is less likely that some directors will be **excluded from making important decisions** and **given restricted access to information**. Boards that take all views into consideration and scrutinise proposals more thoroughly hopefully should end up making better decisions. It also **enhances the role of non-executive directors.**

Reduction of dominance

If all directors are of **equal status**, this **reduces the chances** of the board being **dominated** by a **single individual** or a **small group.** It fulfils the requirement of governance reports such as the Combined Code that there is a **balance of power and authority.**

Better relationships

The **relationships between different directors** may be better as a single board promotes easier co-operation.

Case for JPX adopting a unified board structure

Removal of family dominance

Combining JPX's boards should **dilute the influence of the controlling family** and enable other viewpoints to be heard. At present the family's domination of the upper board appears to be stifling debate.

Involvement of department heads

A unitary head with department heads will mean that their **views are heard when strategy** is devised, which should improve the quality of decision-making.

Consistency with ChemCo

Adopting a unified board structure would make JPX's board structure consistent with ChemCo's. This would help solve the problem of **integrating JPX** into ChemCo's culture and structure. It should also give ChemCo more confidence that JPX's governance is effective.

Signalling

A unitary board would signal to stakeholders such as JPX's managers and employees, also ChemCo's shareholders, that the acquisition would mean that ChemCo intended the **management culture at JPX to alter.**

(d)   The UK's Higgs report summarises the role of non-executive directors under four headings.

Strategy

Non-executive directors should contribute to discussions about the strategic direction of their organisation, and be prepared to **challenge the viewpoints of executive directors.**

Scrutiny

Non-executive directors should **scrutinise the performance of executive management** in **meeting goals and objectives**, and **monitor the reporting of financial performance**. They should ensure that **shareholders' interests** are represented, and that managers are not taking advantage of the agency relationship to under-perform or to reward themselves excessively.

Risk

Non-executive directors have a general responsibility to satisfy themselves that **financial information is accurate and that financial controls and systems of risk** management are **robust**. They will have further, specific, responsibilities if they are members of the **audit or risk management committees**.

People

Non-executive directors are also responsible for **manning the nomination and remuneration committee**. As members of the nomination committee, they will be responsible for considering whether the board is well-balanced in terms of **skills, experience etc**. On the remuneration committee, they should consider overall policies, and the appropriate level of remuneration for each director.

Contribution to JPX

Remove family dominance

From ChemCo's viewpoint, appointment of non-executive directors will **dilute the seemingly reactionary dominance of the family**.

Better balanced board

Non-executive directors could widen the perspectives of JPX's board, which appear to be rather narrow at present, and bring new skills and experience. These extra contributions should **improve the quality of decision-making**. They should also address the point that important views are not being heard when strategy is discussed.

Representing shareholder interests

At present there is little opportunity for external shareholders to **express any concerns** about the direction JPX is taking. Non-executive directors can **put shareholders' viewpoints** in board discussions, and **act as a contact point** for shareholder representatives. This addresses the issue of board **accountability** raised by Leena Sharif.

Monitoring function

Non-executive directors can focus on ensuring the board **monitors risks, controls and operations effectively**, and also monitor the performance of executive directors.

(e)   To: Leena Sharif

From: Chief Accountant

Date: 12 March 20X7

Subject: Environmental footprint and environmental reporting

Introduction

The purpose of this memo is to explain the term environmental footprint and to discuss the importance of environmental reporting.

Environmental footprint

Environmental footprint can be defined as the evidence of the **impact a business's activities have upon the environment.** It can be seen in terms of a business's direct inputs and outputs, also its indirect effects. Input effects relate to the business' **resource usage**, for example water and land usage, and whether it **replenishes the environment** in any way. Output effects relate to matters such as **emissions causing pollution**, also the impact of **using and disposing of any packaging.** Indirect effects include effect on local transport systems of JPX's employees attempting to get to work.

Importance of environmental reporting

Good governance practice

Environmental reporting can be seen as fulfilling the key governance principle of transparency, and the requirement of various governance codes for the board to provide a **balanced and understandable assessment of the company's position**. This includes negative impacts such as environmental impacts.

Impact on operations

The need to **specify the impact on the environment** builds environmental reporting into internal control systems, and hence provides a spur, encouraging reductions in environmental impact.

Stakeholders

Investors and other stakeholders are becoming more interested in the level of environmental disclosure, seeing them as **disclosures** relating to **risk management and strategic decision-making.** This can lead to investors seeing companies as lower risk as more risks are known about and reported, and hence companies' cost of capital falling.

Reputation building

An increasing number of companies see voluntary environmental reporting as a means of demonstrating their commitment to good practice and hence **enhancing their reputation**, leading to **marketing opportunities** as green companies. Surveys such as Sustainability's Tomorrow Value surveys provide useful publicity for companies.

If you have any further questions, please do not hesitate to contact me.

Question 2

Text references. Chapter 3.

Top tips. Directors' remuneration is the type of subject that you are very likely to see in this exam as it is (always) topical and there's lots of corporate governance guidance covering it. In (a) 8 marks is quite a generous allocation for the role of the remuneration committee; the answer brings out what it does, the issues and complexities with which it has to engage, and the key corporate governance responsibilities of accountability (here the reporting requirements) and compliance. Your answer on cross-directorships needs to bring out the key principle (independence) and show how independence is breached.

In (b) the description of remuneration brings out the most important issue of links with performance, but also another important issue, that of directors getting benefits on better terms than employees. Note the stress on trying to balance short and long-term priorities; the weighting of each is not easy to determine, particularly for a sales director whose short-term performance will be significant.

In (c) the arguments for the proposal take an absolutist view of the rules, reinforced by arguments stressing the beneficial consequences (simple solution, better for reputation).

The arguments against the proposal stress that there is doubt about malpractice and also other consequences (loss of experience unbalancing the board). Remember under most governance codes not all non-executive directors have to meet the independence criteria, but there need to be sufficient independent non-executive directors on the board to constitute a strong presence and to staff the key corporate governance committees.

Overall (c) is a good example of weighing up a strong ethical solution against a maybe weaker, but more practical, one.

Easy marks. The descriptive sections on remuneration committee and directors' remuneration certainly offer most of the marks you need to pass this question. Remember however that in your exam, the marks may be more tilted towards application.

Marking scheme

				Marks
(a)	(i)	1 mark for each valid point made for demonstrating an understanding of cross directorships	2	
	(ii)	Award up to 2 marks for each valid point made on roles of remuneration committees	8	
	(iii)	Award up to 2 marks for each valid point on undermining the roles	4	
		max		12
(b)		1 mark for each component of a director's remuneration correctly identified	4	
		1 mark for each relevant point describing how Finn's remuneration might be more aligned to shareholders' interests	5	
		max		8
(c)		Award 1 mark for each point evaluating the proposal from Hanoi House	1	
		Arguments in favour – up to 3 marks	3	
		Arguments against – up to 3 marks	3	
		max		5
				25

BPP
LEARNING MEDIA

(a)   **Complying with laws and best practice**

To ensure that executive directors do not set their own remuneration, governance codes such as the UK Combined Code suggest that the committee should be **staffed by independent non-executive directors**, who have no personal interests other than as shareholders. The committee should also ensure **compliance with any relevant legislation**, for example prohibition of loans to directors.

Establishing general remuneration policy

The remuneration committee is responsible for establishing remuneration policy, acting on behalf of shareholders, but for the **benefit of both the board and shareholders**. They should consider the **pay scales** for directors, including how much the remuneration offered by comparable companies should influence remuneration levels in its own company. It also includes considering what **relation remuneration should have** to **measurable performance** or enhanced shareholder value and **when** directors should receive performance-related benefits.

Determining remuneration packages for each director

The committee needs to establish packages that will **retain, attract and motivate directors** whilst taking into account the interests of shareholders as well. The committee should consider how **different aspects of the package** are balanced, also what **measures** are used to assess the performance of individual directors.

Determining disclosures

The committee should also consider what **disclosures** should be made in the remuneration committee report in the accounts, generally in the corporate governance section. The report normally includes **details of overall policies** and the **remuneration of individual directors.**

Cross-directorship

Cross-directorships are when two or more directors **sit on the boards of the same companies;** there may also be **cross-shareholdings** in both companies. The cross-directorship undermines the role of the remuneration committee because Mr Ng, its chairman, is linked with Frank Finn as fellow directors of another company. He does not have the necessary **independence s**ince Frank Finn, in his role as director of DEF, may be responsible for determining Mr Ng's salary. Both may therefore be tempted to act in their own interests by voting the other a high salary.

(b)   **Basic salary**

Basic salary is the **salary laid down** in the director's contract of employment. The terms are determined by the contract and the original salary is not generally related to performance (although increases in it may be). Shareholder interests can be promoted by ensuring that contracts of employment are **not of excessive length**; however if remuneration packages are heavily weighted towards basic salary, as here, they may be criticised for not providing enough incentives for directors to perform well.

Performance related bonus

Directors may be paid a cash bonus for **good performance.** Performance measures need be determined carefully so that they are in **shareholders' interests**, are not **subject to manipulation of profits**, **do not focus excessively on short-term results** and **reward the individual contribution of Mr Finn.** However given that Mr Finn is a sales director, **rewards based on revenues or profits** would play an important part in rewarding performance, on an annual or more frequent basis.

Shares and share options

Share options give directors the **right to purchase shares at a specified exercise price over a specified time period in the future.** If the price of shares rises due to good company performance so that it exceeds the exercise price, the directors will be able to purchase shares at lower than their market value. Share options can be used to align Mr Finn's interests with shareholder wishes to maximise company value. They can also be used to **reward long-term performance** whereas bonuses can be used to reward short-term performance, by specifying that the options may not be exercised for some years (the UK Combined Code recommends not less than three years).

Benefits in kind

Benefits in kind could include a **car, health provisions** and **life assurance**. It may be difficult to relate these elements to directors' performance and indeed one symptom of the breakdown of the agency relationship is the directors being rewarded with excessive 'perks'. There is also the issue that these measures may be **unpopular with employees** who are not enjoying the same terms. Thus the remuneration committee should ensure that the value of these benefits is not excessive compared with other elements of the package.

Pensions

Some companies pay pension contributions for directors. As pension contributions tend to be linked to **basic salary**, they are not usually connected with performance, and again there may be a concern about directors receiving **preferential treatment,** with Mr Finn and others' pension contributions being paid at a higher rate than those of staff. The UK Combined Code stresses that the remuneration committee should consider the pension consequences and associated costs to the company of basic salary increases and changes in pensionable remuneration.

(c) **Nature of issues**

The issues are how best to deal with a **conflict of interest** and also whether it is fair for the two directors to suffer detriment.

Arguments in favour of Hanoi's House position

Integrity

Resignation of both directors would arguably demonstrate that they are acting with **integrity** and are **putting their companies' interests before their own.** It would also demonstrate **ABC's strict adherence** to the **principles of good corporate governance.**

Removal of threat to independence

Given that corporate governance reports suggest that cross-directorships are a threat to independence, resignation is the **simplest way to remove that threat**.

Reputation risk

ABC and DEF may be vulnerable to criticisms that **'fat cat' directors** are operating on a 'you scratch my back, I'll scratch yours' basis. Resignation would **restore confidence in the remuneration committee.**

Arguments against Hanoi House's position

Evidence of malpractice

Although cross-directorships are against corporate governance best practice, it looks excessive to suggest that there is **evidence of malpractice. Frank Finn's** package may have been poorly designed, but this may not have been deliberate.

Loss of Mr Ng

Swanland Investment make the legitimate point that the two directors' contribution will be lost. It emphasises the complexities of corporate governance, the need to choose between the **better functioning of the board** against the **threat to independence**.

Role of other directors

Swanland's proposals emphasises that the remuneration committee does not just consist of Mr Ng; there should be other **independent non-executive directors** on it who are capable of coming to a fair decision even without Mr Ng.

Question 3

Text references. Chapter 11.

Top tips. In (a) you should get a certain amount of mileage from using Professor Cheung's arguments in the question. Partly the disadvantages of codes is that accountants pay too much attention to the examples and not enough to understanding the basic principles (this point is also picked up in the answer to Question 4 (c)). The impact of regional differences is interesting; you will remember that they impact upon individuals' ethical outlook, so how can codes respond. The arguments against the opinion bring out what codes can achieve, particularly minimum standards of behaviour.

(b) emphasises the key concept of integrity. The definition and the importance of integrity represent knowledge you must have; the examiner has laid a lot of stress on it.

(c) just asks for a definition of these two viewpoints. You may be asked in other questions to apply them to a situation where a deontological (absolute) perspective suggests one course of action, a consequentialist (teleological) perspective another.

Easy marks. (b) is the type of question that should represent easy marks; you need to be able to define key concepts and briefly explain their significance.

Marking scheme

			Marks
(a)	Award 1 mark for each valid point made supporting codes of professional ethics	6	
	Award 1 mark for each valid point made on limitations of codes of professional ethics	6	
	Up to 2 marks for using an actual code of ethics by way of example	2	
	max		12
(b)	Definition of integrity – 1 mark for each relevant point	4	
	Importance of integrity – 1 mark for each relevant point	4	
	max		7
(c)	Explanation of deontology – 1 mark for each valid point	4	
	Explanation of consequentialism – 1 mark for each valid point	4	
	max		6
			25

(a)   **In favour of Professor Cheung's views**

Stress on probity and integrity

Professor Cheung emphasises the **key principles** that should be at the heart of accountants' ethical thinking; arguably professional codes, with their **identification of many different situations** lack this focus.

Treatment as rules

Even if ethical codes stress that they are based on principles, evidence suggests that some treat them as a set of rules to be **complied with and 'box-ticked'**. In particular the examples codes give can be treated as actions to be taken in situations with different sets of circumstances where they may not be appropriate.

Situations outside the codes

Giving a lot of specific examples in codes may give the impression that ethical considerations are **primarily important** only when accountants are facing decisions illustrated in the codes. They may **downplay the importance of acting ethically** when facing decisions that are not clearly covered in the codes.

Limited values of codes

International codes, such as IFAC or ACCA, can **never fully encompass regional differences and variations** and thus are maybe of limited value. Focusing on the key principles of integrity and probity, which in all jurisdictions it is agreed accountants should possess, is a simple solution.

In addition the value of international codes may be limited by their not being legally enforceable around the world (although ACCA can **enforce sanctions** against members for serious breaches).

Against Professor Cheung's views

Building confidence in professions

Codes represent a clear statement that **professionals** are expected to act in the public interest, and act as a **benchmark** against which behaviour can be judged. They thus should enhance public confidence in the professions.

Fundamental principles

Both ACCA and IFAC's codes clearly state that they are based on **fundamental principles**, not a rulebook. These fundamental principles include integrity, also objectivity, professional competence, confidentiality and professional behaviour. Guidance is then in terms of **threats to adherence with these fundamental principles.** They emphasise the importance of professionals considering ethical issues actively and seeking to comply, rather than only being concerned with avoiding what is forbidden.

Minimum standards

The codes state that the ethical principles are **minimum standards** that can be **applied internationally**; local differences are not significant.

Need for application

Although clearly accountants should be following principles of probity and integrity, accountants facing ethical decisions may have difficulty **applying these concepts.** More detailed guidance, based on fundamental principles and with examples, should **assist ethical decision-making.**

Examples

Codes stress that the examples given are **not universal guides for action.** Although accountants may appear to be in very similar situations to those described in the examples, they should exercise their own ethical judgement actively rather than simply following the examples.

Prohibitions

Although a code may be based on principles, it can include explicit prohibitions if principles are not felt to be adequate.

(b) **Definition of integrity**

Integrity is a **strong attachment to morality**. It implies **sticking to principles** no matter what the pressures are to deviate from them. For accountants it implies **probity, professionalism** and **straightforward dealings in relationships** with all the different people in business life. Trust is vital in relationships and **belief in the integrity of others** is the basis of trust. It also implies qualities beyond a mechanical adherence to accounting standard and law; the post-conventional, highest level of Kohlberg's morality.

Integrity in corporate governance

As corporate governance codes cannot cover every situation, **maintenance of good corporate governance** will sometimes depend on judgements not backed by codes; in these instances integrity is particularly important.

As integrity is partly about proper dealing in relationships, it also underpins the principles of **fair and equitable dealings with shareholders** in corporate governance, particularly in relation to directors exercising an **agency relationship** in respect of shareholders. Good corporate governance is also about **maintaining market confidence** that the company is being run honestly; firm belief that directors have integrity will promote confidence in the company.

(c) **Deontological**

Deontology is concerned with the **application of universal ethical principles** in order to arrive at rules of conduct. It lays down in advance conditions by which actions may be judged. The criteria for judgement are separate from the facts of the situation. An action is judged to be right if society would benefit by everyone doing it, or wrong if it would harm society if everyone did it.

Consequentalist

The consequentalist approach to ethics is to make moral judgements about ethical decisions on the **basis of their outcomes.** Right or wrong then becomes a question of **benefit or harm**. One example of a consequentalist approach is **utilitarianism** – the principle that the chosen course of action is likely to result in the greatest good for the greatest number of people.

Contrast between deontological and consequentalist approaches

The main contrast between the two approaches is that the deontological approach takes no account of consequences; the same ethical decision will be made in all situations no matter what the differing outcomes of the decision might be in each situation. Consequentalist ethics by contrast **depend on the situation** and are **not absolute.**

Question 4

> **Text references.** Chapters 4, 6 and 11.
>
> **Top tips.** (a) appears to be in two parts, first description of good control systems and then application to FF. The description paragraphs appear to be quite generously rewarded; don't assume that this will necessarily be the case in your exam where the majority of marks are likely to be given for application of knowledge to the scenario.
>
> You should note a couple of things which the answer to (a) stresses. Firstly the importance of embedding internal control which has been stressed by the examiner; secondly the need for control systems to respond quickly to changing risks. You may well see scenarios in the exam where the company's business situation is changing, hence its risks are altering, and you will need to explain that the control systems have to respond.
>
> (b) stresses the importance of reputation risk. The level of reputation risk is partly determined by the level of other risks, but, as this answer stresses, it also depends on stakeholder responses. Lost sales is the obvious consequence, but note also the non-financial consequences such as recruitment problems or increased regulator attention.
>
> The key question (c) brings out is when the duty of confidentiality might be overridden. The discussions of professional responsibilities brings out how accountants should have recourse to the basic principles of integrity, probity and public interest in situation where the detail in codes isn't helpful.
>
> **Easy marks.** The first parts of (a) and (b) are descriptive rather than application based, requiring knowledge of Turnbull and the definition of reputation risk.

Marking scheme

			Marks
(a)	Description of 'sound' control systems – up to 2 marks for each valid point	6	
	Explanation of shortcomings at FF plc – 1 mark for each valid point made	6	
	max		10
(b)	Definition of 'reputation risk' – 1 mark for each valid point made	3	
	Explanation of the financial effects of poor reputation – 1 mark for each valid point made	4	
	Recognition of the causes of FF's reputation problems – 1 mark for each valid point made	2	
	max		8
(c)	Responsibilities to employer – 1 mark for each valid point made	4	
	Responsibilities to professionalism – 1 mark for each valid point made	4	
	max		7
			25

(a) **Control systems**

The Turnbull report sees control framework as being designed to **achieve a number of objectives** and emphasises the need for the control system to be **sound;** an unsound system can undermine corporate governance. **Control systems** are often defined as being made up of two main elements – the **control environment** and **control procedures**.

BPP
LEARNING MEDIA

Compliance with laws and regulations

Control systems should **ensure compliance with applicable laws and regulations**, also with internal policies.

FF's systems clearly have not done this; FF has **failed to follow fire safety standards** and its accounts have **failed to comply with accounting standards**. Also management have **not been able to enforce the objective** of complying with the highest standards of control.

Ensure the quality of internal and external reporting

This requires the **maintenance of proper records and processes** which generate a flow of timely and relevant information.

The qualified audit report that FF has had may be a **failure of controls**, a lack of awareness within the company of the requirements of accounting standards.

Respond to significant and changing risks

The control system should **identify what the most significant risks** are, and be capable of responding quickly to **evolving risks within the business.**

The **lack of compliance with fire reporting standards** suggests a failure within SS's systems to **identify significant risks**, not just the **direct risks of selling unsafe products** but also the **reputation risk** arising from this.

Control environment

The control environment is the **stress** placed by directors and managers, also the management style and **corporate culture and values shared by all employees.**

The Turnbull report comments that internal control systems should be **embedded in the operations of a company** and **form part of its culture.**

The scenario highlights a number of problems with the control environment within FF. Although the board have sought to promote the highest standards of internal control, the **directors failed to respond** when the issue of product safety was raised. In addition Miss Osula asserted that there was a overall **culture of carelessness** within FF.

Control procedures

Control procedures represent the specific **policies and procedures** designed to achieve objectives.

The scenario highlights a number of failings in the control procedures of FF. The **quality control** relating to the **material testing** clearly failed. The qualified audit report suggests a **failure in accounting controls**. Reporting control failings to management is a management control, part of the **system of accountabilities,** and again that failed to work as no action was taken.

(b) **Reputation risk**

Reputation risk is the risk of a **loss of reputation** arising from the adverse consequence of another risk materialising. Reputation risk levels depend **not only on the levels of other risks** but **the reaction of stakeholders** to those other risks materialising – how much less of the organisation do stakeholders think, and what do they do.

Stakeholders and financial consequences

Thus the level of reputation risk depends on the actions that stakeholders can take that can affect the organisation financially. These actions vary by stakeholder.

Shareholders

Shareholders can ultimately sell their shares, more easily if FF is **listed**, if they lack confidence in the way the company is governed. If shareholders holding a significant proportion of shares do this, FF's **share price will fall.**

Customers

If customers are concerned about the safety of FF's products, they are likely to cease buying them, causing **falls in revenues and profits**.

Law enforcement agencies

FF may face **legal action** as a result of failing to comply with standards. This could lead to **fines** and **lawyers' fees** for defending the action. FF may also be ordered to **cease manufacturing** the product that has not complied with standards, again causing **falls in revenues and profits.**

Auditors

Because of the qualified audit report, auditors are likely to scrutinise FF's records more closely in subsequent years, leading to an **increase in audit fees.**

(c)   **Ethical responsibilities to employer**

Probity

Accountants should act honestly and not be swayed from fulfilling their duty to the employers by considerations of **personal interests** or **illegitimate pressures** to act other than in their employers' interests.

Professional competence

Accountants should **exercise competence and skill** in the service of the employer and maintain knowledge of best practice, legislation and techniques. Accountants should also **exercise due care** when working in the employer's interests.

Confidentiality

Accountants should respect **confidential information** that they have about their employer and should **not disclose it without proper or specific authority** or **unless there is a legal or professional right or duty to disclose.** This should apply during and after their employment.

Responsibilities towards shareholders and stakeholders

Accountants should seek to fulfil the company's objectives of trying to maximise shareholder value, also **maintaining good relationships** with **other relevant stakeholders.**

Responsibilities as an accountant

Public interest

Accountants have a general duty to act in the public interest; at times this may override the **duty of confidentiality.** With FF, Miss Osula's actions could be justified on the grounds that the public needed to know about potential dangers of FF's products.

Professional behaviour

Accountants should **avoid any action that discredits the profession** and **comply with laws and regulations, also ethical codes.** Again Miss Osula's **actions could be justified** on the grounds that to stay silent would have effectively been condoning a breach of regulation.

ACCA
Examiner's answers

The pilot paper questions are Mock exam 3

The supplementary questions are located in the list as follows:

Supplementary question number	Kit question reference
1	26
2	13
3	6

BPP LEARNING MEDIA

1   (a)   JPX's current corporate governance arrangements

Inadequacy of JPX's current corporate governance arrangements

The case highlights a number of ways in which the corporate governance at JPX is inadequate. JPX's history as a privately run family business may partly explain its apparent slowness to develop the corporate governance structures and systems expected in many parts of the world. There are five ways, from the case, that JPX can be said to be inadequate in its corporate governance although these are linked. There is overlap between the points made.

In the first instance, the case mentions that there were no non-executive directors (NEDs) on the JPX board. It follows that JPX would be without the necessary balance and external expertise that NEDs can provide. Second, there is evidence of a corporate culture at JPX dominated by the members of the family. The case study notes that they dominate the upper tier of the board. This may have been acceptable when JPX was a family owned company, but as a public company floated on a stock exchange and hence accountable to external shareholders, a wider participation in board membership is necessary. Third, the two-tier board, whilst not necessarily being a problem in itself (two-tier boards work well in many circumstances), raises concern because the department heads, who are on the lower tier of the board, are excluded from strategic discussions at board level. It is likely that as line managers in the business, the departmental heads would have vital inputs to make into such discussions, especially on such issues as the implementation of strategies. It is also likely that their opinions on the viabilities of different strategic options would be of value. Fourth, it could be argued that JPX's reporting is less than ideal with, for example, its oblique reference to a 'negative local environmental impact'. However, it might be noted that ambiguity in reporting is also evident in European and American reporting. Finally, having been subject to its own country's less rigorous corporate governance requirements for all of its previous history, it is likely that adjusting to the requirements of complying with the European-centred demands of Chemco will present a challenge.

  (b)   Risks of the proposed acquisition

Risks that Chemco might incur in acquiring JPX.

The case describes a number of risks that Chemco could become exposed to if the acquisition was successful. Explicitly, the case highlights a possible environmental risk (the 'negative local environmental impact') that may or may not be eventually valued as a provision (depending on whether or not it is likely to result in a liability). Other risks are likely to emerge as the proposed acquisition develops. Exchange rate risks apply to any business dealing with revenue or capital flows between two or more currency zones. The case explicitly describes Chemco and JPX existing in different regions of the world. Whilst exchange rate volatility can undermine confidence in cash flow projections, it should also be borne in mind that medium term increases or decreases in exchange values can materially affect the returns on an investment (in this case, Chemco's investment in JPX). There is some market risk in Chemco's valuation of JPX stock. This could be a substantial risk because of JPX's relatively recent flotation where the market price of JPX may not have yet found its intrinsic level. In addition, it is not certain that Chemco has full knowledge of the fair price to pay for each JPX share given the issues of dealing across national borders and in valuing stock in JPX's country. All mergers and acquisitions ('integrations') are exposed to synergy risks. Whilst it is expected and hoped that every merger or acquisition will result in synergies (perhaps from scale economies as the case mentions), in practice, many integrations fail to realise any. In extreme cases, the costs arising from integration can threaten the very survival of the companies involved. Finally, there are risks associated with the bringing-together of the two board structures. Specifically, structural and cultural changes will be required at JPX to bring it in line with Chemco's. The creation of a unitary board and the increased involvement of NEDs and departmental heads may be problematic, for example, Chemco's board is likely to insist on such changes post-acquisition.

Assessment of risk

The assessment of the risk exposure of any organisation has five components. Firstly, the identity (nature and extent) of the risks facing the company should be identified (such as considering the risks involved in acquiring JPX). This may involve consulting with relevant senior managers, consultants and other stakeholders. Second, the company should decide on the categories of risk that are regarded as acceptable for the company to bear. Of course any decision to discontinue exposure to a given risk will have implications for the activities of the company and this cost will need to be considered against the benefit of the reduced risk. Third, the assessment of risk should quantify, as far as possible, the likelihood (probability) of the identified risks materialising. Risks with a high probability of occurring will attract higher levels of management attention than those with lower probabilities. Fourth, an assessment of risk will entail an examination of the company's ability to reduce the impact on the business of risks that do materialise. Consultation with affected parties (e.g. departmental heads, stakeholders, etc.) is likely to be beneficial, as information on minimising negative impact may sometimes be a matter of technical detail. Fifth and finally, risk assessment involves an understanding of the costs of operating particular controls to review and manage the related risks. These costs will include information gathering costs, management overhead, external consultancy where appropriate, etc.

  (c)   Unitary and two-tier board structures

Advantages of unitary board structure in general

There are arguments for and against unitary and two-tier boards. Both have their 'place' depending on business cultures, size of business and a range of other factors. In general, however, the following arguments can be put for unitary boards.

One of the main features of a unitary board is that all directors, including managing directors, departmental (or divisional) directors and NEDs all have equal legal and executive status in law. This does not mean that all are equal in terms of the organisational hierarchy, but that all are responsible and can be held accountable for board decisions. This has a number of benefits. Firstly, NEDs are empowered, being accorded equal status to executive directors. NEDs can bring not only independent scrutiny to the board, but also experience and expertise that may be of invaluable help in devising strategy and the assessment of risk. Second, board accountability is enhanced by providing a greater protection against fraud and malpractice and by holding all directors equally accountable under a 'cabinet government' arrangement. These first two benefits provide a major underpinning to the confidence that markets have in listed companies. Third, unitary board arrangements reduce the likelihood of abuse of (self-serving) power by a small number of senior directors. Small 'exclusivist' boards such as have been evident in some corporate 'scandals' are discouraged by unitary board arrangements. Fourth, the fact that the board is likely to be larger than a given tier of a two-tier board means that more viewpoints are likely to be expressed in board deliberations and discussions. In addition to enriching the intellectual strength of the board, the inclusivity of the board should mean that strategies are more robustly scrutinised before being implemented.

Relevance to JPX in particular

If the JPX acquisition was to proceed, there would be a unitary board at Chemco overseeing a two-tier board at JPX. The first specific argument for JPX adopting a unitary board would be to bring it into line with Chemco's. Chemco clearly believes in unitary board arrangements and would presumably prefer to have the benefits of unitary boards in place so as to have as much confidence as possible in JPX's governance. This may be especially important if JPX is to remain an 'arms length' or decentralised part of Chemco's international operation. Second, there is an argument for making changes at JPX in order to signal a departure from the 'old' systems when JPX was independent of the 'new' systems under Chemco's ownership. A strong way of helping to 'unfreeze' previous ways of working is to make important symbolic changes and a rearrangement of the board structure would be a good example of this. Third, it is clear that the family members who currently run JPX have a disproportionate influence on the company and its strategy (the 'family business culture'). Widening the board would, over time, change the culture of the board and reduce that influence. Fourth, a unitary board structure would empower the departmental heads at JPX whose opinions and support are likely to be important in the transition period following the acquisition.

(d)   Non executive directors

Four roles of non-executive directors.

The Higgs Report (2003) in the United Kingdom helpfully described the function of non-executive directors (NEDs) in terms of four distinct roles. These were the strategy role, the scrutinising role, the risk advising role and the 'people' role. These roles may be undertaken as part of the general discussion occurring at Board meetings or more formally, through the corporate governance committee structure.

The strategy role recognises that NEDs are full members of a unitary board and thus have the right and responsibility to contribute to the strategic success of the organisation for the benefit of shareholders. In this role they may challenge any aspect of strategy they see fit, and offer advice or input to help to develop successful strategy.

In the scrutinising role, NEDs are required to hold executive colleagues to account for decisions taken and results obtained. In this respect they are required to represent the shareholders' interests against the possibility that agency issues arise to reduce shareholder value.

The risk role involves NEDs ensuring the company has an adequate system of internal controls and systems of risk management in place. This is often informed by prescribed codes (such as Turnbull) but some industries, such as chemicals, have other systems in place, some of which fall under International Organisation for Standardisation (ISO) standards.

Finally, the 'people' role involves NEDs overseeing a range of responsibilities with regard to the management of the executive members of the board. This typically involves issues on appointments and remuneration, but might also involve contractual or disciplinary issues.

Specific benefits for JPX of having NEDs

The specific benefits that NEDs could bring to JPX concern the need for a balance against excessive family influence and the prior domination of the 'family business culture'. Chemco, as JPX's new majority shareholder, is unlikely to want to retain a 'cabal' of an upper tier at JPX and the recruitment of a number of NEDs will clearly help in that regard. Second, NEDs will perform an important role in representing external shareholders' interests (as well as internal shareholders). Specifically, shareholders will include Chemco. Third, Chemco's own board discussion included Bill White's view that the exclusion of departmental heads was resulting in important views not being heard when devising strategy. This is a major potential danger to JPX and NEDs could be appointed to the board in order to ensure that future board discussions include all affected parties including the previously disenfranchised department heads.

(e) Environmental reporting.

Memorandum

From: Professional Accountant
To: Leena Sharif

Date: DD/MM/YYYY

Re: environmental issues at Chemco and JPX

1. Introduction

I have been asked to write to you on two matters of potential importance to Chemco in respect of environmental issues. The first of these is to consider the meaning of the term, 'environmental footprint' and the second is to briefly review the arguments for inviting JPX (should the acquisition proceed) to introduce environmental reporting.

2. 'Environmental footprint'

Explanation of 'environmental footprint'

The use of the term 'footprint' with regard to the environment is intended to convey a meaning similar to its use in everyday language. In the same way that humans and animals leave physical footprints that show where they have been, so organisations such as Chemco leave evidence of their operations in the environment. They operate at a net cost to the environment. The environmental footprint is an attempt to evaluate the size of Chemco's impact on the environment in three respects. Firstly, concerning the company's resource consumption where resources are defined in terms of inputs such as energy, feedstock, water, land use, etc. Second, concerning any harm to the environment brought about by pollution emissions. These include emissions of carbon and other chemicals, local emissions, spillages, etc. It is likely that as a chemical manufacturer, both of these impacts will be larger for Chemco than for some other types of business. Thirdly, the environmental footprint includes a measurement of the resource consumption and pollution emissions in terms of harm to the environment in either qualitative, quantitative or replacement terms.

3. Environmental reporting at JPX.

Arguments for environmental reporting at JPX

There are number of arguments for environmental reporting in general and others that may be specifically relevant to JPX. In general terms and firstly, I'm sure as company secretary you will recognise the importance of observing the corporate governance and reporting principles of transparency, openness, responsibility and fairness wherever possible. We should invite JPX to adopt these values should the acquisition proceed. Any deliberate concealment would clearly be counter to these principles and so 'more' rather than 'less' reporting is always beneficial. Second, it is important to present a balanced and understandable assessment of the company's position and prospects to external stakeholders. Third, it is important that JPX recognises the existence and size of its environment footprint, and reporting is a useful means if doing this. Fourth, and specifically with regard to JPX and other companies with a substantial potential environmental footprint, there is a need to explain environmental strategy to investors and other interested stakeholders (eg Chemco). Finally, there is a need to explain in more detail the 'negative local environmental impact' and an environmental report would be an ideal place for such an explanation.

Summary:

As JPX's 'environmental footprint' is potentially quite large, it is important that Chemco ensures as far as possible, that any such footprint left by JPX is known and measured. Additionally, in the interests of transparency, openness, responsibility and fairness, it is important that it is also fully reported upon for the information of both investors and other interested stakeholders.

2 (a) Remunerations committees and cross directorships

Remunerations committees

Remunerations committees comprise an important part of the standard board committee structure of good corporate governance.

The major roles of a remuneration committee are as follows. Firstly, the committee is charged with determining remunerations policy on behalf of the board and the shareholders. In this regard, they are acting on behalf of shareholders but for the benefit of both shareholders and the other members of the board. Policies will typically concern the pay scales applied to directors' packages, the proportions of different types of reward within the overall package and the periods in which performance related elements become payable.

Secondly the committee ensures that each director is fairly but responsibly rewarded for their individual contribution in terms of levels or pay and the components of each director's package. It is likely that discussions of this type will take place for each individual director and will take into account issues including market conditions, retention needs, long-term strategy and market rates for a given job.

Third, the remunerations committee reports to the shareholders on the outcomes of their decisions, usually in the corporate governance section of the annual report (usually called Report of the Remunerations Committee). This report, which is auditor reviewed, contains a breakdown of each director's remuneration and a commentary on policies applied to executive and non-executive remuneration.

Finally, where appropriate and required by statute or voluntary code, the committee is required to be seen to be compliant with relevant laws or codes of best practice. This will mean that the remunerations committee will usually be made up of non-executive members of the board and will meet at regular intervals.

Cross directorships

Cross directorships represent a threat to the efficient working of remunerations committees. A cross directorship is said to exist when two (or more) directors sit on the boards of the other. In practice, such arrangements also involve some element of cross-shareholdings which further compromises the independence of the directors involved. In most cases, each director's 'second' board appointment is likely to be non-executive. Cross directorships undermine the roles of remunerations committees in that a director deciding the salary of a colleague who, in turn, may play a part in deciding his own salary, is a clear conflict of interests. Neither director involved in the arrangement is impartial and so a temptation would exist to act in a manner other than for the benefit of the shareholders of the company on whose remunerations committee they sit. It is for this reason the cross directorships and cross shareholding arrangements are explicitly forbidden by many corporate governance codes of best practice.

(b) Mr Finn's remunerations package

Different components of directors' rewards

The components of a director's total rewards package may include any or all of the following in combination. The basic salary is not linked to performance in the short run but year-to-year changes in it may be linked to some performance measures. It is intended to recognise the basic market value of a director. A number of benefits in kind may be used which will vary by position and type of organisation, but typically include company cars, health insurance, use of health or leisure facilities, subsidised or free use of company products (if appropriate), etc. Pension contributions are paid by most responsible employers, but separate directors' schemes may be made available at higher contribution rates than other employees. Finally, various types of incentives and performance related components may be used. Short to medium term incentives such as performance-related annual bonuses will encourage a relatively short term approach to meeting agreed targets whilst long term incentives including share options can be used for longer term performance measures.

Mr Finn's remuneration package

The case mentions that, "Mr Finn's remuneration package as a sales director was considered to be poorly aligned to Swanland's interests because it was too much weighted by basic pay and contained inadequate levels of incentive."

The alignment of director and shareholder interests occurs through a careful design of the performance related components of a director's overall rewards. The strategic emphases of the business can be built into these targets and Mr Finn's position as a sales director makes this possible through incentives based on revenue or profit targets. If current priorities are for the maximisation of relatively short-run returns, annual, semi-annual or even monthly performance-related bonuses could be used. More likely at board level, however, will be a need for longer-term alignments for medium to long-term value maximisation. While Mr Finn may be given annual or even quarterly or monthly bonus payments against budget, longer-term performance can be underpinned through share options with a relevant maturity date or end-of-service payouts with agreed targets. The balance of short and longer-term performance bonuses should be carefully designed for each director with metrics within the control of the director in question.

(c) Evaluation of the proposal from Hanoi House.

The dilemma over what action to take in the light of Mr Ng and Mr Finn's cross directorship is a typical problem when deciding how to address issues of conflicts of interest. Should the situation be 'put right' at minimum cost, or should the parties in the arrangement be punished in some way as Hanoi House suggested? Swanland's more equivocal suggestion (that the remunerations committee reconsider Mr Finn's remuneration package without Mr Ng being present) may be more acceptable to some shareholders. This debate touches on the ethical issues of a pragmatic approach to some issues compared to a dogmatic approach.

For the proposal

Hanoi House's more radical proposal would have a number of potential advantages. Specifically, it could be argued that the resignation of both men from their respective NED positions would restore ABC shareholders' confidence in the remunerations committee. The appearance of probity is sometimes as important as the substance and resignations can sometimes serve to purge a problem to everybody's (except for the director in question's) benefit. The double resignation would signal a clean break in the apparently compromising relationship between Mr Finn and Mr Ng and, certainly as far as ABC was concerned, would resolve the problem decisively. It would signal the importance that ABC placed on compliance with corporate governance best practice and this, in turn, would be of comfort to shareholders and analysts concerned with the threat to the independence of ABC's remunerations committee.

Against the proposal

Hanoi House's proposal was seen as too radical for Swanland. Among its concerns was the belief that only Mr Ng's resignation from ABC's remunerations committee would be strictly necessary to diffuse the situation. Clearly Swanland saw no problem with Mr Finn's position on the ABC board in his executive capacity. Furthermore, it took a pragmatic view of Mr Ng's position as NED on ABC's board. It considered Mr Ng's input to be valuable on the ABC board and pointed out that this input would be lost if Hanoi House's proposal was put into practice. Hanoi House may therefore have been mindful of the assumed deficit of talent at senior strategic level in corporate management and accordingly, wished to retain both Mr Finn's and Mr Ng's expertise if at all possible.

3 **(a)** Professor Cheung's views on codes of professional ethics

Professor Cheung adopts a sceptical stance with regard to codes of ethics. There are arguments both supporting and challenging his views.

Supporting Professor Cheung's opinion

Professional codes of ethics have a number of limitations, some of which Professor Cheung referred to. Because they contain descriptions of situations that accountants might encounter, they can convey the (false) impression that professional ethics can be reduced to a set of rules contained in a code (as pointed out by Professor Cheung). This would be a mistaken impression, of course, as the need for personal integrity is also emphasised. Ethical codes do not and cannot capture all ethical circumstances and dilemmas that a professional accountant will encounter in his or her career and this reinforces the need for accountants to understand the underlying ethical principles of probity, integrity, openness, transparency and fairness. Although codes such as IFAC's are intended to apply to an international 'audience', some may argue that regional variations in cultural, social and ethical norms mean that such codes cannot capture important differences in emphasis in some parts of the world. The moral 'right' can be prescribed in every situation. Finally, professional codes of ethics are not technically enforceable in any legal manner although sanctions exist for gross breach of the code in some jurisdictions. Individual observance of ethical codes is effectively voluntary in most circumstances.

Against Professor Cheung's opinion

There are a number of arguments for codes of professional ethics that challenge Professor Cheung's views. Firstly, professional codes of ethics signal the importance, to accountants, of ethics and acting in the public interest in the professional accounting environment. They are reminded, unambiguously and in 'black and white' for example, that as with other professions, accounting exists to serve the public good and public support for the profession is likely to exist only as long as the public interest is supported over and above competing interests. The major international codes (such as IFAC) underpin national and regional cultures with internationally expected standards that, the codes insist, supersede any national ethical nuances. The IFAC (2003) code states (in clause 4), "the accountancy profession throughout the world operates in an environment with different cultures and regulatory requirements. The basic intent of the Code, however, should always be respected." The codes prescribe minimum standards of behaviour expected in given situations and give specific examples of potentially problematic areas in accounting practice. In such situations, the codes make the preferred course of action unambiguous.

A number of codes of ethics exist for professional accountants. Prominent among these is the IFAC code. This places the public interest at the heart of the ethical conduct of accountants. The ACCA code discusses ethics from within a principles-based perspective. Other countries' own professional accounting bodies have issued their own codes of ethics in the belief that they may better describe the ethical situations in those countries.

(b) Integrity

Meaning of 'integrity'

Integrity is generally understood to describe a person of high moral virtue. A person of integrity is one who observes a steadfast adherence to a strict moral or ethical code notwithstanding any other pressures on him or her to act otherwise. In professional life, integrity describes the personal ethical position of the highest standards of professionalism and probity. It is an underlying and underpinning principle of corporate governance and it is required that all those representing shareholder interests in agency relationships both possess and exercise absolute integrity at all times. To fail to do so is a breach of the agency trust relationship.

Importance of integrity in corporate governance

Integrity is important in corporate governance for several reasons. Codes of ethics do not capture all ethical situations and the importance of the virtue of the actor rather than the ethics of the action is therefore emphasised. Any profession (such as accounting) relies upon a public perception of competence and integrity and in this regard, accounting can perhaps be compared with medicine. As an underlying principle, integrity provides a basic ethical framework to guide an accountant's professional and personal life. Finally, integrity underpins the relationships that an accountant has with his or her clients, auditors and other colleagues. Trust is vital in the normal conduct of these relationships and integrity underpins this.

(c) Deontology and consequentialism

Deontological ethics

The deontological perspective can be broadly understood in terms of 'means' being more important than 'ends'. It is broadly based on Kantian (categorical imperative) ethics. The rightness of an action is judged by its intrinsic virtue and thus morality is seen as absolute and not situational. An action is right if it would, by its general adoption, be of net benefit to society. Lying, for example, is deemed to be ethically wrong because lying, if adopted in all situations, would lead to the deterioration of society.

Consequentialist ethics

The consequentialist or teleological perspective is based on utilitarian or egoist ethics meaning that the rightness of an action is judged by the quality of the outcome. From the egoist perspective, the quality of the outcome refers to the individual ("what is best for me?"). Utilitarianism measures the quality of outcome in terms of the greatest happiness of the greatest number ("what is best for the majority?"). Consequentialist ethics are therefore situational and contingent, and not absolute.

4   (a)   FF plc and a 'sound' system of internal control

Features of sound control systems

The Turnbull code employs the term 'sound' to indicate that it is insufficient to simply 'have' an internal control system. They can be effective and serve the aim of corporate governance or they can be ineffective and fail to support them. In order to reinforce 'soundness' or effectiveness, systems need to possess a number of features. The Turnbull guidance described three features of a 'sound' internal control system.

Firstly, the principles of internal control should be embedded within the organisation's structures, procedures and culture. Internal control should not be seen as a stand-alone set of activities and by embedding it into the fabric of the organisation's infrastructure, awareness of internal control issues becomes everybody's business and this contributes to effectiveness.

Secondly, internal control systems should be capable of responding quickly to evolving risks to the business arising from factors within the company and to changes in the business environment. The speed of reaction is an important feature of almost all control systems (for example a servo system for vehicle brakes or the thermostat on a heating system). Any change in the risk profile or environment of the organisation will necessitate a change in the system and a failure or slowness to respond may increase the vulnerability to internal or external trauma.

Thirdly, sound internal control systems include procedures for reporting immediately to appropriate levels of management any significant control failings or weaknesses that are identified, together with details of corrective action being undertaken. Information flows to relevant levels of management capable and empowered to act on the information are essential in internal control systems. Any failure, frustration, distortion or obfuscation of information flows can compromise the system. For this reason, formal and relatively rigorous information channels are often instituted in organisations seeking to maximise the effectiveness of their internal control systems.

Shortcomings at FF plc.

The case highlights a number of ways in which the internal control at FF fell short of that expected of a 'sound' internal control system. First, and most importantly, the case suggests that the culture of FF did not support good internal control. Miss Osula made reference to, "culture of carelessness in FF" and said that the issue over the fire safety standards, "was only one example of the way the company approached issues such as international fire safety standards." While having systems in place to support sound internal control, it is also important to have a culture that also places a high priority on it. Second, there is evidence of a lack of internal control and reporting procedures at FF. Not only was the incorrect fire-rating labelling not corrected by senior management, the attempt to bring the matter to the attention of management was also not well-received.

Third, there is evidence of structural/premeditated contravention of standards (and financial standards) at FF. In addition to the fire safety issue, the case makes reference to a qualified audit statement over issues of compliance with financial standards. There is ample evidence for shareholders to question the competence of management's ability to manage the internal control systems at FF.

(b)   Reputation risk

Defining reputation risk

Reputation risk is one of the categories of risk used in organisations. It was identified as a risk category by Turnbull and a number of events in various parts of the world have highlighted the importance of this risk. Reputation risk concerns any kind of deterioration in the way in which the organisation is perceived, usually, but not exclusively, from the point of view of external stakeholders. The cause of such deterioration may be due to irregular behaviour, compliance failure or similar, but in any event, the effect is an aspect of corporate behaviour below that expected by one or more stakeholder. When the 'disappointed' stakeholder has contractual power over the organisation, the cost of the reputation risk may be material.

Effects of poor reputation on financial situation

There are several potential effects of reputation risk on an affected organisation. When more than one stakeholder group has reason to question the otherwise good reputation of an organisation, the effect can be a downward spiral leading to a general lack of confidence which, in turn, can have unfortunate financial effects. In particular, however, reputation risk is likely to affect one or more of the organisation's interactions with resource providers, product buyers, investors or auditors/regulators. Resource provision (linked to resource dependency theory) may affect recruitment, financing or the ability to obtain other inputs such as (in extremis) real estate, stock or intellectual capital. Within product markets, damage to reputation can reduce confidence among customers leading to reduced sales values and volumes and, in extreme cases, boycotts. Investor confidence is important in public companies where any reputation risk is likely to be reflected in market value. Finally, auditors, representing the interests of shareholders, would have reason to exercise increased scrutiny if, say, there are problems with issues of trust in a company. It would be a similar situation if the affected organisation were in an industry subject to high levels of regulation.

FF and reputation

At FF, the sources of the potential threat to its reputation arise from a failure to meet an external standard, an issue over product confidence and a qualified audit statement. The failure to meet an external standard concerned compliance with international fire safety standards. The issue over product confidence involved selling one product falsely rated higher than the reality. These would be likely to affect customer confidence and the attitude of any fire safety accrediting body. The qualified audit statement would be likely to intensify the attention to detail paid by auditors in subsequent years.

(c)   Ethical responsibilities of a professional accountant

A professional accountant has two 'directions' of responsibility: one to his or her employer and another to the highest standards of professionalism.

Responsibilities to employer

An accountant's responsibilities to his or her employer extend to acting with diligence, probity and with the highest standards of care in all situations. In addition, however, an employer might reasonably expect the accountant to observe employee confidentiality as far as possible. In most situations, this will extend to absolute discretion of all sensitive matters both during and after the period of employment. The responsibilities also include the expectation that the accountant will act in shareholders' interests as far as possible and that he or she will show loyalty within the bounds of legal and ethical good practice.

Responsibilities as a professional

In addition to an accountant's responsibilities to his or her employer, there is a further set of expectations arising from his or her membership of the accounting profession. In the first instance, professional accountants are expected to observe the letter and spirit of the law in detail and of professional ethical codes where applicable (depending on country of residence, qualifying body, etc.). In any professional or ethical situation where codes do not clearly apply, a professional accountant should apply 'principles-based' ethical standards (such as integrity and probity) such that they would be happy to account for their behaviour if so required. Finally, and in common with members of other professions, accountants are required to act in the public interest that may, in extremis, involve reporting an errant employer to the relevant authorities. This may be the situation that an accountant may find him or herself at at FF. It would clearly be unacceptable to be involved in any form of deceit and it would be the accountant's duty to help to correct such malpractice if at all possible.

Supplementary Section B
Professional Accountant

1   (a)   The normative-instrumental distinction describes two different approaches or underlying ethical motivations. Often applied to the ways in which organisations behave towards stakeholders, it can be applied to any situation in which ethical motivations are relevant.

In the case, Jenny Harris is demonstrating a normative approach to adoption of the corporate code of ethics. It is evident from what she says that she is internally motivated. She described herself as personally driven by high ethical values and appears to see ethical behaviour as an end in itself. She tends not to take the business implications of the proposed code into account and thereby tends towards the altruistic rather than the strategic. Her attitude is informed primarily by internal motivation rather then the pursuit of external reward.

Alan, by contrast, demonstrates instrumental characteristics. He appears to be primarily motivated by business performance and sees the ethical code as a means to further other objectives (not as an end in itself). His attitude to the code of ethics is underpinned by questions about what can be gained, for the business, of the code's adoption. Accordingly, he is strategic rather than altruistic in him motivation.

(b)   This question draws upon two of Kohlberg's three levels of moral development. In particular, it asks how the decision on possible apology for and withdrawal of the image would vary depending on whether Jenny, as the chief executive of JH Graphics, makes conventional and pre-conventional ethical assumptions.

The conventional ethical level views the moral 'right' according to whether it is compliant with the existing legal and regulatory frameworks and/or norms of the society or culture in which the decision is taking place. If the image was generally acceptable and offensive only to the religious group in question, it can probably be assumed that it was otherwise culturally inoffensive. It was certainly not illegal as no laws were broken. From the conventional level, therefore, there is no case for withdrawing the image.

The preconventional moral development level views the moral right as that which attracts the least punishment and the most reward. Whereas in the case of personal morality, such rewards and punishments are likely to be made at the personal level, the issues involved are more complex for organisations. Preconventional morality might ask, for example, whether the company is likely to be rewarded or punished by keeping or withdrawing the image. In this context, rewards or punishments are likely to be viewed in economic terms or in terms of boycotts or increased business arising from the publicity.

(c)   This is a complicated ethical situation and the board of JH Graphics will be considering several factors in attempting to come to a decision over what to do with the offending image.

One factor likely to be considered is the possible effects of the dispute on the reputation of company. It is not at all certain that the row will be damaging. In some industries, possibly including graphic design, to be seen to be capable of producing provocative and challenging imagery could be advantageous whereas in other situations it may be adverse.

The company will also be likely to take into account the level and direction of public/political opinion and support. The case mentions that the controversy was a major news story and it would be necessary to find out whether the independent coverage of the issue was generally critical or generally favourable of JH Graphics. If the majority of public opinion was against JH Graphics and supportive of the religious critics, that may be influential in JH Graphics considering the withdrawal of the image.

Consideration should also be given to the economic importance of the advertisement/client to JH Graphics. The case says that the client is happy with the image (and presumably untroubled by the religious controversy) but from JH Graphics's point of view, the question concerns how much they could possibly lose if they unilaterally withdrew the rights to use the image and thereby upset the client.

The board would also be likely to consider the possible direct influence of offended religious groups on JH Graphics. The Mendelow map, which measures the influence of a stakeholder by considering its power and interest, may be helpful in determining how influential the religious group is likely to be on the wellbeing of JH Graphics. Is it, for example, large and potentially influential (e.g. in terms of mobilising opinion) or small and unlikely to have an effect?

The directors should also assess the value of all the unexpected publicity to JH Graphics? Mr Leroy is clearly of the view that is "was bringing the company free publicity and that was good for the business". Whilst such a profile raising controversy might be damaging to JH Graphics, it might also be advantageous, especially if being seen as being willing to 'push the boundaries' of taste and decency is a potential source of competitive advantage. The publicity received is obviously far more than the company could afford in terms of buying publicity but this needs to be weighed against whether the publicity is good for JH or adverse.

The national culture in which the decision is taking place could have an influence on the outcome. The intensity of the debate over the importance of not causing offence will vary depending upon the national culture, which can, in turn, influenced and underpinned by historical and religious culture.

(e)   This question touches on the debate over stakeholder recognition and the limits of corporate accountability and responsibility. It is in the nature of any stakeholder that they make a 'claim' upon the activities of the organisation. The debate is over whether that claim is recognised and whether, accordingly, the nature of the claim is taken into account in decision-making.

In this instance, it is relatively uncontroversial to recognise the religious group as a stakeholder (Freeman's definition defines a stakeholder as an entity that can 'affect or be affected by...'). The perceived legitimacy of the claim depends on where the limit of accountability is drawn and the reasonableness of the claim. There is a continuum of legitimacy with, perhaps, shareholders being 'entirely legitimate' in making a claim at one extreme and terrorists as 'entirely illegitimate' at the other. The legitimacy of the religious group's claim (they are unlikely to have a direct economic relationship with JH Graphics) depends upon where that line is drawn. It might also be pointed out that offence taken by a stakeholder doesn't necessarily imply a responsibility towards the stakeholder.

2 **(a)** There is an obvious cost involved in setting up internal audit in an organisation and so it is typical to ask what factors signify the need for internal audit before one is established. Several factors influence the need for internal audit:

The scale, diversity and complexity of the company's activities. The larger, the more diverse and the more complex a range of activities is, the more there is to monitor (and the more opportunity there is for certain things to go wrong).

The number of employees. As a proxy for size, the number of employees signifies that larger organisations are more likely to need internal audit to underpin investor confidence than smaller concerns.

Cost-benefit considerations. Management must be certain of the benefits that will result from establishing internal audit and it must obviously been seen to outweigh the costs of doing so.

Changes in the organisational structures, reporting processes or underlying information systems. Any internal (or external) change is capable of changing the complexity of operations and, accordingly, the risk.

Changes in key risks could be internal or external in nature. The introduction of a new product, entering a new market, a change in any of the PEST/PESTEL factors or changes in the industry might trigger the need for internal audit.

Problems with existing internal control systems. Any problems with existing systems clearly signify the need for a tightening of systems and increased monitoring.

An increased number of unexplained or unacceptable events. System failures or similar events are a clear demonstration of internal control weakness.

The case on Franks & Fisher highlights three factors that would underpin its need to establish internal audit. There has been growth in number of products, activities and (presumably) processes in recent times, thereby complicating the internal environment and introducing more opportunity for internal control failure. There have been problems with internal control systems (the line stoppage and Mr Kumas's comment that, "problems with internal control in a number of areas"). Finally, there was an unacceptable event (the line stoppage) that was attributed to poor internal control. Mr Kumas confirmed this with his opinion about a 'great need' for internal audit.

(b) In practice, a decision such as this one will depend on a number of factors including the supply of required skills in the internal and external job markets. In constructing the case for an external appointment, however, the following points can be made. Primarily, an external appointment would bring detachment and independence that would be less likely with an internal one. Firstly, then, an external appointment would help with independence and objectivity (avoiding the possibility of auditor capture). He or she would owe no personal loyalties nor 'favours' from previous positions. Similarly, he or she would have no personal grievances nor conflicts with other people from past disputes or arguments. Some benefit would be expected from the 'new broom' effect in that the appointment would see the company through fresh eyes. He or she would be unaware of vested interests. He or she would be likely to come in with new ideas and expertise gained from other situations. Finally, as with any external appointment, the possibility exists for the transfer of best practice in from outside – a net gain in knowledge for Franks & Fisher.

(c) The first thing to say is that Mr Kumas's belief is inappropriate and it would be an unacceptable for the internal auditor to report to a divisional director who might be the subject of an internal audit. The reasons put forward in favour of his request are spurious. All of Mr Kumas's information and expertise would be available to the internal auditor in any event, with or without his oversight of the function. Reporting to Mr Kumas would be a clear threat to the independence of the internal auditor as he/she would not be objective in auditing the accounting and finance department. The advice from relevant codes and guidelines would also strongly counsel against My Kumas's proposal. The Cadbury code is typical where, point (g) under the 'role of the internal audit committee' emphasised the independence of the internal audit function from management. Mr Kumas's request should be refused.

(d) Objectivity is a state or quality that implies detachment, lack of bias, not influenced by personal feelings, prejudices or emotions. It is a very important quality in corporate governance generally and especially important in all audit situations where, regardless of personal feeling, the auditor must carry out his or her task objectively and with the purpose of the audit uppermost in mind. The IFAC Code of Ethics explains objectivity in the following terms (Introduction, clause 16): "… fair and should not allow prejudice or bias, conflict of interest or influence of others to override objectivity."

It thus follows that characteristics that might demonstrate an internal auditor's professional objectivity will include fairness and even-handedness, freedom from bias or prejudice and the avoidance of conflicts of interest (e.g. by accepting gifts, threats to independence, etc.). The internal auditor should remember at all times that the purpose is to deliver a report on the systems being audited to his or her principal. In an external audit situation, the principal is ultimately the shareholder and in internal audit situations, it is the internal audit committee (and then ultimately, shareholders).

3 **(a)** An agency cost is a cost incurred by the shareholder in monitoring the activities of company agents (i.e. directors). Agency costs are normally considered as 'over and above' existing analysis costs and are the costs that arise because of compromised trust in agents (directors). In this case, the increased agency costs that arise are the increased monitoring and 'policing' costs that Sentosa House (Sonia) will incur because of the irregular behaviour described in the case.

The first problem identified is Eastern's non-compliance with relevant codes/requirements in respect of non-executive directors and committee structure. There are an insufficient number of NEDs to form the normal committee structure for a public company which means that Sentosa may consider itself to have to monitor some of the risks to Eastern that otherwise the risk committee would undertake. The investor relations department shows evidence of being unhelpful and uninformed – an unfortunate combination of failings. The chairman appears to be arrogant and potentially untrustworthy (he saw no need for risk committee and dealt very abruptly with Sonia when she called). Finally, the company is pursuing risky strategies with no obvious explanation as to why such strategies are necessary.

In this situation, then, Sentosa House has the choice of selling its holding in Eastern or incurring increased monitoring costs to ensure that its own investors' interests, in turn, are adequately represented.

(b) Intervention by an institutional investor in a company whose stock it holds is usually considered to be radical step and normally represents a step change in agency costs for the investor. This caveat notwithstanding, it is an important 'last resort' for institutional investors to have available to them as they seek to adequately represent the interests of their own investors.

There are a number of conditions under which it would be appropriate for institutional investors to intervene in a company whose shares it is holding.

The first condition is concerns about strategy in terms of products sold, markets serviced, expansions pursued or any other aspect of the company's overall strategic positioning.

Its operational performance may give rise, especially if there are one or more segments that have consistently underperformed without adequate explanation.

The third condition is when non-executive directors do not hold executive management to account. There may, for example, be evidence of unaccountable 'kitchen cabinets' or curious executive decisions that are not adequately challenged by non-executive directors.

Fourth, consistent or serious failure in internal controls would justify intervention, although this, in turn, may become evident through operational underperformance. Ongoing or unaddressed failures in, for example, quality assurance, health and safety, environmental emissions, budgetary control or information systems might justify intervention.

Fifth, failing to comply with the relevant code, laws or stock market rules is the next situation. If the company is listed in a rules-based jurisdiction, it is a matter of law but in a principles-based country, compliance is only 'optional' under the stock market's 'comply or explain' rules. Consistent or unexplained non-compliance is like to be penalised by the market

Sixth, inappropriate remuneration policies, if extreme or obviously self-serving, might attract intervention. Such a situation would normally also signify a failure of the remunerations committee which would make it a double cause for concern.

Finally, a poor approach to social responsibility is a condition for possible intervention, especially if there is publicly-available evidence that might adversely affect the reputation of the company.

With reference to the case, Eastern Products fail on several counts that might encourage institutional shareholder intervention. Firstly, its failure to comply with relevant code (particularly on number of non-executive directors and lack of risk committee). Second, the non-executive directors are not holding executives to account because there is an insufficient number of them. Third, there are concerns about strategy (which is considered to be very risky).

(c) Risk committees are considered best practice by most corporate governance regimes around the world for a number of reasons. Sonia has, for good reason, doubts over the competence and good faith of the management of Eastern Products and a risk committee made up of non-executive directors could help her confidence in a number of ways.

In the first instance, the information systems put in place to provide information for the risk committee. This would generate awareness of and facilitate review of all relevant risks for discussion by the risk committee, including those arising from the 'very risky' strategy.

It would review and assess the effectiveness of internal controls on risk. A committee made up of independent, non-executive directors would bring scrutiny to Thomas on two fronts. There is evidence that Thomas may be relatively inexperienced, having been in post for only two years, and the way that he dealt with Sonia's entirely legitimate enquiry shows some evidence of immaturity and/or impatience. Non executive presence would be able to challenge and act as a counterweight to this failing. Non-executive directors would also bring scrutiny of Thomas's leadership over strategy, especially (in the context of the risk committee) the wisdom of his 'very risky' strategies.

(d) The opinion shows confusion over the meaning of the term 'compulsory'. Whilst in a principles-based jurisdiction, compliance is not legally compulsory, it is required for the stock market listing. Accordingly, compliance is effectively compulsory if the company wishes to enjoy the benefits of its listing. Companies in principles-based jurisdictions are subject to 'comply or explain' in that non-compliance needs to be explained in terms of specific areas of non-compliance and the reason for non-compliance. Compliance is also necessary for market confidence in the Eastern Products stock in that the market would be likely to devalue a stock that was a consistent non-complier. Finally, shareholders and stock markets are entitled to challenge the explanation for non-compliance if they aren't satisfied with the explanation given in the annual report.